Approaches and Implementation of Multinational Electronic Health Record Interoperability

Sterling K. Carter
SBC Global Consulting, LLC, USA

Christina Anastasia
Colorado Technical University, USA

Barbara Mae Carter
Colorado Technical University, USA

IGI Global
Scientific Publishing
Publishing Tomorrow's Research Today

Vice President of Editorial	Melissa Wagner
Director of Acquisitions	Mikaela Felty
Director of Book Development	Jocelynn Hessler
Production Manager	Mike Brehm
Cover Design	Jose Rosado

Published in the United States of America by
IGI Global Scientific Publishing
701 East Chocolate Avenue
Hershey, PA, 17033, USA
Tel: 717-533-8845 | Fax: 717-533-7115
Website: https://www.igi-global.com E-mail: cust@igi-global.com

Library of Congress Cataloging-in-Publication Data

LCCN: 2025031512 (CIP Data Pending)
ISBN13: 9798369320273
Isbn13Softcover: 9798337373850
EISBN13: 9798369320280

British Cataloguing in Publication Data
A Cataloguing in Publication record for this book is available from the British Library.

Table of Contents

Preface

Electronic Health Records (EHRs) are digitised health record repositories with both clinical and nonclinical applications. Healthcare systems rely on EHRs to document basic patient information, such as blood type, medications, lab results, annual physicals, surgeries, patient care history, medical insurance billing and coding, Durable Medical Equipment (DME), and vaccination history. EHRs are powerful tools and are essential to Medicine. However, EHRs are often siloed and do not exchange data with non-local systems or global health agencies, such as the World Health Organisation (WHO). "Approaches and Implementation of Multinational Electronic Health Records Interoperability" presents concepts of data sharing and multinational interoperability between medical facilities such as hospitals and clinics, and global health and public health organisations, which are crucial in disease surveillance and pandemic preparedness.

The international community continues to recover from the COVID-19 pandemic, which rapidly spread across multiple nations, killing millions. As of May 25, 2025, there have been over 777,950,273 cases of COVID-19, resulting in 7,096,650 deaths, with over 60,000 new cases reported weekly. Fortunately, the World Health Organisation (WHO) is working tirelessly with member states to align global resources and enhance global pandemic preparedness and prevent future outbreak threats through the WHO Pandemic Agreement. On May 20, 2025, the WHO's 78th World Health Assembly approved the WHO Pandemic Agreement, with a vote of 124 in favour, 11 abstentions, and no objections. Sixty nations did not attend the assembly.

Approaches and Implementation of Multinational Electronic Health Records Interoperability, as shown in Figure 1 Deming's PDSA Model, endeavors to contribute to the Body of Knowledge (BOK), narrowing the strategic focus of its predecessor, Multinational Electronic Health Record Interoperability Strategies, to support pandemic preparedness, the WHO's Pandemic Agreement, and UN Sustainable Development Goals (SDGs). During a pandemic, local healthcare providers, public health and global health professionals are on the frontlines fighting the disease, often a great risk to themselves. Closing information gaps between the organizations through multinational data-sharing inoperability allows access to urgently needed information to protect population. Every chapter in this text is relevant to closing data-sharing gaps between global and public health entities with local EHRs in hospitals.

CHAPTER OVERVIEW

Chapter 1: Why Do We Need Multinational EHR Interoperability Strategies?

This chapter lays the foundation by exploring the urgent need for interoperable EHR systems across borders, framing them as essential tools for equity, outbreak preparedness, and global health diplomacy.

Chapter 2: The Mothership – The World Health Organization (WHO)

Positioning the WHO as the central coordinating body, this chapter examines its role in setting standards, convening stakeholders, and operationalizing global health strategies through digital infrastructure.

Chapter 3: Basics of Complexity Theory

Introducing complexity theory, this chapter equips readers with a systems-thinking lens to understand how health, technology, and governance interact in unpredictable and nonlinear ways across multinational contexts.

Chapter 4: Building Health-Oriented Organization Partnerships

This chapter explores how strategic partnerships—across governments, NGOs, and private sectors—can strengthen EHR implementation and foster collaborative resilience in global health systems.

Chapter 5: Environmental Research: Democratic Republic of the Congo

Using the DRC as a case study, this chapter illustrates how environmental and ethnographic research can inform digital health strategies and contextualize outbreak risk in LMICs.

Chapter 6: Environmental Health

Expanding the lens, this chapter connects environmental determinants to health outcomes, emphasizing the need for integrated data systems that support One Health and planetary health frameworks.

Chapter 7: Public Health Functions from a Multinational Perspective

This chapter maps core public health functions—surveillance, response, and prevention—onto a multinational canvas, showing how interoperable EHRs can enhance coordination and accountability.

Chapter 8: WHO-Compatible EHR Systems to Align with Health Sustainable Prevention Measures, UN Sustainable Development Goals, and the WHO Pandemic Agreement

Here, the book synthesizes global mandates and frameworks, demonstrating how EHR systems can be designed to align with SDGs, pandemic preparedness, and WHO's evolving digital health agenda.

Chapter 9: Change Management Models for Multinational Projects

This chapter introduces practical models for navigating change across diverse health systems, offering tools to manage resistance, build consensus, and sustain digital transformation.

Chapter 10: Multinational Teams of Teams

Concluding with a vision for collaborative leadership, this chapter explores how distributed, interdisciplinary teams can drive innovation and equity in global health through shared digital ecosystems.

Figure 1. Multinational electronic health record interoperability strategies

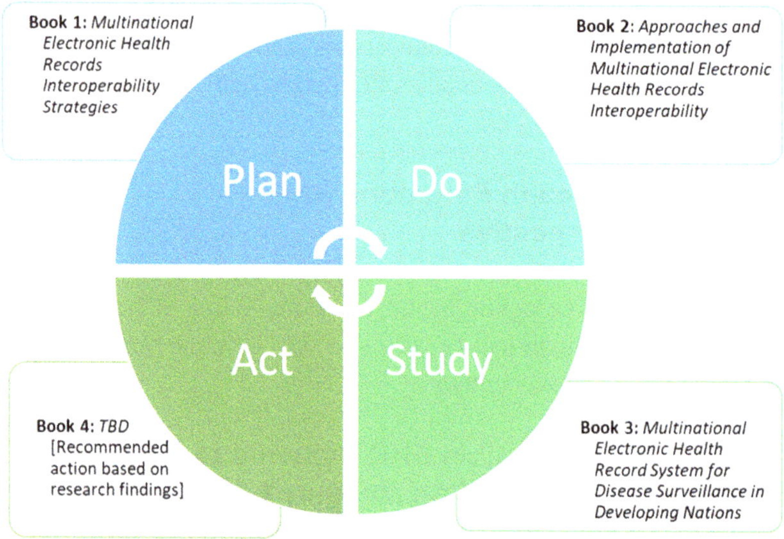

Note: Adapted from Deming's PDSA Model

Chapter 1
Why Do We Need Multinational EHR Interoperability Strategies?

ABSTRACT

This chapter establishes the foundational rationale for multinational electronic health record (EHR) interoperability, emphasizing its role in cross-border disease surveillance, continuity of care for mobile populations, and global pandemic preparedness. Drawing on case studies from LMICs and high-income nations, it explores how fragmented data systems hinder timely diagnosis, outbreak response, and equitable access to care. The chapter argues for harmonized standards and governance frameworks that prioritize both technical feasibility and ethical inclusivity.

INTRODUCTION

Electronic Health Records (EHR) are Patient Health Information (PHI) documents in a digitized format. EHR systems are essential for modern health practices, allowing access to a patient's treatment history. EHRs reduce misinterpretations, prevent medical errors, and enable health systems to share health information across providers (Carter, 2024). EHR systems are used in over 80% of practices in the United States, a developed nation which spends 18% of its Gross Domestic Product (GDP) on healthcare expenditures or $20,000 per capita. The United Kingdom, France, Germany, Russia, China, and other developed nations rely on EHR technology in their healthcare systems. However, EHR systems are not interoperable across international regions and nations and do not share life-saving data in real-time. The world has

DOI: 10.4018/979-8-3693-2027-3.ch001

changed, and the threats are more significant than ever. The threat does not involve a major war breaking between the superpowers and escalating to a nuclear conflict; although possible, there are controls and human decisions that can prevent such a nightmare. The threat is not a significant climate shift, which does not mean that Climate Change is a myth; it is genuine. The danger is not an economic collapse; it is a possibility. The significant threat to human safety is health safety, specifically, the threat of a global disease outbreak.

EHR systems are robust tools that empower providers to work efficiently, reduce errors, and share PHI with other local providers to make decisions quickly and accurately, provided that the patient and provider are on the same network. However, when a patient travels abroad and falls ill, collapsing in Berlin, a limited local EHR system with the traveler's medical history, emergency contacts, and treatment history in Seattle is of little use. A more dangerous scenario occurred at a hospital in Dallas, TX, on September 13, 2014, when America experienced its first travel-associated case of Ebola (Sevilla, 2017). A sick man, returning from a trip to West Africa, was taken to a hospital displaying non-indigenous symptoms. The attending healthcare professionals were unaware of the patient's travel history, the health dangers in the area; only that the patient had recently traveled to West Africa. West Africa, particularly ECOWAS (Economic Community of West African States) nations have strong robust economies, thanks to their wealth of natural resources such as oil, diamonds, gold, cocoa, uranium, timber, and gas. The exponential growth of African economies, attract foreign investors and contribute to globalization.

Globalization opens opportunities for trade, travel, logistics, market expansion, education, and the sharing of human-made or natural resources between nations. It unites the international community and releases the power to share technology, culture, products and services, ideologies, and languages that, without it, are often inaccessible (Lincicome, 2023). Globalization has improved developing countries' living standards, reduced hunger, created multinational companies, and promoted global initiatives such as reducing climate change and preventing or ending wars. Globalization defends the weak, feeds the hungry, holds the guilty accountable, treats the sick, and evangelizes the lost. Globalization is a multinational force that facilitates collaboration among nations to address multinational initiatives. Globalization enhances negotiations between nations, both government organizations and non-government organizations. Globalization promotes cultural exchanges and tolerance. Through student exchanges, globalization educates and emancipates the international community from intellectual and economic poverty. Many well-known scientists, educators, innovators, authors, philosophers, change agents, and professionals in many verticals and the international community have benefited from globalization. However, globalization is a double-edged sword, cutting back and forth, as globalization is the mother of many multinational challenges. The benefits of globalization are self-evident; however, uniting the power of over 8.4 billion people is not without risks and troubles, one of which is global health security (Carter et al., 2024).

When considering the current benefits and future opportunities of globalization, public global health security and protecting interconnected and interdependent, multinational industries and systems with robust, health data-sharing information-sharing technology critical. The international community is inundated with updates on numerous wars and conflicts. These are all considered traditional global concerns, and as previously stated, the international community unites and addresses them. But what waits and lurks in the shadows of our day-to-day multinational travels, cultural exchanges, foreign trade, and transnational endeavors is another threat that we cannot see. The danger is elusive, adaptive, efficient, and often relentless. The threat is unbiased and threatens the multilingual, multi-ethnic, and multicultural. The threat is both religious and irreligious. It threatens the rich and poor. It holds the highly educated in the same contempt as the illiterate. Sexual orientations or political leanings are irrelevant to this threat, and it has absolutely no regard or respect for the wisdom of the aged or mercy to the young. It is a merciless killer and is one billionth our size. The threat is the disease.

Globally, the disease continues to be an existential threat and has killed more people than all the world's wars combined (Norrie, 2016). Annually, nations invest $ trillions on military defense budgets, establishing and funding multinational defense treaties and alliances in preparation for fighting wars, with the United States with an over $900 billion annually defense budget and the most powerful member of the North Atlantic Treaty Organization (NATO). However, the Ebola outbreak of 2014 and the COVID-19 Pandemic of 2019, revealed that the even the most advanced military technology used by highly trained service members cannot contend with the disease, or to prevent its catastrophic impact, and that a global coalition of government leaders, logistics and supply chain professionals, airlines, cruise lines, public and global health organizations, government and non-government organizations, (GO and NGO) academic, doctors, local and international researchers, and scientists from varying fields, with a convergence of technologies and data, saved millions of lives. Therefore, global health security requires a global convergence of all relevant sciences and technologies to protect our nations and cities from disease. Global health security is a non-traditional security and is the responsibility of local, national, and global authorities (Heymann & Rodier, 2004).

OUTBREAK RESPONSE

The global population is 8.4 billion and is projected to grow to 9.7 billion by 2050. Globalization links our societies by increasing international trade, student and cultural exchanges, business and leisure travel, and logistics; and elevating developing nations to developed nations. The unpleasant side of globalization is that it also creates opportunities for cross-border disease proliferation in unsuspecting nations. Therefore, an effective public health system must include outbreak preparedness and preparation for global health emergencies at the national level. Interoperable information-sharing systems are essential to public health systems and support global health initiatives. Advances in data collection and uses- such as enhanced data sharing will impact public health and the healthcare industry (Shah & Sial, 2024).

Prevalence and Incidence of Disease

When considering the quantitative and qualitative data analysis, and perspectives from historians, few could contend that disease, not war, is the greatest threat to human safety and well-being. Although wars have shaken the world to-and-from like a drunkard in a windstorm, it pales compared to disease. Disease has killed more people and ruined more lives than all the world's wars combined. Between 1346 and 1353 (seven years), the Bubonic Plague killed fifty million people: 50% of Europe's population. Between 1939 and 1945 (six years and one day), World War 2 deaths in Europe ranged between fifteen million and twenty million, or 3.76% of the world's population at that time. Fast-forward to the 21st century, the disease remains an existential threat to human safety, especially in large cities in developed nations, often the preferred destinations of migrants and international trade hubs, such as large cities in the United States.

Since December 31, 2019, globally, over seven million people have died from COVID-19, of which 1.2 million, 17%, of the deaths occurred in the United States. America makes up 4% of the global population but suffered over 17% of all Covid 19 deaths. Large cities with international airports and dense immigrant populations suffer the most. They are at greater risk due to hundreds of flights to and from other large international cities, often in developing nations with less robust healthcare and disease surveillance and reporting infrastructure. Insufficient global health data-sharing with local public health systems allows unsuspecting infected business and leisure travelers, logistics professionals, and immigrants to bring infestations to other nations.

PRIORITY POPULATION – LARGE AMERICAN CITIES

Ebola 2014 – Dallas, Texas

On September 30, 2014, the first travel-associated case of Ebola occurred at a hospital in Dallas, TX. Thomas Eric Duncan traveled from Liberia /West Africa to Dallas, and although the Centers for Disease Control and Prevention (CDC) and the WHO were aware that probable and suspected cases of Ebola and Ebola deaths in 2014 occurred in Liberia, Sierra Leone, and Guinea, doctors at a local hospital Dallas, TX were unaware. Dallas is a large city with hundreds of flights to and from West Africa, however, physicians did not consider the patient's travel history. American EHR systems are not interoperable with international disease surveilling systems and do not receive updates on disease outbreaks (Carter, 2024). The patient arrived at the ED of Presbyterian Hospital with a high fever, dizziness, nausea, abdominal pain, headaches, and decreased urination, complaining of pain, travelling from an area known to have outbreaks of Ebola. Still, the doctor misdiagnosed the illness as a sinus infection. The patient died on October 8, 2024, eight days later.

Novel Coronavirus 2020 – Seattle, Washington

On December 31, 2019, the People's Republic of China voluntarily, in compliance with IHR 2005, reported to the WHO pneumonia cases associated with a wholesale seafood market in Wuhan, Hubie Province. On January 7, 2020, Chinese health officials confirmed that the cases of pneumonia were associated with Coronavirus, 2019, $nCoV^2$. Wuhan is large international city of thirteen million people with daily flights to and from the United States. Although the Chinese government reported the infections, by January 30, 2020, 23 days later, over 9976 cases were reported across twenty-one nations, and within that time, $nCov^2$ arrived in the United States.

On January 19, 2020, a 35-year-old man checked into a Snohomish County, Washington hospital, just north of Seattle, after returning from Wuhan, China. The patient disclosed that he had just returned to Washington from visiting family. The patient's travel history inspired local and state health officials to notify the American Centers for Disease Control and Prevention (CDC) Emergency Operations Center. The Chinese government voluntarily reported the infections to the World Health Organization (WHO); however, the virus spread rapidly because local public health systems and hospitals do not receive the WHO's weekly epidemiological reports in EHR systems. The WHO sends outbreak reports to governments. There are over seven hundred million Covid-19 cases to date.

CONTRIBUTING FACTORS

Zoonotic Diseases

Non-communicable diseases, such as cardiovascular disease, cancer, or chronic respiratory disease, are commonly found in wealthy developed nations and Low-to-Middle-Income Countries (LMIC) and develop through behavior, lifestyles, and, in some cases, genetic predispositions. Zoonotic diseases, in contrast, are lethal infestations that endanger wealthy nations and developing countries.

Zoonotic diseases, such as Ebola and Covid-19, transmit from animals to humans and humans to humans. Over 60% of viruses are zoonotic, and 70% of zoonotic pathogens derive from wildlife. Wildlife and domesticated livestock graze in the fields and often drink from the same water source, causing viruses to transfer to domesticated livestock. Over 45% of the earth's usable surface is devoted to livestock, which supplies 24% of the world's meat. Zoonosis, an infection, or virus from an animal infecting a human, occurs in developing nations; 12% of the global population depends on animals for survival. Seeking a better life and employment opportunities and escaping poverty, people from LMICs migrate to developed countries.

Large cities in developed nations, such as Dallas, TX, USA, with a population of 1.3 million, have multi-ethnic cultures, often from developing nations. They are also international hubs for airlines, transporting millions of travelers to and from the city.

Traditional EHR Systems

Traditional EHR systems allow real-time patient data-sharing across a closed network or system. However, EHR systems are not interoperable and do not share information across non-local regions or international borders, which are the traditional migration patterns of infectious diseases. Global trade, international travel, logistics, and interoperability shortfalls have been the source of zoonotic infestations. Zoonotic diseases traverse the globe quickly, and current EHR systems are not interoperable with non-regional or foreign EHR systems or foreign industries and technologies through which diseases travel, impeding effective disease surveillance, which, when coupled with changes in International Health Regulations in 1969 and 2005 makes the global disease burden a national public health problem.

SIGNIFICANT ISSUES- POLITICAL, SOCIAL, AND ECONOMIC FACTORS

A national outbreak response plan is essential to protect societies during global health emergencies. In 1969, the WHO and WHA developed legally binding and initiative-taking disease reporting regulations for UN-recognized states. Nations were legally obligated to report outbreaks to the UN, who, a week later, released an epidemiological report of all nations reporting outbreaks to all UN-recognized states. The infected nation would have to take protective measures to ensure its infected citizens were free of the disease or vaccinated before traveling. Uninfected nations would also ensure that travelers from the infected nations were free of the disease or vaccinated before crossing the uninfected nation's borders. Unfortunately, Low-to-Middle-Income Countries (LMIC) did not have the resources or disease surveillance infrastructure to ensure safety with a robust public health outbreak response plan; however, internationally, their economies suffered and suffered significant losses due the international and social stigmatization from being on the WHO's epidemiological report. In protest, the LMICs either reported outbreaks late or stopped reporting completely. In 2005, the WHO changed the regulations.

Due to changes from 1969 to the 2005 versions of the World Health Organization's (WHO) International Health Regulations (IHR), disease surveillance and reporting are no longer legally binding for UN-recognized member states. The 2005 version removed the legally binding UN mandate to report outbreaks to a voluntary system, making outbreak reporting and responses a local public health matter (Labonte et al., 2021). The shift from disease reporting being an international mandate to a voluntary local public health issue has led to the current public health and disease surveillance. However, disease migration remains a global problem and requires nations, especially with large, densely populated international cities, to have an outbreak response with international considerations.

The Ebola outbreak in 2014 and the COVID-19 pandemic clearly illustrate the need for immediate international engagement with interoperable data-sharing systems for local outbreaks, alerting the global community of the epidemic and the industries by which viruses travel. If an outbreak occurs, a rapid, aggressive response is critical. Public health officials will declare a public health emergency under the local or national Public Health Emergency Preparedness (PHEP) system. A Public Health Emergency is declared to respond to a natural or human-caused public health disaster that can cause mass injuries or deaths, such as a chemical spill or disease outbreak. However, without effective reporting and data-sharing, some local public health emergencies, such as local disease outbreaks, have international ramifications. Additionally, global disease surveillance is challenged without sufficient multinational information-sharing data systems, converting international threats into local public health problems. There is significant data on the prevalence of specific disease migration and the ensuing health challenges.

POLICY IMPACT – HISTORICAL AND CURRENT POLICIES

Due to the changes within the IHR 1969 and 2005 iterations, no current policy demands an international response to EHR interoperability. However, the Health Information Technology for Economic and Clinical Health Act (HITECH) of 2009 is included in the American Recovery and Reinvestment Act (ARRA) of 2009. It promotes leveraging the power of technology to improve American healthcare through enhanced Health Information Exchanges (HIE). The WHO, the WHA, and world leaders convened in March of 2021 to discuss and outline a series of steps and processes for an international treaty for outbreak responses, the WHO Pandemic Agreement (formally known as the Global *Pandemic Preparedness Treaty).* The treaty will include local, regional, and multinational data-sharing if implemented. The treaty shifts from current systems and supports a transition to a global approach to a local public health problem. In the event of an outbreak, under the Pandemic Preparedness Treaty, technologies will be converged from traditionally unrelated verticals to solve public health crises. *Computational convergence and interoperability in electronic health records (EHR)* presents the most relevant technologies from unrelated industries to find solutions to problems (Mishra et al., 2024).

Transitioning to a Global Approach

Carter (2024) stated that globally, the disease has taken more lives than all the world's wars combined. Preventing multinational disease migration requires transitioning from current processes, the traditional EHR systems, to multinational systems that benefit large cities on both a national and global scale, leveraging the power of multiple governments, technologies, and subject matter experts. However, such a change requires careful and thoughtful collaboration among nations, learning from previous mistakes, and ensuring that any multinational solution to disease migration benefits all countries, not just the wealthy nations but the Low-to-Middle-Income Countries.

INITIATIVE EFFECTIVENESS

Outbreak response plans with interoperable EHR systems allow public health officials at the national or local level access to current international outbreak information. The healthcare professionals who addressed the COVID-19 patient from Wuhan, China, lost valuable time contacting the American CDC. Although the Chinese government reported the outbreak to the WHO, which generated the epidemiological report, and the patient acknowledged that they'd travelled to China, the Washington hospital that attended to the patient did not receive the epidemiological report and had to take extra steps and time to contact the WHO. Suppose EHRs were interoperable with the WHO and received data updates, such as the weekly epidemiological reports. In that case, valuable time is saved, the patient can be treated appropriately, and the Dallas, TX, Ebola case is diagnosed correctly.

FACTORS IN IMPLEMENTATION AND SUCCESS

Global trade, immigration, wars, large densely populated cities in developed nations, less developed LMICs, business and leisure travel, dependency on livestock, technological limitations in current health information systems, and nation-state vs global ideologies are all contributing factors to the current state of outbreak response (Carter, 2024). When coupled with fear, misinformation, political polarizations, and a plethora of other barriers and variables invisible to those outside of government, healthcare, and geopolitics, it is self-evident that local public health outbreak response systems must begin with an understanding of how diseases travel from a global perspective and take proactive measures to be prepared for international contingencies, before they become a local public health problem. The COVID-19 pandemic and Ebola outbreak are examples which highlight that data-sharing and EHR interoperability between local, government, and global health systems would have given frontline healthcare professionals critical data needed to respond to the infections and that multinational interoperable systems are essential to combating disease. Therefore, a global effort to design and implement multinational interoperable EHR systems (Figure 1) enhances global and public health systems. However, understanding their differences between the disciplines is vital.

Figure 1. The WHO/ public health / medicine data-sharing and interactions

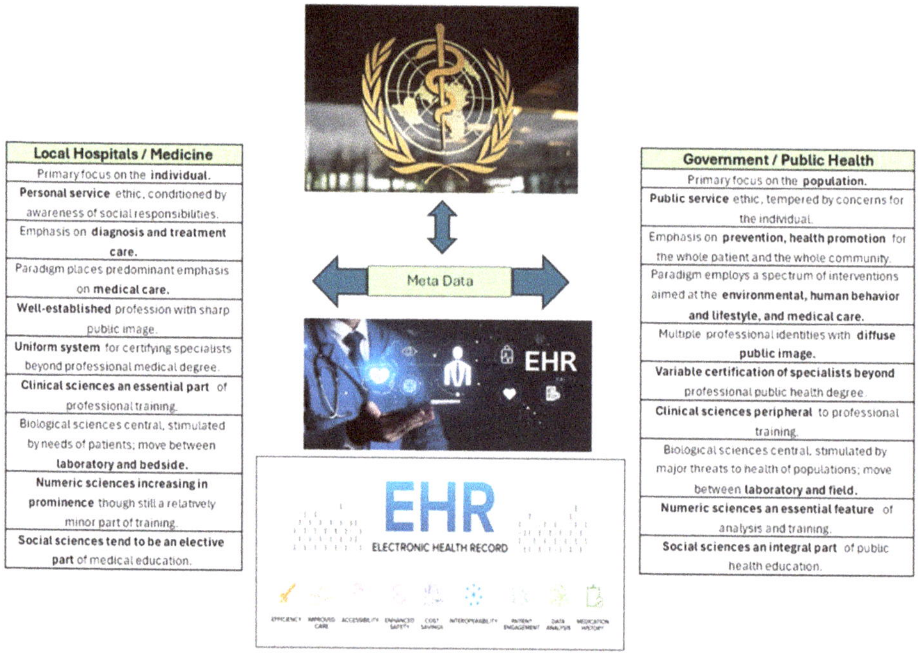

Note. This image explains the interconnectivity between public health, global health, and medicine.

The Disease Migration Cycle

The concept of an interoperable EHR system is not new, but a data-sharing WHO-Compatible EHR system is new and there will be barriers to change in Public Health, Global Health and Medicine. Disease migration follows a cycle, touching three critical areas, Disease Migration Cycle (DMC) of Public Health, Global Health, and Medicine (Figure 2). Surveillance and intervention efforts must understand the DMC and through global collaboration intervene and prevent the pathogen from reaching the next cycle. Public Health problems such disease outbreaks, when unresolved become Public Health Emergencies (PHE). When PHEs are not properly addressed, they become a Global Health threat and can become a Public Health Emergencies of International Concern (PHEIC), which, as experienced during COVID-19, leads to a Global Pandemic. Medicine, where EHR systems are often used in a local hospital in Paris, Moscow, London, or a LMIC, and were the infected and/dying are treated is the gap. Frontline healthcare professionals, as reported in the 2014 Ebola case in Dallas, TX are often unaware or unprepared to treat a sick infected patient with no knowledge of the outbreak, PHEIC, the patient's travel history, or data from the

WHOs Weekly Epidemiological Record (WER). In the 2014 Ebola case in Dallas, the hospital in Monrovia, Liberia was aware of the Ebola outbreak and reported the infections to the WHO, who reported the virus in the WER, and issued a PHEIC. The American CDC, as other national or public health agencies, received the WER and was aware of the PHEIC. Unfortunately, however, the staff at Texas Presbyterian Hospital in Dallas were unaware of the virus and misdiagnosed the patient.

Figure 2. Disease migration cycle

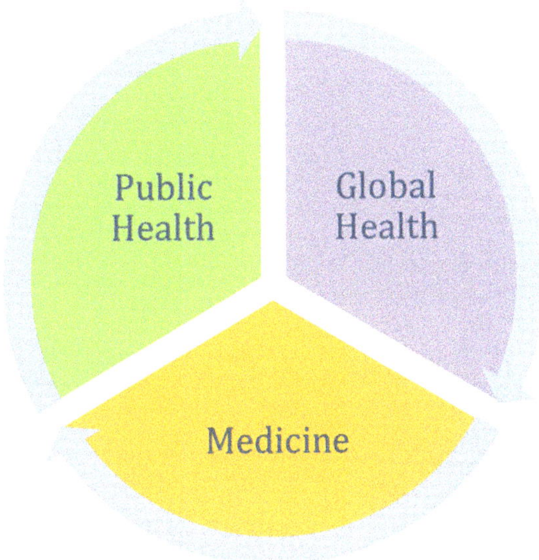

DIFFERENCES: PUBLIC HEALTH, GLOBAL HEALTH, MEDICINE

Public Health

Public Health is preventive and addresses the needs of populations to promote measures to predict and prevent disease outbreaks and protect population well-being through education, policies, and interventions such as vaccinations to prevent the patient from being infected. Public health organizations are commonly found at the city or county levels. Local health departments are essential to preventing the spread of disease, however without sufficient, timely, and accurate data, as revealed in the COVID-19 and Ebola cases, viruses will spread resulting due to misdiagnosis or unnecessary delays. Public Health and Medicine differ in purposes as seen in

Table 1, but they are interconnected (UoP, 2023). Global Health systems are vital to both disciplines.

Table 1. Public health vs medicine, University of Pittsburgh

Medicine	Public Health
Primary focus on the **individual**	Primary focus on **population**
Personal service ethic, conditioned by awareness of social responsibilities	**Public service** ethic, tempered by concerns for the individual
Emphasis on **diagnosis and treatment**, care	Emphasis on **prevention, health promotion** for the whole patient and for the whole community
Paradigm places predominant emphasis on **medical care**	Paradigm employs a spectrum of interventions aimed at the **environment, human behavior and lifestyle, and medical care**
Well-established profession with sharp public image	Multiple professional identities with **diffuse public image**
Uniform system for certifying specialists beyond professional medical degree	**Variable certification** of specialists beyond professional public health degree
Clinical sciences an essential part of professional training	**Clinical sciences peripheral** to professional training
Biological sciences central, stimulated by needs of patients; move between **laboratory and bedside**	Biological sciences central, stimulated by major threats to health of populations; move between **laboratory and field**
Numeric sciences increasing in prominence, though still a relatively minor part of training	**Numeric sciences an essential feature** of analysis and training
Social sciences tend to be an elective part of medical education	**Social sciences an integral part** of public health education

Note: This image explains the difference between Medicine and Public Health.

Global Health

Global health extends outbreak preventions and threats to an international level. Carter (2024) revealed that before a disease becomes a Public Health Emergency of International Concern (PHEIC), it is an outbreak or public health emergency locally. On September 20, 2014, Thomas Eric Duncan, travelled from Monrovia, Liberia, a

LMIC to Dallas, TX. He checked into a hospital displaying a fever, abdominal pain, dizziness, and nausea. The healthcare professionals were unaware of Mr. Duncan's travel history. Mr. Duncan was released from the hospital with antibiotics for a sinus infection. Although the WHO declared a PHEIC for the Ebola outbreak on August 8, 2014, forty-two days before Mr. Duncan's arrival to the United States, those treating him, were unaware of the PHEIC in addition to his travel history. On September 30, 2014, ten days later, Mr. Duncan was diagnosed with Ebola, but it was too late. Thomas Eric Duncan passed away on October 8, 2014. Although the American government was aware of the WHO declaration of the PHEIC for Ebola, the local hospital in Dallas was unaware of where Mr. Duncan had been or the PHEIC declaration for Monrovia, Liberia. Dallas/Fort Worth International Airport (DFW) does not have direct flights from Liberia. Typically, the travelers make connections through Brussels, Paris, or Washington, DC, so how many restaurants did Mr. Duncan eat in? Before arriving in the United States, where was Mr. Duncan's connecting flight? How many doorknobs or elevator buttons did he touch? How many travelers did he encounter? Did he pick up a gift for a family member from the many gift shops commonly found in international airports? The same questions are relevant once he landed in the United States?

Medicine

Medicine is local, individualized care based on the needs of the patient, and is often reactive, managing, diagnosing, and treating diseases once the patient is infected. In Medicine, healthcare professionals collaborate directly with the patient in hospitals or clinics with the goal of healing once the patient is sick, recording patient health information (PHI) in Electronic Health Record systems (EHR).

CONCLUSION

Addressing healthcare through an international perspective with initiatives that empower data-sharing through interoperability is essential to Public and Global Health, as well as Medicine. Although industries rely more on interconnected and interoperable systems than before, the interoperability and data-sharing gaps between medicine, global, and public health systems creates an environment that makes battling disease migration more challenging. There are many opportunities to close the data-sharing gaps, but only if as a society we are open and willing to pursue solutions from an international perspective. Medicine, Public Health, and Global Health are interrelated and must have the ability to share data-sharing relevant data.

REFERENCES

Carter, S. K. (2024). Using Electronic Health Records for Disease Surveillance (EHR-DS) to support UN SDGs. In *Computational Convergence and Interoperability in Electronic Health Records (EHR)* (pp. 137-152). IGI Global Publishing.

Carter, S. K., Anastasia, C., & Carter, B. M. (2024). *Multinational Electronic Health Records Interoperability Strategies*. IGI Global Publishing.

Heymann, D. L., & Rodier, G. (2004). SARS: A global response to an international threat. *The Brown Journal of World Affairs, 10*(2), 185–197. http://www.jstor.org/stable/24590530

Labonte, R., Wiktorowicz, M., Packer, C., Ruckert, A., Wilson, K., & Halabi, S. (2021). A pandemic treaty, revised international health regulations, or both? *Globalization and Health, 17*(128), 1–4. DOI: 10.1186/s12992-021-00779-0 PMID: 34742296

Lincicome, S. (2023, September 12). *Globalization isn't going anywhere.* CATO Institute. https://www.cato.org/publications/globalization-isnt-going-anywhere

Merson, M. H., Black, R. E., & Mills, A. J. (2018). *Global health: Diseases, programs, systems, and policies* (4th ed.). Jones & Bartlett Learning.

Mishra, R., Dwivedi, V., & Saxena, S. (2024). *Computational convergence and interoperability in electronic health records (EHR)*. IGI Global Publishing.

Norrie, P. (2016). *A History of Disease in Ancient Times: More Lethal Than War.* Springer International Publishing AG., DOI: 10.1007/978-3-319-28937

Sevilla, N. L. (2017). *Germs on a plane: The transmission and risks of airplane-borne diseases* [Ph.D., George Mason University]. ProQuest Dissertations & Theses Global.

Shah, I. A., & Sial, Q. (2024). *Advances in computational intelligence for the Healthcare Industry 4.0*. IGI Global Publishing.

UoP. (2023). *Public Health vs. Medicine*. University of Pittsburgh. Retrieved 6/13/2025 from https://www.publichealth.pitt.edu/public-health-vs-medicine

APPENDIX

Chapter 1 Study Questions

1. What are LMICs, and why are they more susceptible to disease outbreaks?
2. Why is a global approach to pandemic preparedness critical to EHR interoperability?
3. What is Zoonosis and why is it relevant to global health now and in the future?
4. What is PHEP, and provide an example?
5. What are International Health Regulations (IHRs) and what are the differences between the 1969 and 2005 versions?
6. How does globalization increase susceptibility to disease outbreaks?
7. How would a multinational interoperable EHR system impact the Ebola case in Dallas, TX and the COVID-19 case in Seattle, WA?
8. How are Medicine and Public Health interrelating?
9. Considering the history of war and disease, which has been more deadly?
10. Globalization has increased international trade and migration. In your opinion, what measures can be considered to promote globalization and migration, while protecting local populations?

Chapter 2
The Mothership:
The World Health Organization (WHO)

ABSTRACT

The COVID-19 pandemic exposed critical gaps in global health preparedness. This chapter traces the virus's spread from China and analyzes global response strategies, highlighting both achievements and failures. Despite the revised International Health Regulations (IHR 2005), responses remained reactive, delaying containment and allowing widespread transmission. The chapter discusses the virus's evolving strains, vaccination efforts, and the need for continued research. It critiques delays in early reporting, inadequate surveillance, and weaknesses in the responses of the WHO and national governments. Emphasis is placed on the necessity of overhauling global health frameworks, particularly improving multinational electronic health record interoperability and strengthening core health system capacities. The pandemic serves as a warning and a catalyst for reform.

INTRODUCTION

The emergence of the COVID-19 pandemic in late 2019 sent shockwaves through the global community, sparking an unparalleled response as nations scrambled to contain the spread of the Virus and mitigate its devastating impact. This chapter offers a comprehensive overview of the global response to COVID-19, tracing its trajectory from the first reported cases to the subsequent evolution of strategies and policies. By examining the successes and shortcomings of international efforts, particularly considering the revisions made to the 2005 International Health Regulations, we aim to glean valuable insights that can inform more effective planning and preparedness for future pandemics. In dissecting the various challenges faced and

DOI: 10.4018/979-8-3693-2027-3.ch002

lessons learned throughout the COVID-19 crisis, we endeavor to lay a foundation for proactive measures that can safeguard against the emergence and proliferation of novel infectious diseases, thereby mitigating the potential for future global health catastrophes.

CURRENT STATE OF COVID-19

As of May 2024, Covid has not been eradicated; however, with the help of global research, vaccinations have slowed down the spread and reduced the number of deaths. While this is great news, the Virus continues to grow into new strains, requiring continued research and testing to prevent new pandemics.

Table 1. Omicron and sub-variants Covid-19

VARIANT	YEAR
Omicron	2020-2024
JN-1	2024
Delta	2022
Alpha	2021/2022
Beta	2020/2021
Gamma	2020/2021
Epsilon	2021
Eta	2021
Iota	2021
Kappa	2021
Zeta	2021
Mu	2021

At the close of 2019, the initial instances of COVID-19 emerged in China, stemming from the SARS-CoV-2 virus and then manifesting with a spectrum of symptoms, ranging from mild to severe. Symptoms included fever, cough, difficulty breathing, fatigue, body aches, loss of taste or smell, sore throat, congestion, nausea, vomiting, and diarrhea. For patients with underlying medical conditions, COVID-19 could last for weeks and, in many cases, can be deadly (cdc.gov; Carter et al., 2023). Mutations in Omicron COVID-19 brought about new strains, including Delta, Alpha, Gamma, and Beta (2020), Omicron (2021), Delta (2021), Alpha, Gamma, and Beta, JN.1 (2023) (CDC, 2023).

VARIANTS OF CONCERN

Omicron and Its Sub-Variants

Omicron first emerged in late 2021 and quickly became the dominant strain due to its high transmissibility. Unlike earlier variants, Omicron was associated with milder symptoms in many cases, although it still posed significant risks to vulnerable populations. Omicron's evolution produced numerous sub-variants, including JN.1, which appeared in 2023 and continued to circulate in 2024. These mutations underscored the virus's capacity to adapt, presenting new challenges for public health responses and vaccine efficacy.

Delta Variant

The Delta variant (B.1.617.2) emerged in India in late 2020 and rapidly spread worldwide, becoming the predominant strain by mid-2021. Delta was characterized by higher transmissibility and increased severity of illness compared to earlier variants. It overwhelmed healthcare systems globally and led to a surge in hospitalizations and deaths until Omicron replaced it as the dominant strain in December 2021 (Katella, 2023; Aleem et al., 2023).

Beta Variant

Beta (B.1.351) was first identified in South Africa toward the end of 2020. This variant raised concerns due to its numerous mutations, which allowed it to partially evade antibodies generated by natural infection or vaccination. Despite these concerns, Beta did not become widely prevalent in the United States (Katella, 2023; Aleem et al., 2023).

Alpha Variant

Alpha (B.1.1.7), identified in Great Britain in late 2020, became the first highly publicized variant. Its rapid spread led to a surge in cases worldwide, prompting its classification as a variant of concern by the CDC. However, the emergence of Delta gradually rendered Alpha less dominant (Katella, 2023; Aleem et al., 2023).

Gamma Variant

The Gamma variant, first identified in Brazil, emerged in early 2021 and was estimated to be 1.7 to 2.4 times more transmissible than earlier strains of the virus.

Despite its increased transmissibility, Gamma's global impact was less pronounced than that of Delta and Omicron (National Library of Medicine, 2021).

The Ongoing Impact of COVID-19

COVID-19 and its variants have not disappeared. According to the Johns Hopkins Coronavirus Resource Center, the pandemic's weekly case rates reached over 200,000 at their peak, with an average fatality rate of 3,000 in 2021. By 2022, weekly cases declined to 116,000, with fatalities averaging 2,500. By December 2022, these numbers dropped further to 60,000 cases per week and 600 fatalities. The decline in cases and fatalities reflects the success of global vaccination efforts, improved treatment protocols, and widespread public health measures.

Despite these achievements, the cumulative toll of COVID-19 remains staggering. By December 2021, there were over 103 million reported cases and more than three million deaths worldwide. By the end of 2022, fatalities had decreased to 244,000 annually. While these reductions signify progress, they also serve as a reminder of the pandemic's devastating impact and the importance of sustained vigilance.

While the Omicron variant was restrained, this did not stop the mutation into Delta, Beta, and Alpha strains of COVID-19) Delta (B.1.617.2) first emerged in India in late 2020 before rapidly spreading worldwide, becoming the predominant strain of the coronavirus until Omicron replaced it in mid-December 2021 (Katella, 2023; Aleem et al., 2023). The Beta variant, or B.1.351, was initially identified in South Africa toward the end of 2020 and subsequently spread to other areas. Experts expressed concerns regarding its numerous mutations and potential to evade antibodies. However, Beta was not widely prevalent in the United States (Katella, 2023; Aleem et al., 2023). Alpha (B.1.1.7) gained considerable attention as the earliest highly publicized variant. Originating in Great Britain in November 2020, cases surged in December of that year before becoming dominant in the U.S., prompting CDC classification as a variant of concern. However, as the more aggressive Delta variant emerged, Alpha gradually diminished (Katella, 2023; Aleem et al., 2023). According to the National Library of Medicine (2021), the Gamma strain, which showed up in 2021, was estimated to be 1.7–2.4 times more transmissible than other illnesses such as the flu or common cold.

Covid-19 and its variants have not gone away. According to the Johns Hopkins Corona Virus Resource Center, COVID-19 and its variants saw over two hundred thousand cases weekly, with an average fatality rate of three thousand in 2021. In 2022, the average number of cases declined to one hundred sixteen thousand cases and two thousand five hundred fatalities per week. By December of 2022, another decline was seen, with an average of sixty thousand cases per week and a fatality rate of six hundred. While this decline is excellent news, the world must prepare for the next pandemic. The final number of cases as of December 2021 was over one hundred and three million cases and over three million fatalities. As of December 2022, fatalities dropped to two hundred and forty-four thousand.

While the declining cases and fatalities attributed to COVID-19 are great news, new viruses are beginning to take center stage. In April of 2024, the World Health Organization (WHO) announced the outbreak of Lassa fever in Nigeria, with over five thousand cases and over one hundred deaths from January to April. While this may seem irrelevant to most people outside of Nigeria, it is essential to remember that COVID-19 began in a small province in China and is believed to have originated from human interactions with animals in the Wuhan Province. The Virus's rapid spread led to thousands of infections, prompting China to impose quarantine measures affecting over 60 million people (who.int; Carter et al., 2023). Despite efforts by the Chinese government, the Virus continued to spread and soon crossed international borders. By March 2020, the World Health Organization declared COVID-19 a global pandemic (who.int). The Virus spreads through contaminated air, via tiny droplets expelled through sneezing or coughing, and by touching the eyes, nose, or mouth with contaminated hands (cdc.gov). To understand a spread such as this, it is necessary to understand how the world responded to the spread.

THE GLOBAL COVID-19 RESPONSE (REACTIVE VS PROACTIVE)

The response to Covid-19 presented a new understanding of how disease can quickly spread. The last significant pandemic prior to COVID-19 was the Ebola virus, which began in 2013 and was maintained in West Africa and European nations, creating a psychological sense of protection for Western countries. Prior to this, most pandemics had negligible impact on the West, apart from the Swine Flu (2010), Avian Flu (2010), and SARS (2003). While these pandemics had the potential to grow, they were sustained in countries outside of the West (Carter et al., 2023). This means that when COVID-19 began, most Westerners did not think twice because, in most pandemic cases, countries such as the United States were minimally impacted. While countries in the East were proactively calling for immediate action, this Laissez-faire perspective created a bottleneck to action in Western nations. This “we can think about it later” approach allowed the spread of COVID-19 in the United States and its borders, forcing a reactive approach to the pandemic. Had a global plan been in place at the time, the spread of the Virus could have been maintained.

The proactive response to the pandemic began in China, the Virus's origin, and spread throughout Europe and Africa. Although the origins of COVID-19 are subject to much speculation, it is widely accepted that the Virus originated in China due to human interactions with animals in the Wuhan Province. The first cases were reported in December 2019; despite the efforts made by the Chinese government, the Virus continued to spread and swiftly crossed international borders. By March 2020, the World Health Organization declared COVID-19 a global health pandemic (who.int). The Virus spreads through three primary means: inhaling contaminated air, exposure to tiny droplets expelled during sneezing or coughing, and direct contact with the eyes, nose, or mouth when the Virus is present (cdc.gov; Carter et al., 2023).

One area that remains problematic is that there has yet to be a reporting structure globally to prevent the spread of disease globally, meaning that there still is not an acceptable approach to implement solutions such as multinational electronic health records (EHR) interoperability (Carter et al., 2022) even with the IHR of 1969 and the revisions to the IHR in 2005. A review of how the world responded to COVID-19 reactively and proactively is warranted to understand the importance of building and implementing a global EHR.

While predicting what type of disease or Virus may appear is complex, one of the big problems associated with a situation such as Covid Response is to be proactive rather than reactive. Both proactive and reactive responses can be expected with the onset of a potential pandemic; however, as shown in Table 2 below, throughout 2020, most of the pandemic responses were reactive, not proactive. COVID-19 was detected in China on December 12, 2019, to understand the pandemic response timeline better. The WHO office in China reported their suspicions on December 31, giving the Virus over 19 days to travel in any number of directions from China. Even though the WHO was informed of the potential outbreak, they did not deploy any emergency management notification until January 2, 2020, adding two more days for the Virus to continue spreading without mitigation. Eight days later, on January 10, the Virus was named "2019 Novel Coronavirus" or "2019-nCoV" to show the world it originated in China. No proactive steps were taken from when China recognized the Virus on December 12 to a mass forced sequestration on January 23, which could be considered the first proactive step in preventing the spread of the Virus. However, it is essential to note that the Virus had 11 days to spread before the forced quarantine in China. The WHO and the CDC took another proactive step to issue mandates for screening airports for flights to and from China on January 17. At this point, the Virus had 37 days to travel out of China and into other countries. There were breakdowns at both the micro and macro levels.

To understand the worldwide response to the COVID-19 pandemic, the actions taken by governments, organizations, and scientists in the first six months need to be evaluated. It began with the first reported case of Covid-19 on December 12, 2019, through January 23, 2020. There was a delayed response globally that allowed the Virus to spread quickly. The first notification of a problem occurred when several

Chinese individuals displayed pneumonia-like symptoms. It took 19 days for the WHO to be notified. Two days after learning of the coronavirus, the Who sent out an announcement 21 days after the onset of the new Virus, which entailed deploying the Incident Management Support team. This gap in time allowed COVID-19 to begin spreading throughout China, into surrounding countries, and globally due to unrestricted travel from China. Fifteen days later, the CDC responded and drew on the preparedness plan created during the Middle East Respiratory Syndrome Coronavirus (MERS-CoV). This happened over thirty days after the first reported incident. The delays in response from the WHO and the CDC provided over a month for the Virus to spread, and it did. Forty-two days after the first reported incidents of COVID-19, China sequestered eleven million citizens into a lockdown to prevent further spread.

Figure 1. Covid-19 response 12/12/2020 - 1/23/2020

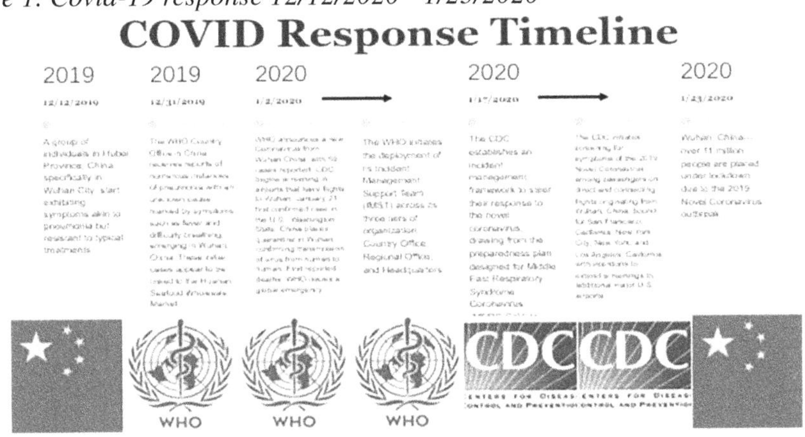

In Figure 2, the timeline starts on January 28, 2020. An additional five days were lost before the CDC issued a Level 3 Travel Health Notice and mandated a 14-day federal quarantine for anyone who returned from China. It should be noted that this impacted just 195 individuals. Three more days passed before the WHO, DHH, and CDC announced that the COVID-19 outbreak had reached emergency status globally and placed travel restrictions.

Figure 2. Covid response timeline 1/28-2/4

In Figure 3, the timeline starts on February 3, 2020, fifty-three days after the first reported cases were found in China. COVID-19 finally gets an official name, and twenty days later (71 days after the first reported cases), Italy deploys a lockdown. On March 1, 2020, the Whitehouse signed the CARES Act into law, and it was on March 11, 2020, the WHO finally declared COVID-19 as a pandemic, ninety-one days after the first reported cases.

Figure 3. Covid response timeline 2/3/20-3/14/20.

The Covid-19 pandemic serves as a harsh reminder of the global failures to safeguard the world from such crises. Due to the reactive stance of both the WHO and most member countries, the pandemic's outcome resulted in over one million deaths from the 99 million cases in the United States and 3.4 million fatalities globally (WHO, 2021). This failure can be traced back to the very onset of the pandemic. According to de Souza et al (2022), although the WHO followed protocol by declaring the pandemic, this announcement failed to spur many nations into implementing robust preparedness and response strategies. To draw greater attention to the severity of the situation, the WHO officially declared COVID-19 a pandemic on March 11, a scenario that had been anticipated in the International Health Regulations (IHR-2005).

The WHO Health Emergencies Program, established in 2016, identified several critical obstacles in combating COVID-19. These included inadequate surveillance, monitoring, and risk management measures, such as early detection, contact tracing, and isolation of cases. Additionally, gaps in risk communication and the absence of a global genomic surveillance framework further hindered efforts. Weaknesses within national healthcare systems, particularly regarding the care of infected individuals and protection of healthcare workers, were glaring. The failure to provide adequate equipment and supplies, coupled with inequitable access to vaccines, exacerbated the crisis. These systemic issues underscored the global unpreparedness for a pandemic of this scale.

The failure of multiple systems during the COVID-19 pandemic cannot be attributed solely to a single organization or country. Instead, a series of global events and actions contributed to the outcome. One of the first issues was the delay in China reporting the virus to the WHO (Gostin, 2021). This delay created a critical window for the virus to spread unchecked. While China's actions were a significant factor, many other countries, including the United States, also failed to respond adequately. Even after the Public Health Emergency of International Concern (PHEIC) was announced, numerous nations were slow to act. Compounding this was a global shortage of resources, which allowed the virus to continue its rapid transmission.

Gostin (2021) highlighted this period as a "collapse in global solidarity" (p. 1132). The pandemic exposed a profound lack of preparedness for an event of this magnitude. Despite the restructuring of the International Health Regulations in 2005 (IHR-2005) to address emerging threats, these changes failed to account for the realities of a pandemic on this scale. Analyzing the transition from IHR-1969 to IHR-2005 offers valuable context to understand the shortcomings and missed opportunities.

The Covid-19 pandemic's trajectory revealed fundamental gaps in global health governance. The initial response was marred by delays and inaction. China's late reporting of the outbreak, coupled with a lack of transparency, hampered early efforts to contain the virus. The subsequent delay in declaring a PHEIC gave the virus ample time to spread internationally. This series of events set the stage for a crisis that overwhelmed healthcare systems, disrupted economies, and claimed millions of lives.

Despite the WHO's efforts to coordinate a global response, systemic weaknesses undermined its effectiveness. The WHO Health Emergencies Program had flagged potential vulnerabilities years earlier, but these warnings went unheeded. Insufficient investment in surveillance and risk management, coupled with fragmented healthcare systems, left many countries ill-equipped to manage the surge in cases. Risk communication—critical for ensuring public compliance with health measures—was inconsistent and often politicized, further eroding trust.

The lack of a global genomic surveillance framework also proved detrimental. As the virus mutated into variants like Alpha, Beta, Delta, and Omicron, the absence of coordinated genomic monitoring delayed the identification and containment of these strains. This oversight underscores the need for a unified approach to genomic surveillance, which could have facilitated more effective responses to emerging variants.

Healthcare systems around the world faced unprecedented challenges during the pandemic. Many were unprepared for the sheer volume of cases, resulting in overwhelmed hospitals, shortages of medical supplies, and inadequate protection for healthcare workers. The inequitable distribution of vaccines further highlighted global disparities. While wealthier nations secured copious quantities of vaccines, low- and middle-income countries struggled to access even basic supplies, prolonging the pandemic and allowing the virus to continue mutating.

The transition from IHR-1969 to IHR-2005 was intended to enhance global health security by emphasizing early detection and response to health emergencies. However, the framework fell short in addressing the complexities of a pandemic like COVID-19. The IHR-2005's reliance on member states' compliance and self-reporting created vulnerabilities that were exploited during the crisis. Many countries prioritized national interests over global solidarity, undermining the collective response.

The pandemic also exposed a lack of accountability within the global health system. The WHO's inability to enforce compliance with IHR-2005 regulations limited its effectiveness. Member states' reluctance to share critical data, coupled with geopolitical tensions, further hampered efforts to contain the virus. This highlights the need for stronger mechanisms to ensure transparency and cooperation during health emergencies.

Moving forward, addressing these systemic issues requires a multifaceted approach. Strengthening the WHO's mandate and resources is essential to enable it to respond more effectively to future crises. Investing in global surveillance systems, improving risk communication, and ensuring equitable access to vaccines and medical supplies are critical priorities. Additionally, revising the IHR framework to address its shortcomings and enhance accountability will be key to building a more resilient global health system.

The COVID-19 pandemic has underscored the interconnectedness of global health and the need for collective action. While the failures of the past cannot be undone, they offer valuable lessons for the future. By addressing the systemic weaknesses exposed during the pandemic, the world can better prepare for the next global health crisis. Ensuring that these lessons are translated into action will be critical to safeguarding the health and well-being of future generations.

IHR 1969 VS IHR 2005

The World Health Organization (WHO), established in 1948, is one of the most influential global health bodies, with universal membership encompassing all nations. Its mission is to achieve the highest attainable standard of health for all people worldwide (Relman et al., 2021). The International Health Regulations (IHR) of 1969 initially aimed to control the cross-border spread of infectious diseases while minimizing disruptions to global commerce. This was achieved through sanitation guidelines for ports and airports (Relman et al., 2021). Recognizing the need for improvement in disease surveillance and response, the mid-1990s marked the beginning of a revision process aimed at addressing diverse infectious threats and leveraging advancements in communication technologies. These revisions led to initiatives such as the Global Public Health Information Network (GPHIN) and the Global Outbreak Alert and Response Network (GOARN) (Relman et al., 2010).

Before 1996, the WHO primarily acted on reports of infectious disease outbreaks from affected nations. However, the limitations of this reactive model became apparent, prompting the organization to adopt a more proactive approach. This shift led to the establishment of GPHIN by Health Canada and GOARN through collaboration between WHO and its partners. GPHIN, an internet-based surveillance tool, and GOARN, which facilitates coordinated international outbreak responses, played crucial roles during health crises such as the SARS outbreak (Relman et al., 2010).

Empowered to provide technical assistance and critical aid during emergencies, the WHO is tasked with coordinating global health efforts and combating both epidemic and endemic diseases. The organization's central governing body, the World Health Assembly (WHA), comprises delegates from member states and serves as the principal decision-making body. It holds the authority to adopt regulations aimed at preventing the international spread of diseases (Merianos & Peiris, 2005; Broberg, 2020).

The IHR underwent a significant overhaul in 2005 to address emerging epidemics and strengthen global coordination. The revised regulations aimed to prevent, protect against, control, and respond to the international spread of diseases (WHO, 2005). Despite progress in implementing the IHR, challenges persist due to varying levels of health and economic development across nations (Merianos & Peiris, 2005; Broberg, 2020). The shortcomings of the IHR were particularly evident during the COVID-19 pandemic, as the regulations failed to anticipate or adequately manage a crisis of this magnitude. To address these gaps, the WHO issued EB150(3) in 2022, inviting member states to propose amendments to the IHR-2005. While several working groups are currently developing new amendments, much remains to be done to address reporting structures and processes specific to pandemics.

IHR 1969: A HISTORICAL PERSPECTIVE

The original IHR, adopted in 1969, focused narrowly on controlling specific infectious diseases such as cholera, plague, and yellow fever. The regulations emphasized preventing international disease spread through measures like sanitation at points of entry, including ports and airports. However, this framework was limited in scope and effectiveness. It relied heavily on affected countries to report outbreaks, which often led to delays in the global response. Furthermore, the regulations lacked mechanisms to address new and emerging infectious threats, highlighting the need for modernization (Relman et al., 2021).

THE EVOLUTION TO IHR 2005

The limitations of the IHR-1969 became increasingly apparent in the face of emerging infectious diseases like HIV/AIDS and SARS. The mid-1990s marked a turning point, as the WHO initiated a revision process to address the changing landscape of global health threats. This process culminated in the adoption of IHR-2005, which represented a change in thinking in global health governance. Unlike its predecessor, IHR-2005 adopted a broader scope, encompassing all public health emergencies of international concern (PHEIC), regardless of the specific pathogen involved (WHO, 2005).

Key features of IHR-2005 included:

- Enhanced Surveillance and Reporting: Member states were required to develop and maintain core capacities for surveillance and response, including the ability to detect, assess, and report public health events.

- Timely Communication: The revised regulations emphasized the importance of timely communication between member states and the WHO to facilitate rapid response.
- Expanded Scope: The IHR-2005 applied to a wider range of public health threats, including biological, chemical, and radiological hazards.
- Collaboration and Coordination: The regulations called for increased international collaboration, including the sharing of resources and expertise to address public health emergencies. Strengths and Weaknesses of IHR-2005.

While the IHR-2005 represented considerable progress, its implementation revealed persistent challenges. The regulations' reliance on member states to self-report outbreaks created vulnerabilities, as some nations delayed or withheld critical information. This issue was exemplified during the COVID-19 pandemic, when delays in reporting and transparency hindered the global response.

Moreover, disparities in health system capacities among member states limited the effectiveness of the IHR. While wealthier nations were better equipped to meet the regulations' requirements, low- and middle-income countries struggled to build the necessary infrastructure. These disparities undermined the collective ability to respond to global health emergencies and highlighted the need for greater equity in resource distribution.

The COVID-19 pandemic also exposed gaps in global coordination and accountability. Despite the WHO's efforts to coordinate a unified response, geopolitical tensions and competing national interests often hindered collaboration. The lack of enforceable mechanisms within the IHR further limited its effectiveness, as member states were not held accountable for failing to meet their obligations.

Figure 4. IHR amendments and revisions

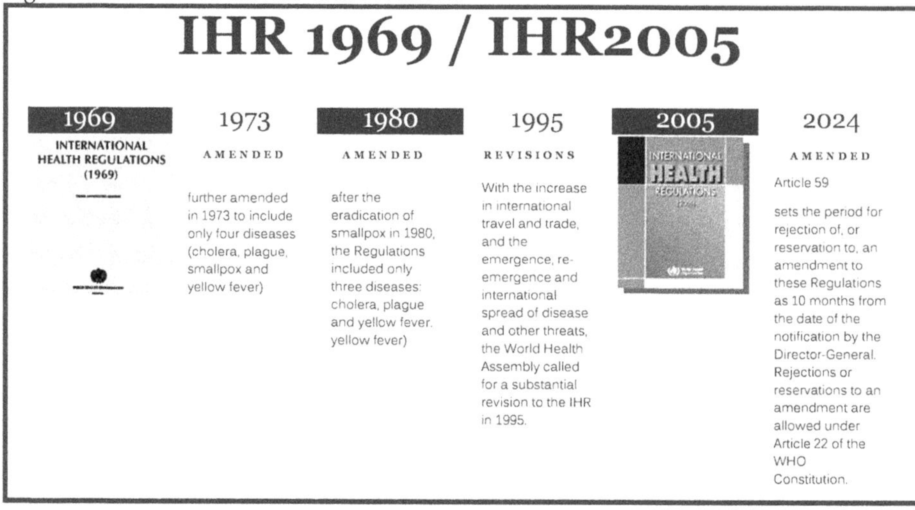

Despite the changes, amendments, and revisions, the world and IHR2005 are still being prepared for a new pandemic. No new plans have been initiated to prevent the spread of disease. This leaves the question, "What will we do if a new pandemic starts?"

Significant deficiencies in reporting mechanisms were observed during the COVID-19 pandemic. Primarily, some Member States needed more resources to adhere to the regulations. Additionally, certain states need to inform the WHO about disease outbreaks promptly. Furthermore, WHO Member States may impose their own travel and trade restrictions, even if such measures are deemed unnecessary or contradict WHO recommendations (Broberg, 2020). Even in a post-COVID world, these same problems remain, leaving a gap for identifying and slowing future potential pandemics.

In their study, Suthar et al. (2018) identified eight core capacities within the International Health Regulations (IHR) 2005, emphasizing the need for their enhancement to prevent future pandemics like COVID-19 (Figure 1). The first four capacities focus on national legislation, policy, and financing. Core Capacity 1 stresses the importance of sustaining political commitment across government levels and integrating global health security priorities into policies. It also emphasizes the collaborative development of national strategic plans for sustained financing and resource allocation, with the establishment of a national secretariat for continuous support. Core Capacity 2 highlights the necessity of effective coordination and communication at national and international levels, utilizing existing organizations and robust programmatic structures. Core Capacity 3 underscores the significance of surveillance in disease management, advocating for strategic planning, legislation, capacity building, and standardized surveillance systems. Core Capacity 4 emphasizes the need for efficient responses to public health emergencies, with clear criteria, multidisciplinary coordination, stakeholder engagement, and optimization of health facilities to reduce transmission (Suthar et al. 2018).

Figure 5. 8 core capacities

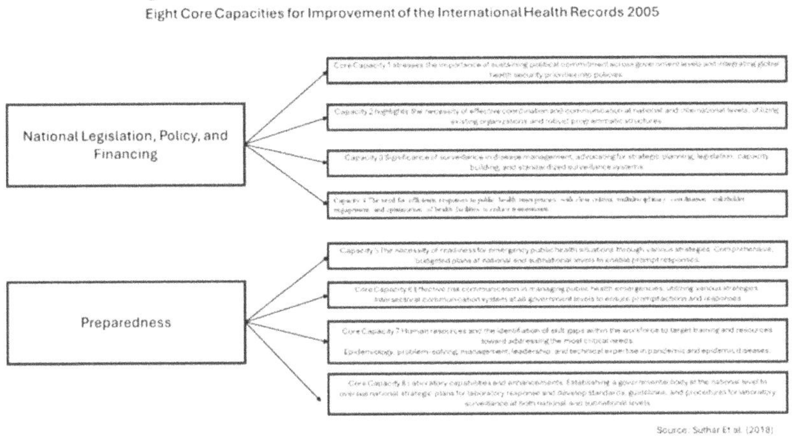

(Suthar et al., 2018)

Core capacities 5 to 8 address global preparedness and the need for substantial changes to the 2005 IRH (Figure 5). As presented by Suthar et al. (2018), this would include Core Capacity 5, which emphasizes the necessity of readiness for emergency public health situations through various strategies. This includes creating comprehensive, budgeted plans at national and subnational levels to enable prompt responses. Evaluating the implementation capacity of response plans through exercises, drills, assessments, and evaluations is essential to ensure their effectiveness. Also, maintaining a national stockpile of medicines, vaccines, and laboratory supplies is vital for efficiently managing public health emergencies (Suthar et al., 2018).

Core Capacity 6 underscores the importance of effective risk communication in managing public health emergencies, employing various strategies. This includes establishing an intersectoral communication system across government levels to ensure prompt responses and connecting with national and international partners for information exchange (Suthar et al. (2018). Regular dissemination of information to stakeholders helps maintain robust communication channels, supported by standard operating procedures to ensure personnel readiness for emerging epidemics and early warning system activation. This is also where the implementation of Electronic

Health Records could be incorporated to slow the spread of disease. Utilizing diverse media enhances information accessibility.

Core Capacity 7 highlights the significance of human resources and suggests multiple approaches for improvement. This involves identifying workforce skill gaps and targeting training to address critical needs like epidemiology and leadership. Adapting training methods to suit cultural contexts enhances competency development, while oversight mechanisms sustain training efforts. Nationally agreed-upon recruitment, training, and retention strategies can enhance competency development across all healthcare levels. Core Capacity 8 stresses the importance of laboratory capabilities. It offers strategies for enhancement, including establishing a governmental body for oversight, utilizing reference laboratories, implementing accreditation criteria, and improving training and communication between national and subnational levels. Instituting specific policies for high-containment biosafety laboratories ensures safety and efficacy in testing (Suthar et al. 2018).

CONCLUSION

The COVID-19 pandemic underscored global vulnerabilities in pandemic preparedness and response, resulting in over one million deaths out of ninety-nine million cases in the United States and 3.4 million globally (WHO, 2021). Despite the World Health Organization's (WHO) declaration of the pandemic on March 11, 2020, as foreseen in the International Health Regulations (IHR) of 2005, the response remained reactive rather than proactive (deSouza, 2023). The WHO Health Emergencies Program, established in 2016, identified critical obstacles, including inadequate surveillance, monitoring, and risk management efforts, gaps in risk communication, and deficiencies in global healthcare systems (Merianos & Peiris, 2005; Broberg, 2020). The delay in China reporting the Virus to the WHO exacerbated the situation, allowing for unchecked spread globally (Gostin, 2021). The pandemic exposed a "collapse in global solidarity," highlighting a lack of preparedness for a crisis of this scale (Gostin, 2021). While the IHR underwent significant revision in 2005, shifting from reactive to proactive measures, its implementation faced challenges, particularly ensuring all countries met core capacity requirements (Merianos & Peiris, 2005; Broberg, 2020). Despite progress, disparities in health and economic development hindered full compliance. The 2005 revision aimed to address modern infectious threats and enhance global coordination, yet it fell short in effectively managing the COVID-19 crisis (Merianos & Peiris, 2005).

REFERENCES

Aleem, A., Akbar Samad, A. B., & Vaqar, S. (2023, May 8) Emerging variants of SARS-CoV-2, and novel therapeutics against Coronavirus (COVID-19). In: StatPearls [Internet]. Treasure Island (F.L.): StatPearls Publishing; 2024 Jan–. PMID: 34033342.

Broberg, M. (2020). A critical appraisal of the World Health Organization's International Health Regulations (2005) in Times of Pandemic: It Is Time for Revision. *European Journal of Risk Regulation: EJRR, 11*(2), 202–209. DOI: 10.1017/err.2020.26

CDC. (2023). Summary of Variant Surveillance Str https://covid.cdc.gov/covid-data-tracker/#variant-summary

de Souza, L. E. P. F., de Castro, M. C., Hage Carmo, E., & Polidoro, M. (2022). December 31). The global failure of facing the pandemic. *Global Health Action, 15*(1). Advance online publication. DOI: 10.1080/16549716.2022.2124645 PMID: 36285582

Global Covid-19 Response (Reactive vs Proactive) IHR 1969 vs IHR 2005, proactive to reactive? *International Health Regulations (1969)*. (1982, January 1). PAHO/WHO | Pan American Health Organization. https://www.paho.org/en/documents/international-health-regulations-1969

Gostin, L. O. (2021). The Coronavirus Pandemic 1 Year On—What Went Wrong? *Journal of the American Medical Association, 325*(12), 1132–1133. DOI: 10.1001/jama.2021.3207 PMID: 33755061

Johns Hopkins University. (2023). Covid-19 data timeline through 2023.0 https://coronavirus.jhu.edu/region/united-states

Katella, K. (2023). *Omicron, Delta, Alpha, and more: What to know about the Coronavirus Variants*. Yale Medicine.

Merianos, A., & Peiris, M. (2005). International Health Regulations (2005). *Lancet, 366*(9493), 1249–1251. DOI: 10.1016/S0140-6736(05)67508-3 PMID: 16214586

Relman, D. A., Chofnes, E. R., & Mack, A. (2010, January 1). *Infectious Disease Movement in a Borderless World: Workshop Summary*. The National Academies Press. https://nap.nationalacademies.org/read/12758/chapter/6

Suthar, A. B., Allen, L. G., Cifuentes, S., Dye, C., & Nagata, J. M. (2018). Lessons learnt from implementation of the International Health Regulations: A systematic review. *Bulletin of the World Health Organization*, *96*(2), 110–121E. https://doi-org.library.capella.edu/10.2471/BLT.16.189100 PMID: 29403114

World Health Organization. (n.d.). *The true death toll of COVID-19 estimating global excess mortality*. World Health Organization. https://www.who.int/data/stories/the-true-death-toll-of-covid-19-estimating-global-excess-mortality The World Health Organization (1983) International Hth Regulation 1969 Regulations 1969 3rd ed.

APPENDIX

Chapter 2 Study Questions

1. What were the major successes and shortcomings of the global response to COVID-19, and how did the revisions to the 2005 International Health Regulations impact these efforts?
2. How did the different variants of COVID-19, such as Delta, Alpha, Gamma, Beta, and Omicron, influence the global pandemic response strategies and outcomes?
3. What were the primary obstacles identified by the WHO Health Emergencies Program in tackling COVID-19, and how did these obstacles contribute to the spread of the virus?
4. How did the delay in reporting the COVID-19 outbreak by China affect the global spread and management of the pandemic, and what lessons can be learned from this for future pandemic preparedness?
5. What are the key recommendations for improving multinational electronic health records interoperability, and how can these improvements enhance global health security and pandemic preparedness?

Chapter 3
Basics of Complexity Theory

ABSTRACT

This chapter deepens the exploration of complexity theory by focusing on its application across diverse organizational contexts, including but not limited to global health systems. Rather than viewing complexity as a barrier, the discussion reframes it as a vital resource for innovation, particularly when organizations face unpredictable challenges. The analysis highlights how complexity theory supports decentralized decision-making, flexible system architecture, and adaptive leadership models. In the case of Electronic Health Records (EHR), the theory encourages the development of modular, interoperable platforms that can evolve with shifting global demands. It also emphasizes the value of cultural intelligence and system resilience, particularly when operating across international boundaries. The chapter further evaluates case-based implementations and policy-level insights, offering guidance for integrating complexity principles into strategic planning and system design. This discussion shows that embracing complexity enables more responsive, equitable, and sustainable solutions.

INTRODUCTION

Complexity theory in organizations, also known as complexity strategy or complex adaptive organizations, applies insights from the study of complex systems to strategic management and organizational studies. The theory "is "the scientific study of systems with many interacting parts that exhibit a global behavior not reducible to the interactions between the individual constituent parts" (Thietart & Forgues, 2011, p. 53). It draws upon research from natural sciences that explores uncertainty and nonlinear dynamics. Emphasizing interactions and feedback loops, complexity

DOI: 10.4018/979-8-3693-2027-3.ch003

theory highlights the continuous evolution of systems. While it suggests that systems are unpredictable, they are also governed by rules that generate order.

In strategic management and organizational studies, complexity theory finds application in understanding how organizations or firms adapt to their environments and navigate uncertainty. Organizations are characterized by dynamic networks of interactions rather than mere aggregations of static entities. They exhibit adaptive behaviors, where individual and collective actions evolve and self-organize in response to micro-events or sequences of events that trigger change.

COMPLEXITY THEORY

Modern organizations operate within increasingly complex and dynamic social systems. Even before the onset of the COVID-19 pandemic, they faced challenges posed by disruptive technologies, blurred organizational boundaries, and rapidly evolving customer demands (Pavlov & Micheli, 2023). These conditions have pushed conventional management theories and frameworks to their boundaries, especially concerning organizational performance management, encompassing strategies to enhance process efficiency and overall organizational performance through implementing performance measurement systems that facilitate gathering, analyzing, and disseminating pertinent data.

Several complexity features are considered when applying Complexity Theory (McGuire, 2011), beginning with the understanding that complex systems are diverse systems (Figure 1).

Figure 1. McGuire's features of complex systems

McGuire (2011) Constructing and appreciating complexity

- ✓ Complex systems consist of a large number of diverse elements
- ✓ These elements interact dynamically
- ✓ Interactions are rich: elements can influence each other
- ✓ Interactions are nonlinear
- ✓ Interactions are typically short-range
- ✓ Interactions have positive and negative feedback loops
- ✓ Complex systems are open to their environment
- ✓ Complex systems operate under conditions far from equilibrium
- ✓ Complex systems have histories
- ✓ Individual elements are typically ignorant of the behavior of the system as a whole

Pavlov and Micheli (2023) suggest that to understand the importance of Complexity Theory, two insights should be considered, "the view of organizations as complex systems and the understanding of organizational performance as an emergent property of these systems. Organizations have long been recognized as complex systems" (p. 903). The authors argue that organizational performance cannot be reduced to the sum of individual or team efforts. While individuals and teams constitute an organization, their contributions do not directly translate into collective organizational performance. Instead, the ongoing interactions among them shape the organizational-level performance outcomes.

The Complexity Theory body of knowledge is shaped by four main theories, which include Systems Theory, Chaos Theory, Network Theory, and Adaptive Systems Theory (Figure 2).

Figure 2. Theories associated with complexity theory

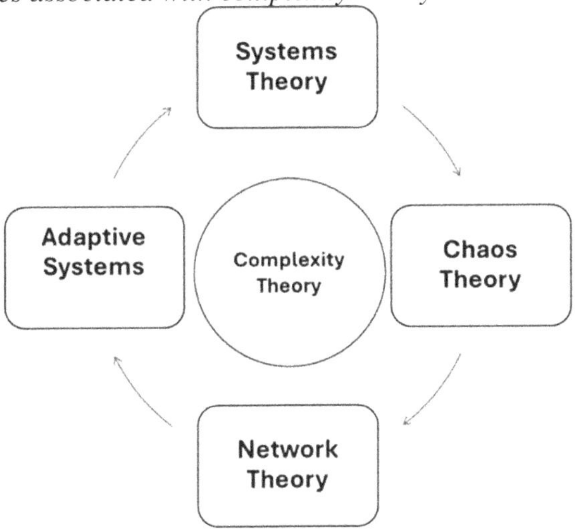

Systems Theory

Often referred to as the foundation of Complexity Theory, Systems Theory explores concepts of self-organization and adaptability. Systems Theory significantly contributes to our understanding of Complexity Theory in computer science. Systems theory sees environments as open and closed systems (Bustamante-Ubilla & Arenas-Torres,2022).

Figure 3. Systems theory and complexity theory

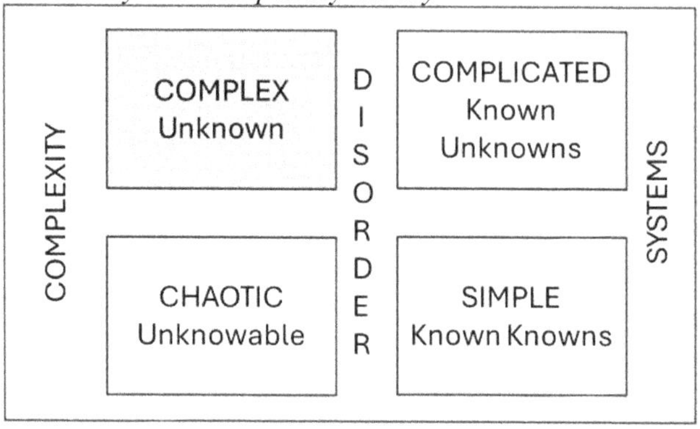

(adapted from Turner, 2019)

In systems theory, the term 'environment' refers to all entities whose attributes affect the system or are influenced by the system's actions (Hall & Fagen, 1956). According to Ackoff (1981), every social system operates within an environment that encompasses three levels of purpose: its purpose, the purposes of its parts, and the overarching purpose of the supra-system to which it belongs, prompting the question of how systems thinkers define social reality in terms of systems and their environments. Observers within systems science view themselves as integral parts of the social systems they study (Ackoff, 1981). When conducting a systems analysis of a problem or situation, they examine the problem rather than starting with a predetermined model. Once they identify and describe the problem, they analyze the subsystems within the system and consider the broader external environment.

An open system interacts with its environment, a concept emphasized in systems theory as the most prevalent type. This universality arises because anything can be conceptualized as a system. For instance, a business functions as an organizational system, while society can be viewed as a system (Bustamante-Ubilla & Arenas-Torres, 2022). In observing a business, one considers it the overarching system with its departments as subsystems. Similarly, a country represents a more extensive system within which organizations like businesses serve as subsystems.

Given that most organizations, whether businesses or others depend on varying degrees on their external environments, they are classified as open systems. Such entities rely on their environments for inputs, labor resources, and product markets. Even nationally, countries operate as open systems by engaging in international trade.

In contrast, a closed system has minimal interaction with its external environment. According to systems theory, closed systems are rare because it is challenging for any entity to function independently of its surroundings (Bustamante-Ubilla & Arenas-Torres,2022). While its internal subsystems remain interdependent and interact continuously, the system operates independently and self-sufficiently without relying on external inputs. This independence can lead to limitations, such as constraints on resources. A closed system exemplifies autarky, where minimal exchange occurs between it and external systems.

Chaos Theory

Chaos Theory, focusing on nonlinear systems that exhibit random behavior with underlying causes, elucidates concepts like feedback loops and system behavior (Englund, 2009). This theory embodies a positive sense of unpredictability and disorder, essential for renewal and revitalization, showing how slight changes in initial conditions can lead to significant outcomes, resonating across scales through fractal geometry. Applied in organizations as complexity science (Lewin & Regine, 2000), it underscores information sharing as a central organizing force, advocates for fostering diverse relationships, and recognizes vision as a powerful but intangible influencer. It emphasizes collaboration as a profound source of meaning and purpose, facilitating the establishment of a collective organizational purpose.

These principles guide organizational behavior by fostering conditions that promote interpersonal connections critical for innovation and problem-solving. Despite challenges such as limited in-person meetings, creating opportunities for people to come together and build relationships is crucial. Initiating project start-up meetings is pivotal as they enable team members to understand each other's strengths and goals, facilitating stages of team development (Englund, 2009). Valuing diversity is essential for nurturing groundbreaking ideas. Moreover, addressing people's need for purpose through a transparent, enduring purpose statement, like leading continuous improvement in project management across the company, enhances motivation and alignment. Crafting a vision statement outlining desired future practices for project success encourages ongoing improvement and excellence in project management by identifying, documenting, understanding, adopting, adapting, and applying best practices.

Two essential ideas are associated with Chaos and Complexity theories. First, change and creativity cannot occur without experiencing chaos. Second, inability is desirable in a system or organization, as it fosters Change and higher levels of functioning (Polifko, 2007).

Figure 4. Chaos theory and complexity theory

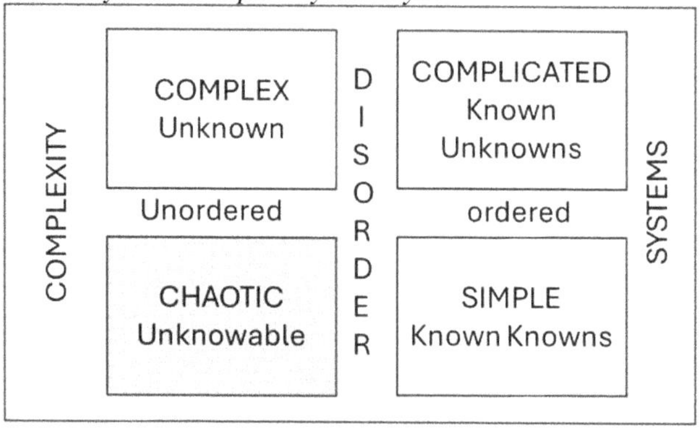

(adapted from Turner, 2019)

Complexity sciences encompass various process-oriented fields of study that delve into nonlinear dynamics within intricate systems (Wahl, 2019). A straightforward definition of a complex system includes any system with more than three interacting variables, making complexity a prevalent characteristic of our world. As shown in Figure 4, chaos is unknowable but can be moved to the simple with the proper steps.

In discussions about chaos theory, it is crucial to clarify that chaos does not denote complete disorder but rather "refers to an underlying interconnectedness that exists in apparently random events" (Briggs & Peat, 1999, p. 2). Briggs and Peat elaborate that chaos science focuses on uncovering hidden patterns, nuances, and the sensitivity of systems, exploring how unpredictability can lead to innovation.

Chaos theory offers a markedly different approach to understanding complex dynamics, challenging the limitations of reductionistic and mechanistic analyses rooted in linear cause-and-effect relationships within complex systems.

Network Theory

Unlike theoretical models, Network Theory relies on real-world data to understand complex systems. It encompasses studies of global supply chains, communication networks, and social networks, providing practical insights into interconnected systems. According to Schirmer et al. (2023), network theory is an increasingly popular field in contemporary science, with diverse applications in social interactions, economics, recipes, and gene-disease associations. Familiar concepts like the "six degrees of separation" highlight its relevance. In 1969, Travers and Milgram conducted a seminal experiment demonstrating that a message could traverse a social network with surprisingly few intermediaries. In a global context, specifically looking at the possibilities of pandemic prevention, Network theory offers a complex yet logical view of actions that can be taken at the onset to prevent the spread of disease.

However, what exactly constitutes a network? At its core, a network can be understood as a collection of objects linked together. These objects could represent humans, products, ingredients, diseases, or brain regions, while the links signify relationships or structural connections. Mathematically, each object is a node, and the links are edges in a graph or network.

Graphs depict networks using nodes (represented as circles) and edges (represented as arrows), where edges may have directionality and weight. Directionality mirrors relationships (e.g., who is friends with whom), while weight indicates the strength of these connections, reflecting differing perceptions in social networks. Nodes within a network can be characterized by their degree, which counts the number of edges connected to them. For instance, a node might have incoming and outgoing edges, distinguishing between in-degree and out-degree. Alternatively, networks can be simplified by disregarding directionality, focusing solely on the number of connections each node has. Beyond degree, various measures describe nodes or entire networks, providing insights into their structure and behavior. These measures are crucial in understanding complex networks in vast systems such as the human brain, which consists of billions of neurons connected by trillions of synapses.

Complexity theory and Network theory share three main elements: (a) both networks and complex systems consist of multiple interdependent components (actors or agents); (b) they exhibit relatively stable patterns of relationships, although complex systems are described with more dynamic terms; and (c) they are characterized by self-organization (Morçö & Wachhaus, 2009). Complex adaptive systems add two additional crucial elements: Change and emergence. Complexity theory focuses more on system dynamics, while network studies emphasize stability. Complex systems also possess emergent and holistic properties that are not observable in their components. While each common element and the unique aspects of complex systems merit detailed analysis, our discussion will concentrate on selected themes with significant potential for integration: stability versus change, self-organization, and uncertainties in knowledge processes.

As presented by Morçö and Wachhaus (2009), network theorists recognize networks' complexity and dynamic nature. However, some also acknowledge the limitations of network theories in fully explaining how Change occurs. These dynamic interactions lie at the heart of complexity theorists' frameworks, which, akin to earlier systems theories, view systems as compositions of structures and processes (Capra, 1996, p. 42).

Complexity theorists advance upon systems theory by refining the understanding of structure-process transformations through concepts such as nonlinearity and dissipative structures. Nonlinearity, originating from mathematics, describes disproportionate relationships between variables where a slight change in one can lead to a significant, disproportionate change in another concept contrasting with the linear cause-effect assumptions often prevalent in policymaking (Perrow, 1986, pp. 146-154). Prigogine and Stengers (1984) pioneered the Dissipative Structure Theory, which posits that natural open systems tend towards dynamic, far-from-equilibrium conditions rather than stable equilibria. Under these conditions, systems exhibit nonlinear behaviors and may undergo bifurcations, potentially leading to new, higher-order structures through self-organization (Morçö & Wachhaus, 2009). In conjunction with Network theory, Complexity theory brings a dynamic and evolutionary viewpoint to the study of networks. It enriches our understanding of how structures and processes transform by introducing concepts such as nonlinearity and dissipative structures. Furthermore, complexity theorists offer methodological tools like agent-based simulations to explore these dynamics in depth.

Figure 5. Global network illustration

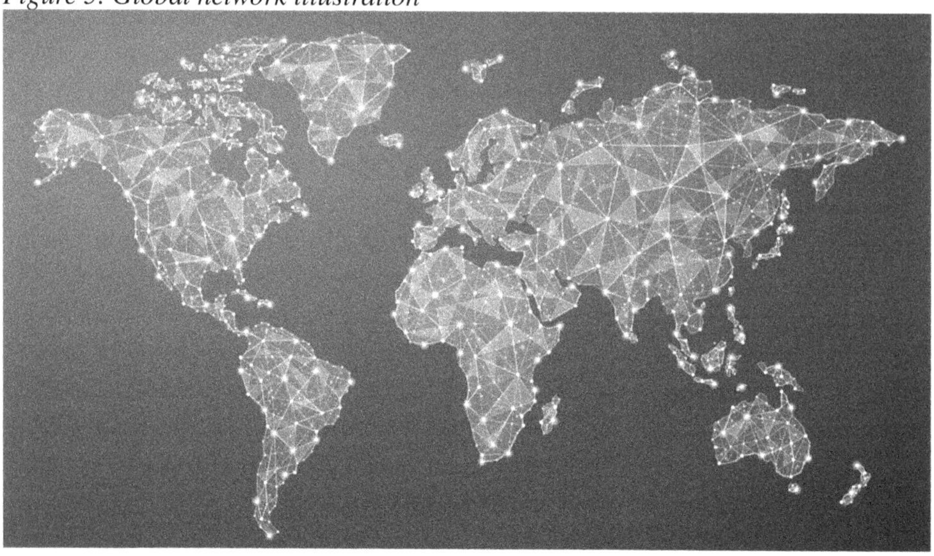

(Dreamstime.com)

Of all the theories associated with Complexity theory, Network theory provides a foundation for a global application of electronic health records, which includes a network of countries, cities, organizations, and people.

Adaptive Systems Theory – Adaptive Self-Organization Theory

The final theory associated with Complexity theory is Adaptive Systems Theory, which examines how systems react and adapt to the behaviors of other elements within the system. Complex adaptive systems would take place globally to implement electronic health records successfully. As argued by Borghi et al. (2022), globalization has changed the world in terms of addressing global health in a way that protects and prevents the spread of disease. This is due to increased travel and global interactions did not address only 25 years ago. Today, however, is a different story, and to prevent pandemics such as COVID-19, systems throughout the globe need to be restructured and built so that everyone is protected. Borghi argues that this can be done by applying complex adaptive systems (CAS) in conjunction with system thinking (p. 1147).

Understanding complex adaptive systems (CAS) is important to appreciate the potential. A CAS is composed of interconnected elements that operate with a specific purpose. A defining feature of CAS is the emphasis on these interconnections among its elements, highlighting their adaptability in response to changing conditions. CASs are characterized by self-organization, where the properties of individual elements and their relationships can give rise to entirely new behaviors within the system, a phenomenon known as emergence. These systems are dynamic, as their elements learn, adapt, and evolve, influenced by interactions, past behaviors, and external environmental factors (Borghi et al., 2022).

The Global Health System (GHS) serves as an example of a complex system due to several critical factors: the involvement of numerous global health actors, the extensive networks that link them, and their interconnections with other sectors such as food, trade, and the environment (Borghi et al., 2022). While Borghi et al. (2022) focused their research on vaccinations, the underlying concepts can be applied to EHRs by incorporating hierarchical multi-level systems; CAS properties manifest across various levels, both higher and lower, each demonstrating characteristics that depend on its position within the system (Borghi et al., 2022).

To incorporate appropriate CAS, global power must be understood through the lens of "physical, economic, structural, institutional, moral, expertise, discursive, and network" (Moon, 2019; p. 5). For example, physical considerations include military powers and economic status, such as wealth. Not all countries are part of an even playing field. Government and leadership, as well as non-government organizations, will impact CAS. Additionally, moral differences and religious beliefs may create problems in networking through complex systems. Even "academics, scientists, and lawyers" can steer processes in specific directions that can prevent adaptation (Moon, 2019; p. 5). Power is only one aspect of determining if CAS can be applied globally. Janssen (1998) argued that most CAS global applications tend to fail but suggested that modeling could be one way to incorporate CAS globally. Building on the Holling (1986) adaptive cycle model, Figure 6 provides an overview of adaptation, showing Gunderson and Holling's adaptive cycle as a descriptive framework for understanding the evolution of dynamic and complex systems. According to this metaphor, complex systems cyclically transition between phases characterized by stability and predictability and phases marked by reorganization and stochasticity.

Figure 6. Hollan 1986 adaptive cycle model

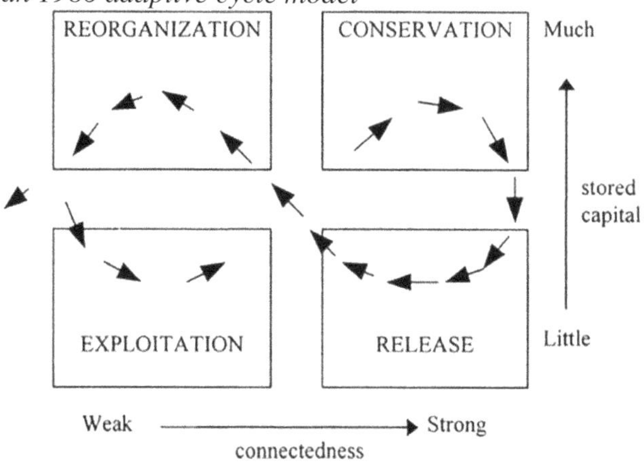

A COMMON THREAD OF SELF-ORGANIZING

Growing interest is in comprehending the dynamics of self-organizing systems, driven by the need to navigate rising complexity and sustainably manage these systems. This interest spans various critical societal domains, including addressing climate change, managing economic crises, and adapting to digital transformation, or, in this case, a global solution to the spread of disease. A significant challenge in managing such complex systems, where agents interact, is bridging the gap between qualitative theories that describe system evolution and quantitative methods capable of accurately assessing these systems' current state and trajectory. As stated by Do (2012), with self-organization, "emergence" represents the interactions between individuals and is essential in understanding how we address systems in response to situations stemming from the simplest, such as a traffic jam, to the most essential, a global pandemic. Self-organizing systems require "collective order" to function. Specifically, Do states, "It is conceivable that combining network science with concepts from statistical physics and methods from nonlinear dynamics can lead to a detailed analytical understanding of emergence that will prove essential for the future analysis and design of complex self-organizing systems" (p. ix). One way to embrace self-organization is to understand how it can be utilized in a situation that leads to a dynamic critical state.

Patterns of cooperation are built on the social structure that evolves through collaborative behaviors (Do, 2012), suggesting that cooperative behaviors in terms of a critical state rely on proactively building collaboration between individuals, communities, and nations. For example, a population of N individuals, such as people, firms, or nations, participates in bilateral collaborative interactions to address a critical situation. Each interaction adheres to a continuous snowdrift game (Do, 2012; p. 29), a fundamental model in game theory. In this setup, an agent "I" can allocate several resources (time, money, effort) to collaborate with another agent "j."

Cooperative investments yield equal benefits BBB to both parties but incur a cost CCC for the investing agent. Essential to this ideology is the collaboration and cooperation between communities and nations focusing on the shared common good. To accomplish this, synchronization must occur within and between the systems.

THE HOFSTEDE MODEL

The Hofstede Model constructs five cultural dimensions, including the Power Distance Index, Individualism vs. collectivism, Masculinity Vs. Femininity; Uncertainty Avoidance Indes, Long Term Vs. Short Term Normative Orientation, and a sixth dimension identified as Indulgence Vs. Restraint.

Power-Distance Index

The Power-Distance Index measures the extent to which individuals with less authority are in an organization or institution. For example, families who accept and expect an unequal distribution of power. While inequality exists in every society, Hofstede notes that some societies display significantly greater equality than others (Hofstede. 1980, 1991).

In high power-distance cultures, hierarchies are accepted as natural, with individuals believing everyone has a defined position that does not require explanation. In contrast, low power-distance cultures strive for a more balanced distribution of authority. These societies promote consultative, democratic, and egalitarian relationships (Hofstede. 1980, 1991).

For example, in low power-distance cultures, parents are more likely to accept open discussions or disagreements with their children. Similarly, workplaces foster environments where employees at all levels expect to provide input, and managers actively seek their perspectives. On the other hand, high-power-distance cultures tend to emphasize unquestioning obedience to authority. Parents expect compliance from children, and subordinates regularly display deference to superiors. In such workplaces, decisions are typically made by those at the top, with little input from lower levels. The emphasis on status and hierarchy in high power-distance societies creates a marked distinction from the more egalitarian approaches of low power-distance cultures (Hofstede. 1980, 1991).

Collectivism vs. Individualism

The distinction between individualism and collectivism reflects how individuals relate to groups within their society. In individualistic societies, personal achievement and self-reliance are prioritized, with individuals focusing on their needs and those of their immediate family. Identity is rooted in the "I." Conversely, collectivist cultures value the well-being and goals of the group above individual interests, shaping a self-image aligned with the "We" (Hofstede, 1980, 1991).

People in collectivist societies place a higher emphasis on relationships and loyalty. They may belong to fewer groups but derive much of their identity from those associations. Additionally, communication in individualistic cultures is often more direct, while in collectivist cultures, it tends to be more nuanced and indirect (Hofstede. 1980, 1991).

Uncertainty Avoidance Index

The Uncertainty Avoidance Index measures how societies handle uncertainty and ambiguity. This dimension examines the extent to which people attempt to minimize unpredictability. At its core, it reflects how cultures perceive and respond to Change or the unknown. High uncertainty avoidance indicates a low tolerance for ambiguity, with individuals and institutions striving for stability through strict rules, regulations, and structured environments. Such cultures may also display higher levels of emotionality.

In contrast, low uncertainty avoidance cultures embrace change and unstructured situations, favoring flexibility and minimal regulation. These societies are more comfortable with ambiguity and tolerate a lack of definitive answers (Hofstede. 1980, 1991). For instance, in a low uncertainty avoidance culture, students may find it acceptable for a teacher to admit they do not know the answer. At the same time, this might be less acceptable in high uncertainty avoidance cultures.

Femininity vs. Masculinity

The femininity vs. masculinity dimension explores how societies traditionally value masculine or feminine traits. Masculine societies prioritize assertiveness, competitiveness, and achievement. Feminine societies, on the other hand, emphasize nurturing, cooperation, and quality of life. A society with a high femininity score will prioritize policies supporting caregiving roles, such as generous maternity leave and affordable childcare. In contrast, societies with lower femininity scores often see more women in leadership roles and higher levels of female entrepreneurship, reflecting a reduced emphasis on traditional gender roles (Hofstede. 1980, 1991).

Short-Term vs. Long-Term Orientation

This dimension reflects how cultures balance immediate needs with future goals. Long-term-oriented cultures emphasize perseverance, thrift, and planning for long-term success. They are willing to delay immediate rewards to achieve more significant outcomes in the future. Short-term-oriented societies focus more on immediate results, valuing tradition, quick achievements, and the present moment, often leading to spending patterns driven by social or environmental pressures. Long-term orientation encourages patience and forward-thinking, while short-term orientation emphasizes tradition and immediate gratification (Hofstede. 1980, 1991).

Restraint vs. Indulgence

This dimension assesses how societies regulate the fulfillment of desires. Indulgent cultures allow individuals to freely satisfy their needs and prioritize enjoyment, leisure, and luxury. In contrast, restrained cultures emphasize self-discipline, saving, and practicality, often curbing gratification through societal norms. For example, people in indulgent societies might spend more on leisure activities and luxuries, while those in restrained societies prioritize frugality and essential needs (Hofstede, 1980, 1991, 2010, 2011).

Table 1. Hofstede's model and HER

Hofstede's Six Dimensions and EHR

Power Distance Index	**high power-distance cultures** - Top Down Flow of Information **low power-distance cultures** - Vertical Flow of Information
Collectivism vs. Individualism	**individualistic cultures** - may prioritize patient autonomy collectivist cultures - shared access, community centered
Uncertainty Avoidance Index	**high uncertainty avoidance cultures** - extensive guidelines, strict protocols, and robust security features to reduce ambiguity **low uncertainty avoidance cultures** - flexibility and ease of use
Femininity vs. Masculinity	**high masculinity orientation cultures** prioritize competitive outcomes, performance metrics, efficiency focused workflows **feminine-oriented cultures** - patient care, nurturing interactions, and quality-of-life improvements
Short Term vs. Long-Term Orientation	**Long-term oriented cultures** - future healthcare needs, predictive analytics, preventive care and resource conservation **short-term oriented cultures** - immediate results, streamlined workflows, rapid diagnosis
Restraint vs. Indulgence	**indulgent cultures** - user-friendly interfaces, enhanced patient engagement and satisfaction **restrained cultures** - practicality and compliance, adherence to rules and protocols

Table 2 provides the application of Hofstede's six dimensions to EHR. Using Hofstede's cultural dimensions in electronic health records (EHRs) reveals how cultural values influence their design, implementation, and adoption. For example, in high power-distance cultures, the hierarchical nature of decision-making may lead to EHR systems with top-down workflows, where only senior healthcare professionals have full access and decision-making capabilities. Conversely, in low power-distance cultures, EHRs incorporate features that encourage input from all levels of healthcare providers, fostering collaboration. Similarly, individualistic cultures may prioritize patient autonomy by integrating features that allow individuals to control and access their medical records directly.

In contrast, collectivist cultures may emphasize shared access, facilitating a more community-centered approach to healthcare. In high uncertainty avoidance societies, EHR systems will include extensive guidelines, strict protocols, and robust security features to reduce ambiguity. In contrast, low uncertainty avoidance cultures might focus on flexibility and ease of use.

In societies with a high masculinity orientation, EHR systems may prioritize competitive outcomes, such as performance metrics for healthcare professionals and efficiency-focused workflows. Conversely, feminine-oriented cultures may design EHRs to emphasize patient care, nurturing interactions, and quality-of-life improvements, such as features that support holistic treatment plans. Long-term-oriented societies might develop EHR systems focusing on future healthcare needs, incorporating predictive analytics and features that encourage preventive care and resource conservation. In contrast, short-term-oriented cultures may prioritize immediate results, such as streamlined workflows for rapid diagnosis and treatment, potentially valuing efficiency over long-term adaptability. Similarly, indulgent societies might design EHR systems with user-friendly interfaces and features that enhance patient engagement and satisfaction. At the same time, restrained cultures may focus on practicality and compliance, favoring systems that enforce strict adherence to rules and protocols. Understanding these cultural dimensions enables the tailoring of EHR systems to align with societal values, improving their acceptance and effectiveness in diverse healthcare environments.

THE GLOBE MODEL

The GLOBE researchers identified nine cultural dimensions, building on Hofstede's foundational work. Five of these dimensions align closely with Hofstede's findings: uncertainty avoidance, power distance, future orientation (valuing long-term planning), assertiveness orientation (similar to masculinity), and gender egalitarianism (similar to femininity). They also introduced two unique dimensions: performance orientation, which emphasizes achievement and excellence, and humane orientation, reflecting the importance placed on fairness, altruism, and care. For example, gender egalitarianism assesses the degree to which a society minimizes gender inequality. While Russia scores low in valuing gender equality, its practices often contradict this, with women holding many positions of power (House et al., 2004; Javidan et al., 2006). In contrast, the U.S. highly values gender equality but practices lag, as men still dominate leadership roles.

Power distance reflects how much a society accepts authority and inequality; for instance, Russia shows high power distance in its organizational culture, with strict respect for hierarchy, whereas the U.S. values lower power distance but often practices otherwise. In-group collectivism emphasizes loyalty and cohesiveness within groups, as seen in Russia, where in-groups are distinct and integral, compared to the U.S., which scores moderately. Performance orientation focuses on rewarding achievement, with the U.S. and China scoring high in practice, though the U.S. values it more than it practices. Uncertainty avoidance measures reliance on rules to manage unpredictability, as evidenced by China's high score and the U.S.'s moderate score. Institutional collectivism relates to how organizations reward collective action in cultures like China (House et al., 2004; Javidan et al., 2006). Future orientation emphasizes planning and delayed gratification, a value seen in the U.S., where moderate practices support long-term goals. Humane orientation captures how societies encourage fairness and altruism, with the U.S. valuing it highly but practicing it moderately. Assertiveness, which reflects directness and confrontation in communication, varies globally, with some cultures prioritizing harmony and others unapologetically.

The GLOBE study also examined leadership styles across seven cultural clusters—Anglo, Confucian Asia, Germanic Europe, Latin America, Middle East,

Nordic Europe, and Sub-Saharan Africa—based on six leadership profiles: charismatic (inspiring and motivating others), team-oriented (building effective teams), participative (involving others in decisions), humane-oriented (showing compassion and generosity), autonomous (independent and individualistic leadership), and self-protective (focusing on self-interest and face-saving). Preferences for leadership styles varied by cluster, reflecting cultural priorities (House et al., 2004; Javidan et al., 2006). For instance, charismatic and team-oriented leadership were more valued in Anglo cultures, while Confucian Asia emphasized humane-oriented leadership, consistent with their respective cultural values. The GLOBE framework's strength lies in its ability to group societies with shared characteristics, providing insights into how cultural dimensions shape leadership preferences worldwide.

Table 2. Globe model and HER

Globe Dimensions and their Impact on HER Systems		
Globe Dimension	**High Impact on EHR**	**Low Impact on EHR**
Uncertainty Avoidance	Strict rules and protocols, risk aversion	Flixible and experiemental approaches
Power Distance	Centralized Decision-making	Participatory decision-making
Future Orientation	Investment in long-term EHR infrastructure	Short-term benefits priortized
Performance Orientation	Emphasis on efficency and performacne tracking	Basic needs over competitive metrics
Hamne Orientation	Patient-centered features and inclusivity	Operational efficiency over inclusivity
Gender Egalitarianism	Equal access and training for users	Disparities in access and usage
In-Group Collectivism	Focus on local networks and team collaboration	Individual-focused interoperability
Institutional Collectivism	Centralized, government-regulated systems	Fragmented systems with private roles
Assertiveness	Direct Communication and transparent Policies	Focus on harmony and minimizing conflict

As outlined in Table 3, cultural dimensions significantly influence the design, implementation, and adoption of Electronic Health Record (EHR) systems across different regions. High uncertainty avoidance cultures like China emphasize strict rules and protocols to minimize unpredictability. Low uncertainty avoidance cultures, like the U.S., favor flexible, adaptive approaches that may face resistance to Change. Power distance also plays a critical role: high power distance societies, exemplified by Russia, rely on top-down decision-making for EHR adoption, whereas low power distance cultures, such as Nordic Europe, involve diverse stakeholders in participatory planning. Future-oriented societies prioritize sustainable and scalable EHR investments, while performance-oriented cultures like the U.S. focus on efficiency and outcome tracking. Humane-oriented regions, such as Sub-Saharan Africa, value patient-centered care and inclusivity, with systems incorporating multilingual support and culturally sensitive interfaces.

As shown in Table 3, factors like gender egalitarianism and collectivism further shape EHR strategies. Cultures with high gender equality ensure equitable access to EHR systems for all users, while societies with strong in-group collectivism, like Russia, design systems favoring tightly integrated local networks over broader interoperability. Institutional collectivism, prominent in cultures like China, fosters centralized, government-regulated EHR frameworks, whereas more individualist societies favor fragmented, private-sector-led systems. Assertiveness impacts communication and enforcement, with high-assertiveness cultures prioritizing transparent data-sharing policies, while low-assertiveness societies focus on harmony, potentially compromising strict adherence to standards. These cultural dimensions, highlighted in Table 2, underscore the importance of tailoring EHR implementation to regional values and operational practices.

THE HOLONIC MODEL

The holonic enterprise model supports global virtual organizations by enabling autonomous management of information and resources interconnected via the internet (Koestler, 1967; 1978). Koestler's work explored the self-organizing behaviors of social and biological systems, introducing the term "holon" to define an entity that simultaneously functions as a self-sufficient unit and as a component of a more extensive system. In this sense, a holon exists as a whole and a subsystem within a more significant framework.

The holonic enterprise operates across three distinct levels:

Global Inter-Enterprise Collaborative Level

In business, enterprises form collaborative networks to produce goods or services. Traditionally, this structure is seen as a linear supply chain flowing from producer to customer. However, within the holonic enterprise model, each holon, supplier, or customer maximizes efficiency (Koestler, 1967; 1968).

Each holon operates independently while maintaining collaboration with the broader enterprise network. For instance, customers aim to engage with the most efficient and responsive suppliers, while suppliers seek partnerships with the most profitable customers. This dynamic interaction leads to the optimization of the entire inter-enterprise collaboration (Koestler, 1968).

Intra-Enterprise Level

Within each organization, resources must be structured to align with the needs of the more extensive collaborative system. Effective management at this level involves strategic planning and adaptable resource allocation, often requiring real-time adjustments (Koestler, 1967; 1978). For example, disruptions such as machine failures necessitate reallocating and reorganizing internal resources, ensuring the enterprise can continue meeting its commitments within the collaborative network.

Machine (Physical Agent) Level

The final level addresses the decentralized control of machines and systems performing operational tasks such as agile manufacturing processes, employing intelligent, self-reconfiguring automation components to ensure flexibility and responsiveness in production (Koestler, 1967; 1978).

By integrating these three levels, the holonic enterprise creates a dynamic, self-organizing system that enhances efficiency and adaptability within complex networks.

Figure 7. Holonic model and EHR

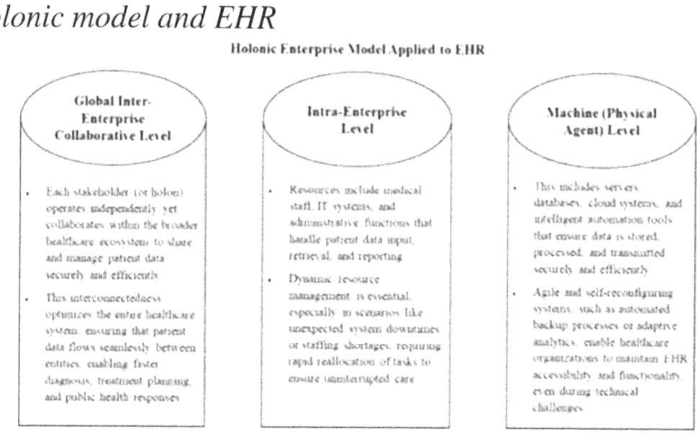

As shown in Figure 7, The holonic enterprise model can be effectively adapted to Electronic Health Records (EHR) systems, providing a framework for enhanced information sharing, resource management, and operational efficiency across the healthcare ecosystem. At the Global Inter-Enterprise Collaborative Level, the model supports a network of healthcare providers, insurers, laboratories, and public health organizations working together to share and manage patient data securely and efficiently. At the Intra-Enterprise Level, organizations such as hospitals, clinics, and specialized practices must strategically organize their internal resources—staff, IT systems, and workflows—to align with the broader EHR network's requirements.

Finally, at the Machine (Physical Agent) Level, the focus shifts to the decentralized control and integration of machines and software systems, including servers, databases, and intelligent automation tools, ensuring the EHR infrastructure's secure, efficient, and adaptive functionality. This integrated approach mirrors the principles of the colonic model, creating a dynamic and resilient EHR system.

Applying the holonic model to EHR systems fosters enhanced stakeholder collaboration, improving coordination and data accuracy and reducing redundancies across entities. It also enables resilience and adaptability, allowing organizations to dynamically address challenges such as system failures or surges in patient volume without disrupting care delivery. Furthermore, advanced automation and intelligent systems ensure secure and efficient data management, supporting scalability across diverse healthcare networks. This integration positions EHR systems as a self-organizing and adaptable ecosystem, aligning with the principles of the holonic enterprise model to enhance healthcare delivery and operational efficiency.

CONCLUSION

Complexity theory, grounded in systems science, explores how organizations navigate uncertainty and change through adaptive behaviors and emergent outcomes. It draws upon foundational theories—systems, chaos, network, and adaptive systems—highlighting the importance of nonlinear dynamics, feedback mechanisms, and self-organization. Organizational performance is understood as an emergent property resulting from dynamic interactions, emphasizing the need for adaptability in complex environments. Network theory provides practical insights into interconnected systems, while adaptive systems theory underscores the importance of resilience and global collaboration, particularly in healthcare.

Applying complexity theory to EHR systems underscores the necessity of tailoring designs to cultural and organizational contexts. The Holonic Enterprise Model offers a framework for managing information and resources within global EHR networks, focusing on three levels: collaborative networks among healthcare providers, internal resource management within organizations, and decentralized control of technological systems. This approach enables organizations to improve coordination, adapt to challenges, and ensure scalability. Combined with understanding cultural dimensions such as power distance, uncertainty avoidance, and collectivism, complexity theory fosters the development of resilient, efficient, and inclusive EHR systems that enhance healthcare delivery globally.

Complexity theory, grounded in systems, chaos, network, and adaptive systems theories, provides a comprehensive framework for understanding the dynamic, nonlinear, and emergent behaviors of modern organizations. It emphasizes the importance of feedback loops, adaptability, and self-organization in navigating uncertainty and disruption. Whether applied to global systems like Electronic Health Records or broader organizational structures, complexity theory underscores the value of innovative, emergent solutions over traditional linear approaches. Through models such as the Holonic Enterprise and cultural frameworks like Hofstede's dimensions and the GLOBE study, organizations can design adaptive, interconnected systems that reflect both local and global needs. By embracing principles of self-organization, network collaboration, and cultural sensitivity, leaders are better equipped to build resilient infrastructures that respond to crises and foster meaningful, sustainable changes in an increasingly complex world.

REFERENCES

Ackoff, R. L. (1981). *Creating the corporate future*. John Wiley & Sons.

Borghi, J., Ismail, S., Hollway, J., Kim, R. E., Sturmberg, J., Brown, G., Mechler, R., Volmink, H., Spicer, N., Chalabi, Z., Cassidy, R., Johnson, J., Foss, A., Koduah, A., Searle, C., Komendantova, N., Semwanga, A., & Moon, S. (2022). Viewing the global health system as a complex adaptive system - implications for research and practice [version1; peer review: 2 approved]. *F1000 Research*, *2022*(11), 1147. DOI: 10.12688/f1000research.126201.1 PMID: 37600221

Bustamante-Ubilla, M., & Arenas-Torres, F. (2022). Epistemological foundations of Complexity Theory. *Sustainability*, *14*(20), 13316. DOI: 10.3390/su142013316

Capra, F. (1996). *The web of life: A new scientific understanding of living systems*. Anchor Books.

Do, A.-L. (2012). *Self-Organization in Continuous Adaptive Networks*. River Publishers. *ProQuest Ebook Central*, https://ebookcentral-proquest-com.library.capella.edu/lib/capella/detail.action?docID=3400129

Englund, R. L. (2009). Applying chaos theory in a project-based organization. Paper presented at PMI® Global Congress 2009—EMEA, Amsterdam, North Holland, The Netherlands. Newtown Square, PA: Project Management Institute.

Hall, A.D., & Fagen, R.E. (1956). Definition of system. General Systems, Yearbook of the Society for General Systems Research (SGSR - now ISSS)

Hofstede, G. (1980a). Culture and organizations. *International Studies of Management & Organization*, *10*(4), 15–41.

Hofstede, G. (1980b). Culture's Consequences. *Sage (Atlanta, Ga.)*.

Hofstede, G. (1991). *Cultures and organizations: Software of the mind*. McGraw-Hill.

Hofstede, G. (2011). Dimensionalizing cultures: The Hofstede model in context. *Online Readings in Psychology and Culture*, *2*(1), 2307–0919.

Hofstede, G., & Minkov, M. (2010). Long-versus short-term orientation: New perspectives. *Asia Pacific Business Review*, *16*(4), 493–504.

Holling, C. S. (1986). The resilience of terrestrial ecosystems: local surprise and global Change. In: Clark, W.C., & Munn, R.E., editors. *Sustainable development of the biosphere*. Cambridge University Press/IIASA Laxenburg

House, R. J., Hanges, P. J., Javidan, M., Dorfman, P. W., & Gupta, V. (Eds.). (2004). *Culture, Leadership, and Organizations: The GLOBE Study of 62 Societies*. Sage.

Janssen, M. (1998). Use of complex adaptive systems for modeling global change. *Ecosystems (New York, N.Y.)*, *1*(5), 457–463. DOI: 10.1007/s100219900041

Javidan, M., Dorfman, P.W., de Luque, M.S., House, R.J. (2006). In the eye of the beholder: Cross-cultural lessons in leadership for project GLOBE. *The Academy of Management Perspectives*, February, *20*(1), pp. 67–90.

Koestler, A. (1967). *The ghost in the machine*. Arkana.

Koestler, A. (1978). *Janus: A summing up*. Random House.

Lewin, R., & Regine, B. (2000). *The soul at work: Listen…respond…let go*. Simon & Schuster.

Moon, S. (2019). Power in global governance: An expanded typology from global health. *Globalization and Health*, *15*(Suppl 1), 74. DOI: 10.1186/s12992-019-0515-5 PMID: 31775779

Pavlov, A., & Micheli, P. (2023). Rethinking organizational performance management: A complexity theory perspective. *International Journal of Operations & Production Management*, *43*(6), 899–915. DOI: 10.1108/IJOPM-08-2022-0478

Perrow, C. (1986). *Complex organizations: A critical essay* (3rd ed.). McGraw-Hill.

Polifko, K. A. (2007). *Concepts of the nursing profession*. Change Agent Leadership, Theories Transformational Leadership. Thomson Delmar Learning.

Schirmer, M., Arichi, T., & Chung, A. W. (2023). *Connectome analysis: Characterization, methods, and analysis*. Academic Press.

Thietart, R. A., & Forgues, B. (2011). Complexity science and organization. In Allen, P., Maguire, S., & McKelvey, S. (Eds.), *The Sage Handbook of Complexity and Management* (pp. 53–64). Sage.

Turner, J. R. (2019). Complexity Theory: An overview with potential applications for the social sciences. *Systems*, *7*(1), 4. DOI: 10.3390/systems7010004

Wahl, D. C. (2019). A brief history of systems science, chaos, and complexity. *Resilience*.

APPENDIX

Chapter 3 Study Questions

1. How does Complexity Theory differ from traditional management theories in explaining organizational performance, and what role do emergent properties play in this framework?
2. What are the key components of the Holonic Enterprise Model, and how can this model be adapted to improve the design and implementation of Electronic Health Records (EHR) systems?
3. How do cultural dimensions, as outlined in the GLOBE and Hofstede models, influence EHR systems' adoption, design, and functionality in different regions?
4. In what ways do systems theory, chaos theory, network theory, and adaptive systems theory contribute to our understanding of complex organizational dynamics and the implementation of global solutions like EHR?
5. What challenges and opportunities are associated with applying adaptive systems theory and self-organization principles to address global health crises, such as pandemics, through systems like EHR?

Chapter 4
Building Health-Oriented Organization Partnerships

ABSTRACT

This chapter examines the strategic formation of partnerships among health-oriented organizations—including ministries of health, NGOs, academic institutions, and multilateral agencies—to advance interoperable EHR systems. It highlights successful models of collaboration in resource-constrained settings and identifies key enablers such as trust, shared governance, and capacity-building. The chapter also critiques partnership failures rooted in power asymmetries and misaligned incentives, offering recommendations for equitable and sustainable engagement.

INTRODUCTION

As discussed in Chapter 1, the Ebola epidemic of 2014 that eventually resulted in America's first travel-associated case of the infection in Dallas, TX (Molinari et al., 2018; Sevilla, 2017); and the Covid-19 pandemic, that reached Seattle, WA, underscores that local public health systems, particularly in large international cities such as Dallas and Seattle, are vulnerable to foreign contagions, and that the term Global Burden of Disease (GBD) is not a casual term or misnomer, and is truly global regardless of the infections' point of origin and local public health systems must have contingencies for public health emergencies of international concern (PHEIC), such as outbreaks of unknown or nonindigenous diseases threaten global health (Turnock et al., 2022).

Five years post-Ebola, the Coronavirus disease pandemic of 2019 also revealed that zoonotic diseases at the local or public health level can, and often cross interna-

DOI: 10.4018/979-8-3693-2027-3.ch004

tional borders, creating examples of the importance of local outbreak preparedness for global health emergencies (Carter et al., 2024). Increases in global trade, travel, and immigration fueled by globalization expose local public health systems to global threats. Globalization allows access to foreign markets to provide goods and services to non-local societies (McCloskey, 2023). The current global population is 8.4 billion people. The population is projected to reach 9.8 billion by the year 2050 and, by the year 2100, 11 billion (Mishra et al., 2024). The global population will increase by 30 per cent over the next 76 years, increasing the need for goods and services, travel, and immigration. Globalization is growing, not declining, as economies in LMICs expand with the help of economic and multinational trade agreements, globalization is here to stay (Lincicome, 2023).

The global community comprises 8.4 billion people across an international family of 195 countries, 193 of which are recognized by the United Nations. The complexities of maintaining order by ending or preventing wars, addressing global problems such as climate change, and alleviating poverty in low-to-middle-income countries (LMIC) are, without question, high priorities, and international leaders must collaborate to overcome these traditional security concerns. However, while powerful and influential global leaders work vigilantly to solve conventional problems such as the war between Russia and Ukraine or the conflicts between Israel, Iran, and Hezbollah, a more significant security threat lurks among populations without regard to land ownership or religious affiliations. It is a threat to Muslims and Jews. The threat has no bias for or against military alliances such as NATO. The danger is fair and impartial, whether its prey is from the developed West or the developing Global South. The threat does not differentiate nor display any preference to G20 nations over the BRICS nations. It is an equal opportunity killer. It is resilient, resourceful, resistant, and resolute. The threat is one billionth our size and has taken more lives than all the world's wars combined. The danger is the disease, the most critical non-traditional threat to health security (Heymann & Rodier, 2004).

Globalization increases trade, logistics coordination, and immigration, and travel to large international cities, such as Seattle, WA and Dallas, TX. However, there is a gap in data-sharing between national and international health-oriented organizations with local public health systems in large cities such as Dallas and Seattle (Carter et al., 2024). Heyman and Rodier (2004) suggested that health security is the responsibility of local, national, and global leaders. The COVID-19 and Ebola pandemics began as public health emergencies; however, when there is a gap in data-sharing between national and international health-oriented organizations with local public health systems, airports, logistics systems in large international cities, outbreak preparedness for international contingencies suffers, the contagion will proliferate across international borders. Local or national public health emergencies become public health emergencies of international concern (PHEIC) (Carter et al., 2024). Therefore, outbreak preparedness in public health systems for large international cities must include partnerships with health-oriented organizations to develop strategies to respond to outbreaks from both national and international organizations, such as the World Health Organization (WHO) and the Centers for Disease and Prevention (CDC).

HEALTH-ORIENTED ORGANIZATION PARTNERSHIPS; THE WORLD HEALTH ORGANIZATION (WHO) & THE CENTERS FOR DISEASE CONTROL AND PREVENTIONS (CDC)

The World Health Organization (WHO)

The World Health Organization (WHO) is a global health organization with the United Nations (UN) system. The WHO declares outbreaks, PHEICs, global pandemics, and collaborates and exchange data with nations to monitor health crisis and manage global health initiatives such as increased diseased surveillance. When a disease outbreak occurs, according to the International Health Regulations of 2005, the infected nation voluntarily reports the contagion to the WHO, which generates a weekly epidemiological report to all UN recognized countries. The is WHO governed by the World Health Assembly (WHA), which is a forum of the 194 UN member states. When the WHO releases its weekly report to UN member states, the member state's national public health system initiates appropriate measures and protocols. In the United States, the national public health system is the Centers for Disease Control and Prevention (CDC). In addition distributing a weekly epidemiological report to UN member states, the WHO has offered a plethora of resources in partnership with public health agencies since 1951 through the Global Health Observatory (GHO) to the UN member states (Aschengrau & Seage III, 2020).

The Centers for Disease Control and Prevention (CDC)

The Centers for Disease Control and Prevention (CDC) is United States' national public health agency. Based out of Atlanta, Georgia, the CDC is a federal agency and provides direction to the US government and organizations to prevent the spread of disease and responds to public health emergencies (Turnock et al., 2022). Although the CDC is based out of Atlanta, Georgia, it has an extensive international reach with offices and resources in sixty-five countries staffed with scientists and researchers that track epidemiological threats around the world. The CDC is a resource for large international cities as it partners with foreign governments, sharing data on potential threats such as disease outbreaks. The CDC and the WHO's services are critical to global health security and endeavor to address the prevalence and disparities in disease surveillance, which is essential to large international cities such as Seattle, WA and Dallas, TX.

DISEASE, ORIGIN, AND DESTINATION

Increased human mobility, specifically air travel between large international cities such as Shenzhen, Moscow, Dallas, Seattle, London or Brussels increases the risk of infectious disease outbreaks (Findlater & Bogoch, 2018). Findler and Bogoch (2018) reveal in Table 1 numerous cases of disease migration to large cities highlighting the virus, point of origin, and destination. Many of the destinations have no direct flights, requiring connections from other international cities, as revealed in the 2014 case between Monrovia, Liberia and Dallas, TX.

Table 1. Cell press reviews

Disease	Origin (Year)	Destination
Influenza H1N1	Mexico (2009) [48]	Pandemic [50]
Vibrio cholerae	South Asia (2002, 2008)	Haiti epidemic (2010) [117]
NDM-1 carbapenem-resistant Gram-negative bacteria	India (2009) [84]	Australia, Austria, Belgium, Canada, China, Croatia, Czech Republic, Denmark, France, Germany, Ireland, Italy, Japan, Kuwait, Lebanon, The Netherlands, New Zealand, Norway Oman, Singapore, South Africa, Spain, Sweden, Switzerland, Taiwan, Turkey, United Kingdom, USA [85]
mcr-1 colistin-resistant Gram-negative bacteria	China (2014) [118]	Algeria, Argentina, Belgium, Brazil, Cambodia, Canada, China, Denmark, Egypt, France, Germany, Great Britain, Italy, Japan, Laos, Lithunia, Malaysia, The Netherlands, Nigeria, Poland, Portugal, South Africa, Spain, Switzerland, Taiwan, Thailand, Tunisia, USA, Vietnam [87]
Dengue virus	Primarily Southeast Asia (1950s) [55]	Global emergence over the past five decades [55]
MERS-CoV	Saudi Arabia (2012) [25]	Epidemics in South Korea and Saudi Arabia, with cases detected in Algeria, Austria, China, Egypt, France, Germany, Greece, Iran, Italy, Jordan, Kuwait, Lebanon, The Netherlands, Oman, Philippines, Qatar, Thailand, Tunisia, Turkey, Turkey, United Arab Emirates, United Kingdom, USA, Yemen [119]
Zika virus	Africa and Asia [69]	First detected in Latin America and the Caribbean in 2015 with ongoing transmission in the South Pacific, Latin America and the Caribbean [71]
Chikungunya virus	Asia and Africa [8,121]	Latin America and the Caribbean in December 2013 with ongoing transmission in this region [120], and autochthonous cases in Europe [60]
SARS-CoV (2002)	Southern China (2002) [22]	Epidemics in Hong Kong, Canada, USA, Vietnam, Singapore, Philippines, and Mongolia [22]
Schistosomiasis	Africa	Epidemic in Corsica (2013), with ongoing transmission [20]

Each case in Table 1 reveals a virus leaving one international city and traveling to several others. However, it is critical to note that due to globalization, large international cities have diverse populations with citizens who travel to and from and have business transactions with the nations listed in the origin/ year column, which can increase the risk for disease.

The first American travel-associated case of the 2014 Ebola outbreak (West Africa) occurred in Dallas, TX. Although there is debate in the literature as to the point of origin, the Covid-19 Virus originated in Wuhan Province, China in December of 2019 and reached the United States in January of 2020, a few miles outside of Seattle, WA (Carter et al., 2024). The carriers took transcontinental flights, one crossing the Pacific Ocean and the other the Atlantic Ocean, but neither city or public health officials were adequately prepared to respond to the viruses and due to a lack of data on potential viruses coming into their cities, lost valuable time contacting tracking down resources for guidance and support such as the CDC Emergency Operations Center, or in the Ebola case, misdiagnosed the patient's symptoms as a sinus infection. An initiative-taking, partnership between large international cities and national and global resources will facilitate health information and data-sharing and enhance outbreak preparedness by educating local populations of potential virus threats.

EDUCATION CAMPAIGNS AND RAISING AWARENESS – PUBLIC SERVICE ANNOUNCEMENTS PSAS

The WHO and the CDC offer resources to public health officials. However, educating the public on potential or actual threats must be data-driven and done with care and compassion. In addition to informing and protecting the traveling and non-traveling public, any education and awareness campaign must consider all audiences and stakeholders such as the economies and industries that depend on or facilitate air travel, and the public health and healthcare systems that respond to public health emergencies. Public Service Announcements (PSA) are powerful, tools to inform the public of the threat of the specific disease, the symptoms, and measures to reduce exposure such as masking, the use and importance of hand sanitizer, and social distancing at airports, train stations, or other public. The objective is to protect the public but avoid a panic or panic behaviors such as panic buying or the stigmatization of a specific demographic group. Educating and raising awareness through PSAs enhances awareness but prevents ostracization of the innocent. PSAs may also be used to discuss general protective measures applicable to all contagions such as vaccinations for annual flu or Covid virus campaigns. PSAs may be in multiple languages depending on the demographics of the city with the appropriate message for the specific audience. A large international city like Dallas or Seattle, are vital to globalization; global trade, immigration, and tourism, and may require a different and more focused message than a PSA for the public. Globalization promotes transoceanic shipping and logistics, international business travel, tourism, and immigration from LMICs to developed and wealth nations, increasing the risk of disease proliferation. The WHO and the CDC provide outbreak and disease surveillance data nations to the public and are useful in developing two outbreak preparedness response strategies. However, an outbreak preparedness plan for a large city must include a strategy that address domestic and international threat.

STRATEGY #1 CDC DOMESTIC STRATEGY PUBLIC HEALTH DATA STRATEGY (PHDS)

A pandemic preparedness plan for a large city or any population must be data driven. A data driven plan supports goal setting, promotes accuracy, prevents stigmatization of the innocent, and measures progress. The Covid-19 outbreak revealed shortfalls in decision making and policies due to a lack of information and data, or disinformation and data. The data shortfall resulted in stigmatization and discriminatory policies against demographics and nations, hurting economies and trade as many nations experienced under 1969 version of the IHR (Carter et al., 2024). The CDC adopted a Public Health Data Strategy (PHDS), Figure 1, is an effective strategy for large cities to ensure accurate disease data collection, provide accurate information, and empower public health agencies to respond to outbreak effectively (CDC, 2024). The PHDS consists of four public health goals:

- *Strengthen the core of public health.*
- *Accelerate access to analytic and automated solutions to support public health investigations and advance health opportunities for all people to attain their highest level of health.*
- *Visualize and share insights to inform public health action.*
- *Advance more open and interoperable public health data.*

During an outbreak, large cities work with state and federal public health agencies, therefore adopting a pandemic preparedness plan like or mirroring state and federal agencies is essential to save time, eliminating wasted resources, and maximizing efficiency. City officials, government officials, and the public are working together to overcome the outbreak.

Figure 1. Centers for disease control and prevention

STRATEGY #2 UNITED STATES (INTERNATIONAL THREATS) NATIONAL BIODEFENSE STRATEGY AND IMPLEMENTATION PLAN COUNTERING BIOLOGICAL THREATS, ENHANCING PANDEMIC PREPAREDNESS, AND ACHIEVING GLOBAL HEALTH SECURITY.

The National Biodefense Strategy and Implementation Plan for Countering Biological Threats, Enhancing Pandemic Preparedness and Achieving Global Health Security is an effective strategy for large cities as it unites a multiple agencies and resources across the US Government to protect American populations and American interests from biological agents or threats. The objective of the Federal Government is to suffering, save lives, and protect the environment and property (House, 2022). A large international city must also be prepared to respond to international threats. Domestic efforts alone are not enough. Outbreak response strategies that align with or mirror the *National Biodefense Strategy and Implementation Plan* prepares a large city to receive support from the government as city leaders, government officials, and the public work together with similar or mirroring strategies and work toward similar or matching goals. The goals for the *National Biodefense Strategy and Implementation Plan* are:

- *Enable risk awareness and detection to inform decision-making across the biodefense enterprise.*
- *Ensure biodefense enterprise capabilities to prevent bio-incidents.*
- *Ensure biodefense enterprise preparedness to reduce the impacts of bio-incidents.*
- *Rapidly respond to limit the impacts of bio-incidents.*
- *Facilitate recovery to restore the community, the economy, and environment after a bio-incident.*

The Covid-19 outbreak stretched human, financial, and technological resources to their limits. An effective outbreak response initiative also requires appropriate allocation of resources.

ALLOCATION OF RESOURCES

Financial

An outbreak preparedness strategy for a large city requires a substantial financial. Commitment. During an outbreak, many cities may be affected, thus state and federal financial support may be limited. A large city such as Dallas or Chicago may devote a portion of its annual budget to outbreak response and preparedness. Municipal bonds are an option to augment cash reserves to purchase urgently needed PPE and other supplies. The first goal for the *National Biodefense Strategy and Implementation Plan* and the CDC's PHDS promotes detection, awareness, information-sharing, and monitoring are the first line of defense and priority in resource allocation. Detection, information-sharing, and monitoring require special equipment and technology, and should be the second priority in resources allocation.

Technology

During the Covid-19 pandemic, many cities, large and small, experienced a shortage of ventilators and N95 masks because vendors outsourced the manufacturing. However, an even greater shortage was in interoperability and data-sharing between government health agencies and local hospitals and clinics. Although the Chinese government followed the IHR 2005 protocols and reported Covid to the WHO, which distributed the weekly epidemiology report to all UN member states, in the first US Covid case in Seattle, the medical staff lost valuable time contacting the WHO's emergency response center. The Ebola case in Dallas also reflects the data-sharing and interoperability. The WHO was aware of the Ebola outbreak in Liberia, as was the CDC, however, the hospital in Dallas, a large international city with hundreds of flights to and from West Africa, was unaware of the outbreak and misdiagnosed the infected patient's symptoms, mistaking hemorrhagic with a sinus infection. A large city like Dallas or Seattle should allocate a percentage of its outbreak preparedness and response budget, to initiate launch Public Private Partnerships (PPP) to research innovative technologies to enhance data-sharing and interoperability (Carter et al., 2024).

Human Resources

Although funding, PSAs, and innovative technologies or innovations are essential to an outbreak response plan, the effects are limited without human community engagement. Protective measures such as masking and social distancing measure met strong resistance during the Covid-19 pandemic. There was distrust, conspiracy theories, and misinformation. Active community engagement from locals within the community is an effective method to gain trust and cooperation. During a crisis, a friendly or trusted member of a community championing the public health measures and policy recommendations will have a greater impact than others from outside of the community. The Covid pandemic sparked fear, anxiety, and mistrust so there are ethical considerations to weigh in implementing an outbreak preparedness plan.

ETHICAL CONSIDERATIONS - THE AMERICAN PUBLIC HEALTH ASSOCIATION (APHA)

When initiating an outbreak response plan, ethical, inclusive, and culturally sensitive conduct are critical. The virus has no biases, yet its carriers do. Thankfully, the Public Health Code of Ethics outline 12 codes (Figure 2) of ethical standards and obligatory practices in public health (Thomas et al., 2002). During an outbreak, public trust is just as essential as PPE and failure to protect the public trust can have devastating consequences.

Rule #10 Protect the confidentiality of information that can bring harm to others.

During the Covid-19 pandemic, although the PRC followed the 2005 IHR protocols, the President of the United States, Donald Trump, labeled the contagion as the "China Virus" which resulted in harassment and attacks on Chinese Americans, and Asians from other countries. The first travel ban was to and from Muslim countries, although Covid-19 is believed to originate in China. Chinese Americans and Muslims of Middle Eastern decent were harassed and attacked during an already very troubling time.

Rule # 12 Build and protect public trust.

During the Covid-19 pandemic, the gross misinformation or disinformation (Rule #5) was rampant and eroded public trust in protective measures such as masking, social distancing, hand sanitizing, and vaccines. The misinformation or disinformation came from polarized political parties on both sides of the aisle, whom their constituents trusted unto death. Many suffering Covid patients left their loved ones, exhausting their final breaths pleading for the vaccine, that by that time, would not help them because they were already infected. They refused the vaccine after receiving inaccurate information from social media or people who had no medical training of any kind.

Goal setting is essential to implementing an outbreak response plan. The SMART acronym is an effective method to emphasize intended outcomes and measure improvement. SMART ensures that the goals are Specific, Measurable, Achievable, Realistic, and Time specific. Using the SMART approach responding to an outbreak, the public health official will:

Specific – Create a process map of the current outbreak response plan in MS Visio and find specific points to streamline.
Measure - Measure the time or cost of each process, and the end-to-end time and cost of the process.
Achievable – Determine what changes or enhancements are achievable or possible.
Realistic – Determine what is legal, sustainable, and operationally realistic.
Timely – Determine a time to implement the new process and measure the progress with miles stones.

Figure 2. American public health association

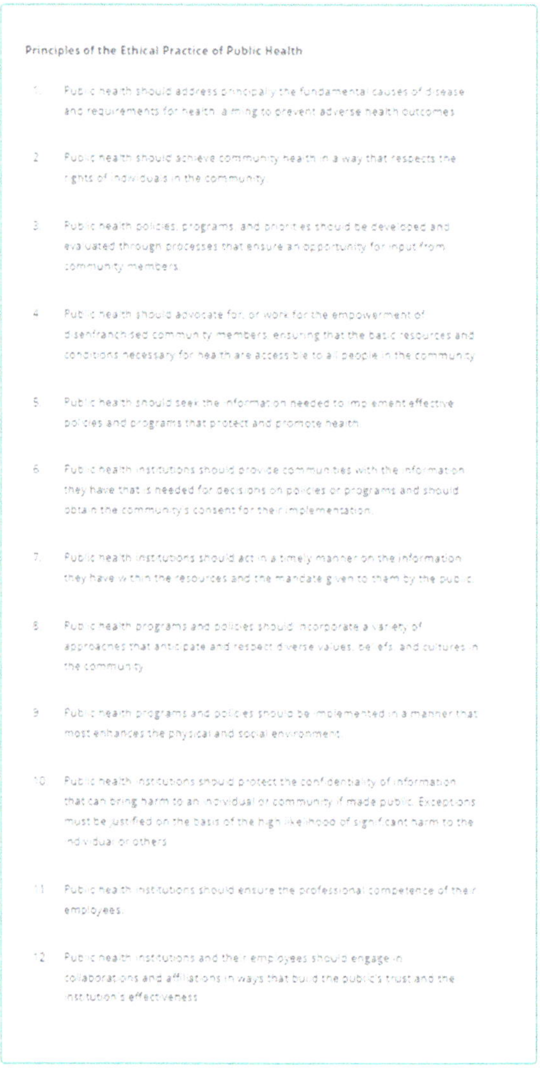

Principles of the Ethical Practice of Public Health

1. Public health should address principally the fundamental causes of disease and requirements for health, aiming to prevent adverse health outcomes.
2. Public health should achieve community health in a way that respects the rights of individuals in the community.
3. Public health policies, programs, and priorities should be developed and evaluated through processes that ensure an opportunity for input from community members.
4. Public health should advocate for, or work for the empowerment of, disenfranchised community members, ensuring that the basic resources and conditions necessary for health are accessible to all people in the community.
5. Public health should seek the information needed to implement effective policies and programs that protect and promote health.
6. Public health institutions should provide communities with the information they have that is needed for decisions on policies or programs and should obtain the community's consent for their implementation.
7. Public health institutions should act in a timely manner on the information they have within the resources and the mandate given to them by the public.
8. Public health programs and policies should incorporate a variety of approaches that anticipate and respect diverse values, beliefs, and cultures in the community.
9. Public health programs and policies should be implemented in a manner that most enhances the physical and social environment.
10. Public health institutions should protect the confidentiality of information that can bring harm to an individual or community if made public. Exceptions must be justified on the basis of the high likelihood of significant harm to the individual or others.
11. Public health institutions should ensure the professional competence of their employees.
12. Public health institutions and their employees should engage in collaborations and affiliations in ways that build the public's trust and the institution's effectiveness.

CONCLUSION

Covid-19 and Ebola are highlighting how large international cities are at risk of outbreaks and can benefit from a robust outbreak preparedness plan. The Ebola and Covid-19 cases in Dallas, TX and Seattle, WA did not originate in the United States, yet over 1.2 million died from Covid-19 alone. Therefore, a disease problem somewhere is a disease problem everywhere. An outbreak response is not a neat paper and pencil exercise with all the variables and formulas ready for use, however, with proper planning, and investments in data-sharing and interoperable systems, lives can be saved.

REFERENCES

Aschengrau, A., & Seage, G. R.III. (2020). Essentials Of Epidemiology. In *Public Health* (4th ed.). Jones & Bartlett Learning.

Carter, S. K., Anastasia, C., & Carter, B. M. (2024). *Multinational Electronic Health Records Interoperability Strategies*. IGI Global.

CDC. (2024). *CDC Public Health Data Strategy: About The Public Health Data Strategy (PHDS)*. United States Centers For Disease Control And Prevention. Https://Www.Cdc.Gov/Public-Health-Data-Strategy/Php/About/Index.Html

Findlater, A., & Bogoch, I. I. (2018). Human Mobility And The Global Spread Of Infectious Diseases: A Focus On Air Travel. *Trends in Parasitology*, *34*(9), 772–783. Https://Doi.Org/Https://Doi.Org/10.1016/J.Pt.2018.07.004 PMID: 30049602

Heymann, D. L., & Rodier, G. (2004). SARS: A Global Response To An International Threat. *The Brown Journal of World Affairs*, *10*(2), 185–197. Http://Www.Jstor.Org/Stable/24590530

House, T. W. (2022). *National Biodefense Strategy And Implementation Plan For Countering Biological Threats, Enhancing Pandemic Preparedness, And Achieving Global Heatlh Security*. The United States Retrieved From., Https://Www.Whitehouse.Gov/Wp-Content/Uploads/2022/10/National-Biodefense-Strategy-And-Implementation-Plan-Final.Pdf

Lincicome, S. (2023, September 12). *Globalization Isn't Going Anywhere*. Cato.Org. Https://Www.Cato.Org/Publications/Globalization-Isnt-Going-Anywhere

Mccloskey, D. N. (2023, September 12). *Globalization Creates A Global Neighborhood, Benefiting All*. Cato.Org. Https://Www.Cato.Org/Publications/Globalization-Isnt-Going-Anywhere

Mishra, R., Dwivedi, V., & Saxena, S. (2024). Computational Convergence And Interoperability. In *Electronic Health Records (EHR)*. IGI Global.

Molinari, N. M., Leblanc, T. T., & Stephens, W. (2018). The Impact Of A Case Of Ebola Virus Disease On Emergency Department Visits In Metropolitan Dallas-Fort Worth, TX, July, 2013-July, 2015: An Interrupted Time Series Analysis. *PLoS Currents*, *10*, •••. Https://Doi.Org/10.1371/Currents.Outbreaks.E62bdea371ef5454d56f71fe217aead0 PMID: 29623242

Sevilla, N. L. (2017). *Germs On A Plane: The Transmission And Risks Of Airplane-Borne Diseases* [Ph.D., George Mason University]. Proquest Dissertations & Theses Global., Https://Proxy.Cecybrary.Com/Login?Url=Https://Search.Proquest.Com/Docview/1958954996?Accountid=26967

Thomas, J. C., Sage, M., Dillenberg, J., & Guillory, V. J. (2002). *A Code Of Ethics For Public Health* (Vol. 92). American Public Health Association.

Turnock, B. J., Birkhead, G. S., Morrow, C. B., & Pirani, S. (2022). *Turnock's Public Health: What It Is And How It Works*. Jones & Bartlett Learning.

Uop. (2023). *Public Health Vs. Medicine*. University Of Pittsburgh. Retrieved 6/13/2025 From Https://Www.Publichealth.Pitt.Edu/Public-Health-Vs-Medicine

APPENDIX

Chapter 4 Study Questions

1. How Can The Multinational Interoperable EHR Model Shown In Figure 1 From Chapter 1 Be Used For Global Health And Disease Prevention In Large International Cities?
2. Considering The Challenges Within Then 1969 And 2005 Versions Of The IHR, How Can The WHO Use The Model Shown In Figure 1 From Chapter 1 To Communication With Not Just Governments, But Directly To Hospitals?
3. How Can Public Health Organizations Apply Principles From The Model In Figure1 From Chapter 1 To Predict And Ensure Proper Allocation Of PPE Resources Such As N95 Masks?
4. There Were Many Communication Gaps Between Organizations At The Global And National Level, How Would A Multinational Interoperable EHR System, As Seen In Figure 1 Resolve Some Of The Public Trust Challenges?
5. How Can Public Health Agencies At The Municipal And Local Level Benefit From WHO Outbreak Data Through A Multinational Interoperable EHR System?
6. Relevant To The Cdcs Strategies One And Two, How Would A Multinational Interoperable EHR System Shown In Figure 1 Chapter 1, Help Predict Outbreaks In A Large International City With Numerous International Flights?
7. When Revieing Table 1, How Would A Multinational Interoperable EHR System As Shown In Figure 1 Chapter 1, Be Used To Prevent Disease Outbreaks In Large International Cities?
8. In Your Opinion, How Would A Multinational Interoperable EHR System As Shown In Figure1 Chapter 1, Been Useful During The COVID-19 Pandemic And The Ebola Outbreak?
9. How Can Knowledge Of Patient's Travel History Be Useful?
10. In Your Opinion, How Important Is Access To Outbreak Data To Treating A Potentially Infected Patient?

Chapter 5
Environmental Research: Democratic Republic of the Congo

ABSTRACT

Focusing on the Democratic Republic of the Congo (DRC), this chapter explores the intersection of environmental degradation, zoonotic spillover, and health system fragility. It synthesizes research on deforestation, mining, and biodiversity loss as drivers of infectious disease emergence, including Ebola and Nipah-like viruses. The chapter advocates for integrated surveillance systems that combine environmental data with health records, positioning EHR interoperability as a tool for early warning and cross-sectoral response.

INTRODUCTION

The Democratic Republic of the Congo (DRC) is the largest country in Sub-Saharan Africa (SSA) and has a land mass comparable to Western Europe. The DRC is exceptionally favored with precious natural resources such as cobalt and copper and has the second-largest rainforest in the world. Although the DRC has a wealth of natural resources, it is plagued with many challenges related to water and foodborne illnesses (indexmundi, 2020).

In 1972, Alfred Crosby Jr coined the phrase *Columbian Exchato* which describes the transfer of plant and animal disease between Europe, Africa, and the Americas dating back to Columbus' voyages in 1492 (Horgan & Netchev, 2022). The world has changed exponentially since 1492; however, the threat of food and waterborne illnesses persists and presents environmental health concerns in low-to-middle-income (LMICS) African nations, specifically the Democratic of the Congo (DRC). Foodborne diseases (FBDs) are infections and pathogens derived from unsafe food and water (Grace, 2023). FBDs globally cause disease outbreaks and impose health, economic, and social burdens on LMICS that often lack medical, technical, and

DOI: 10.4018/979-8-3693-2027-3.ch005

financial resources to develop and sustain efficient pandemic response programs (Carter, 2024).

In 2015, the World Health Organization (WHO) estimated that numerous global and regional diseases develop from 31 food and waterborne sources and traced 1 out of every 10 illnesses to contaminated food or water (Grace, 2023). Inadequate funding, poor public health infrastructure, and resource shortfalls in LMICs increase susceptibility risks and are ideal for outbreaks as environments substantially impact a disease's ability to infect, survive and proliferate (WGU, 2020a). Carter (2024) opined that unless addressed at the international level, local disease outbreaks in LMICS will continue to develop into multinational pandemics. Current local disease surveillance and data-sharing systems are inefficient in combating multinational outbreaks. Disease outbreaks are a global problem and require global solutions.

On September 15, 2015, the United Nations identified 17 opportunities to improve the quality of life, safety, health, and well-being of 8.4 billion global citizens; it also labeled the objectives of the Sustainable Development Goals (SDG). The SDGs are 17 agendas with 169 deliverables to address interconnected social, economic, and environmental challenges (Ravn Boess et al., 2021). Sweden, Denmark, and Finland are making significant progress and have achieved three-quarters of the objectives (Carter, 2024). Sweden, Denmark, and Finland are wealthy and developed nations with a plethora of accessible resources. However, many Low-to-middle-income countries (LMICs) struggle to improve their quality of life and remain at risk for disease outbreaks and pandemics. Although for centuries, wars have ravaged and wreaked havoc across nations and regions, the disease has taken more lives than all the world's wars combined (Norrie, 2016). In addition to Sweden, Denmark, and Finland, many developed nations have made significant progress in SDG accomplishment, how LMICs such as the Democratic Republic of the Congo (DRC) struggle with poverty, health, and sanitation and their causation to disease outbreaks (Mufungizi et al., 2024). UN SDGs 1,3,6, & 8 (No poverty, Good Health, Clean water, and Decent work & economic growth) are interrelated and influence environmental health. In a 2016 report, the WHO revealed that 23% of all deaths are associated with air pollution, poor sanitation, radiation exposure, and other environmental threats (Egbende et al., 2023). The purpose of this research is to call to action to address poor environmental health that leads to outbreaks due to water contamination and food safety in the Democratic Republic of Congo (DRC).

DRC: WATER CONTAMINATION AND FOODBORNE ILLNESSES

In 2010, the World Health Organization stated that 31 million disability-adjusted life years (DALYs) were attributed to 31 hazards from food and waterborne diseases linked to the environment and climate change (Cissé, 2019). A DALY measures time that calculates years of life lost (YLL) due to premature mortality and time lived with poor health due to disease (Hoffmann & Havelaar, 2019). African nations (Figure 1) have the highest rate of water and foodborne DALYs per 100,000 people, particularly among the high child and adult mortality and high child mortality and remarkably high adult mortality categories. Food safety and clean water are vital to SDG attainment in African nations (Morse et al., 2018).

Figure 1. United States department of agriculture

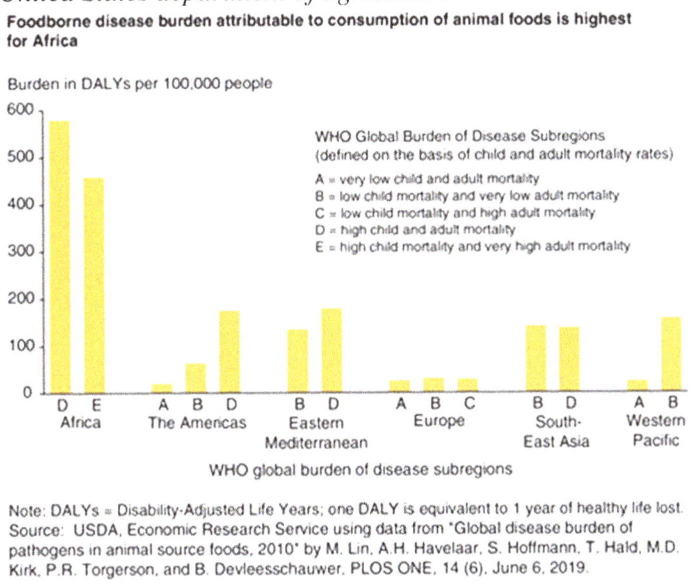

The University of Washington's Institute for Health Metrics and Evaluation (2021) (Figure 2) revealed additional communicable, maternal, neonatal, and nutritional diseases attributed to DALYs in the DRC, many of which are nutritional. The data in Figure 2 reflects a high-altitude perspective of the environmental health problems in the DRC. However, in-depth research reveals interconnections and correlations between economics, health systems, and political landscapes that influence DRC environmental health.

Figure 2. GBD compare tool the University of Washington

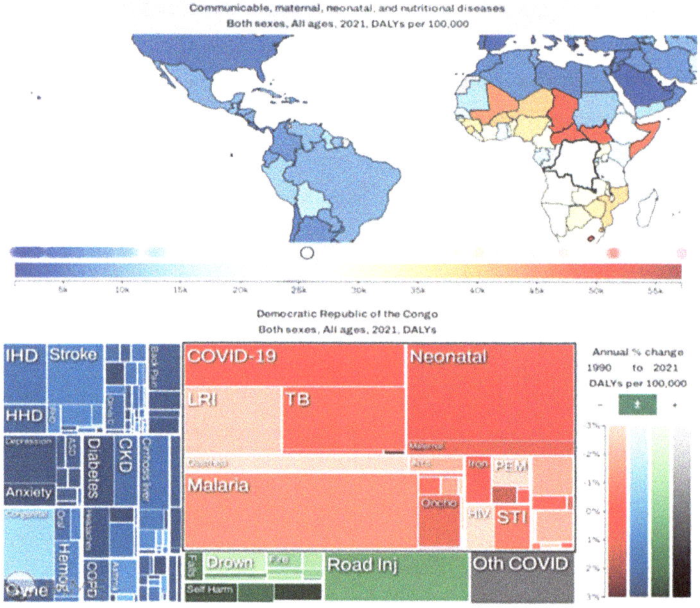

DRC: ECONOMY, HEALTH SYSTEM, AND POLITICAL LANDSCAPE

Economy

Although in 2022, DRC GDP growth peaked at 8.9%, and in 2023 sustained an 8.4% growth (*The World Bank in DRC*, 2025), the DRC is listed among the top five poorest countries with an estimated 73.5% of the DRC population surviving on less than $2.15 per day (indexmundi, 2020). The economic conditions in the DRC impede attaining SDGs 1,3,6 and 8, imposing health risks on the Congolese people. Poor economic conditions limit the DRC's ability to invest in the necessary resources and technologies to improve sanitation, provide clean water, promote good health, and facilitate UN SDGs 1,3,6 & 8 attainment, which reduce environmental risks and reduce disease outbreaks (Mufungizi et al., 2024).

Health System

The UN created 17 SDGs to improve the quality of life, safety, health, and well-being for all nations (Carter, 2024). Although well-meaning, the 2005 version of the International Health Regulations (IHR) did not adequately address the needs of LMICs who lacked the resources to fund, staff, equip, and sustain robust health systems (Carter et al., 2024). The SDGs are a global approach to address interconnected social, economic, and environmental challenges (Ravn Boess et al., 2021); challenges commonly found in the DRC, including poverty.

The Congolese health system is overwhelmed by poverty. Seventy per cent of the DRC's population lives at or below the poverty level (Ravn Boess et al., 2021). SDGs 1(No poverty) will provide the Congolese the needed financial resources to improve the DRC's environmental health and facilitate the attainment of SDGs 3, 6, & 8 (Good Health, Clean Water & Sanitation, and Economic Growth). Health nations are prosperous nations (Raimi et al., 2021). Environmental health initiatives improve the quality of life for nations, and the UN can play an essential role in influencing the Congolese political landscape to bring SDG attainment to fruition.

Political Landscape and Colonization

The DRC has significantly suffered for decades dating back to Leopold II, who colonized the Congo, and declared it as his personal property from 1885 to 1908, killing between 10 and 15 million men, women, and children, and later colonized by the state of Belgium from 1908 to 1960, just 65 years ago. The DRC has yet to recover from colonization. Colonization and foreign interference impoverish nations, destabilize political systems, disrupt self-governance, and obstruct a nation's ability to develop environmental health infrastructures such as food, safe water, and adequate health care, and provide other urgent services for an oppressed and occupied nation. Colonization strips nations of their natural resources and the personal identities of their people. The political landscape of the DRC is intertwined and correlated to its poverty and limited healthcare system.

IMPACT OF WATER AND FOOD SAFETY ON THE DRC

The DRC is listed among the world's poorest countries and faces many challenges in combating environmental threats that contribute to food and waterborne illnesses correlated to anthropogenic action. In 2022, the DRC had the highest rate of typhoid, with 315 cases per 100,000 people. In 2022, the DRC National Malaria Control Program reported 21 million cases of malaria, resulting in 13,000 deaths, and over 30,000 cases of cholera, resulting in hundreds of deaths (Mufungizi et al., 2024). Although FBDs are existential threats to agriculture. Waterborne illnesses are a significant source of disease because they are used for agriculture, human hydration, and cooking and is therefore critical to safe food chains. FBDs were not a global agenda item until 2015 (Grace, 2023). Several years after establishing SDGs, the Congolese people continue to fight food and waterborne diseases such as:

1. **Cholera**, a waterborne illness that causes severe diarrhea and dehydration, frequently causes outbreaks in areas with poor sanitation.
2. **Typhoid,** a contagious food, and waterborne sickness caused by the bacterium Salmonella typhi that generates symptoms of high fever, abdominal pain, appetite loss, and weakness.
3. **Hepatitis A,** a very contagious and dangerous liver disease spread from contaminated food and water, and causes fever, jaundice, and gastrointestinal irritations.
4. **Hepatitis E,** like Hepatitis A, is spread through contaminated water and leads to liver inflammation.
5. **Bacterial and Protozoal Diarrhea** commonly spread through contaminated food and water, leading to gastrointestinal illnesses (indexmundi, 2020).

ANTHROPOGENIC IMPACT ON WATER AND FOOD SAFETY ON THE DRC

Surviving on less than $2.15 per day, the Congolese live in poverty, have poor health infrastructures, and unstable governments, which leave few options to make healthy or safe food or water choices. Citizens of LMICs are forced to drink water and prepare and consume food from untested and unsafe sources. While developed nations have the luxury of government oversight of food sources such as the US Department of Agriculture or the US Food and Drug Administration, the impoverished LMICs often survive on what is available when it is available. The UN has an opportunity to begin the healing process and restoration of the Congo with two prevention strategies.

CONCLUSION

SDG 18 – Environmental Health

The UN SDGs are 17 agendas with 169 deliverables to address a range of interconnected. social, economic, and environmental challenges (Ravn Boess et al., 2021). Water and food safety are closely related to UN SDGs; however, due to the state of environmental health and the projected increase of the global population from 8.4 billion to 10 billion by 2050, which will increase human mobility, demand on systems and needs for resources such as safe food and water, it is recommended that the UN proactively establish an 18th SDG specifically for environmental health.

WASH and African Union Support

Water Sanitation and Hygiene (WASH) is a powerful tool that promotes sound environmental health. The African Union (AU) is a powerful resource that can help African nations develop and sustain safe food and water systems. Developed SSA nations such as South Africa, Nigeria, and Ghana have a wealth of knowledge, resources, and expertise that may benefit other African countries. Additionally, AU nations understand the cultures and traditions within the African continent, which increases trust and promotes unity within SSA. An ideal situation is a partnership between the AU and the UN to develop and sustain critical WASH programs for SSA nations.

REFERENCES

Carter, S. K. (2024). Using Electronic Health Records (EHR) For Disease Surveillance (EHR-DS) To Support UN Sdgs. In *Computational Convergence And Interoperability In Electronic Health Records (EHR)* (Pp. 137-152). IGI Global.

Carter, S. K., Anastasia, C., & Carter, B. M. (2024). *Multinational Electronic Health Records Interoperability Strategies*. IGI Global.

Cissé, G. (2019). Food-Borne And Water-Borne Diseases Under Climate Change In Low-And Middle-Income Countries: Further Efforts Needed For Reducing Environmental Health Exposure Risks. *Acta Tropica*, *194*, 181–188. PMID: 30946811

Egbende, L., Helldén, D., Mbunga, B., Schedwin, M., Kazenza, B., Viberg, N., Wanyenze, R., Ali, M. M., & Alfvén, T. (2023). Interactions Between Health And The Sustainable Development Goals: The Case Of The Democratic Republic Of Congo. *Sustainability*, *15*(2), 1259. Https://Www.Mdpi.Com/2071-1050/15/2/1259

Grace, D. (2023). Burden Of Foodborne Disease In Low-Income And Middle-Income Countries And Opportunities For Scaling Food Safety Interventions. *Food Security*, *15*(6), 1475–1488. Https://Doi.Org/10.1007/S12571-023-01391-3

Hoffmann, S., & Havelaar, A. (2019). Measuring The Burden Of Global Foodborne Disease From Animal And Fish Sources. *Amber Waves: The Economics Of Food, Farming, Natural Resources, And Rural America, 2019*(10).

Horgan, J., & Netchev, S. (2022). *Columbian Exchange*. World History.

Indexmundi. (2020). *Democratic Republic Of The Congo Major Infectious Diseases*. Https://Www.Indexmundi.Com/Democratic_Republic_Of_The_Congo/Major_Infectious_Diseases.Html

Morse, T. D., Masuku, H., Rippon, S., & Kubwalo, H. (2018). Achieving An Integrated Approach To Food Safety And Hygiene—Meeting The Sustainable Development Goals In Sub-Saharan Africa. *Sustainability*, *10*(7), 2394. Https://Www.Mdpi.Com/2071-1050/10/7/2394

Mufungizi, I., Okon, I., Nkundakozera, M., & Akilimali, A. (2024). Supporting Health Systems And Environment In The Democratic Republic Of Congo: A Call For Action. *Health Science Reports*, *7*(7), E2257. PMID: 39027365

Norrie, P. (2016). *A History Of Disease In Ancient Times: More Lethal Than War*. Springer International Publishing AG. Https://Doi.Org/10.1007/978-3-319-28937

Raimi, M. O., Vivien, O. T., & Oluwatoyin, O. A. (2021). Creating The Healthiest Nation: Climate Change And Environmental Health Impacts. In *Nigeria: A Narrative Review. Morufu Olalekan Raimi, Tonye Vivien Odubo & Adedoyin Oluwatoyin Omidiji (2021) Creating The Healthiest Nation: Climate Change And Environmental Health Impacts In Nigeria: A Narrative Review.* Scholink Sustainability In Environment. ISSN.

Ravn Boess, E., Kørnøv, L., Lyhne, I., & Partidário, M. R. (2021). Integrating Sdgs In Environmental Assessment: Unfolding SDG Functions In Emerging Practices. *Environmental Impact Assessment Review, 90*, 106632. Https://Doi.Org/Https://Doi.Org/10.1016/J.Eiar.2021.106632

The World Bank In DRC. (2025). Https://Www.Worldbank.Org/En/Country/Drc/Overview#1

WGU. (2020). *Environmental Health: Lesson 1:1 Environmental Health As Interconnectedness Of Risks [MOOC].* Https://Apps.Cgp-Oex.Wgu.Edu/Wgulearning/Course/Course-V1:Wgux+OEX0355+V01/Block-V1:Wgux+OEX0355+V01+Type@Sequential+Block@A6abd0761688459bba15ffe73a977ebd/Block-V1:Wgux+OEX0355+V01+Type@Vertical+Block@Fea22b1e58da4c1eb6ef136a4518b70e

APPENDIX

Chapter 5 Study Questions

1. A WHO compatible multinational data-sharing EHR system would enable governments and global health systems to measure and monitor disability-adjusted life years. How would measuring disability-adjusted life years (DALYs) benefit LMICs such as the Democratic Republic of the Congo?
2. Why are Foodborne Diseases (FDB) in the DRC potentially dangerous to surrounding nations or the international community?
3. Cholera, Typhoid, Hepatitis A, Hepatitis E, and Bacterial Protozoal Diarrhea are dangerous illnesses, some of which are contagious. How can the WHO and government health systems benefit from an interoperable WHO compatible EHR system to battle these infections?
4. How can government and global health organizations benefit from the metadata generated from a WHO-Compatible multinational EHR system to support UN SDGs?
5. How would the African Union (AU) benefit from a multinational EHR data-sharing system in support the DRC and other member states?
6. In your opinion, how can a multinational EHR system be used in the DRC to measure anthropogenic events and their impact on food and water safety?
7. Belgium ruled the Republic of the Congo, today known as the Democratic Republic of the Congo (DRC), from 1908 – 1960, which many researchers contend has contributed the poverty in the DRC. In your opinion, how can integrating health systems and promoting health-data sharing increase global awareness and prevent future atrocities?
8. What are some of the correlations and causations between poor sanitation, FBDs, and poverty?
9. The Congolese Health system is overrun with underfunding and staffing challenges. Based on what you have learned in this chapter, how can technology make a difference and promote change?
10. Please explain Alfred Crosby Jr's terminology *Columbian Exchato* and explain whether it is relevant today?

Chapter 6
Environmental Health

ABSTRACT

This chapter, titled "Environmental Health," expands the lens to global environmental health, analyzing how climate change, pollution, and ecological disruption exacerbate disease burdens in LMICs. It argues that interoperable EHR systems can support environmental health monitoring by linking clinical data with geospatial and exposure metrics. The chapter also discusses ethical considerations in data collection and use, particularly in marginalized communities disproportionately affected by environmental hazards.

INTRODUCTION

By 2030, the global population will increase from 8.4 billion to 10 billion (Carter, 2024). Globalization increases human mobility, links communities, cultures, and industries by sharing access to foreign markets, leverages the benefits of multinational human and natural resources, cultural exchanges, innovations and technologies, and helps organizations establish or increase an international presence (McCloskey, 2023). Technological advancements in integrated digitized processes and interoperable systems have made the world smaller, making conducting transactions between organizations thousands of miles apart as easy as making a few keystrokes (Winslett, 2023). However, one of the challenges of globalization and global population growth is its increased demand for food chains and the use of glyphosate.

Globalization increases the demand for farmers for agricultural products, more standardized farming processes, and integrated agricultural systems. Glyphosate is a globally used herbicide that promotes food quality, increases crop yields, and protects agriculture from pests and diseases (de Morais Valentim et al., 2024). Glyphosate is an herbicide, and although commonly used in developed and developing countries, there are concerns about its toxicity and potential health risks to humans. Toxicology is crucial to public health and safety, and understanding gly-

DOI: 10.4018/979-8-3693-2027-3.ch006

phosate's Dose-Response Relationship (DRR) is essential to reducing the dangers and consequences of exposure. The DRR is an area of toxicology that promotes the understanding of the interaction of chemicals and living organisms and potential health impacts (WGU, 2020b).

DOSE-RESPONSE RELATIONSHIPS AND GLYPHOSATE

Glyphosate was introduced under the trade name Roundup in 1974 by the Monsanto organization as an herbicide designed to kill living pests and diseases while protecting food sources (Valavanidis, 2018). There is, however, debate in the literature on the product's safety, as some science suggests excessive exposure to glyphosate is potentially dangerous to humans. The United States Department of Health and Human Services (DHHS) Agency for Toxic Substances and Disease revealed in Tables 1(Human) and Table 2 (Animals) several health risks and potential DRR correlations (Pohl et al., 2019).

Table 1. US DHHS agency for toxic substances and disease registry (humans)

• **Gastrointestinal effects:** Clinical signs and/or pathological evidence of glyphosate-induced irritation were observed in several animal studies; the lowest dose level resulting in gastrointestinal effects was 175 mg/kg/day for diarrhea and few feces in pregnant rabbits administered glyphosate acid by gavage. Gastrointestinal disturbances are signs and/or symptoms following ingestion of substantial amounts of glyphosate-containing products.
• **Developmental effects:** Glyphosate treatment-related developmental effects were noted in a few studies at dose levels (≥1,234 mg/kg/day), resulting in maternal toxicity as well.
• **Body weight effects:** Depressed body weight and/or depressed body weight gain resulted from repeated dosing of glyphosate technical at dose levels ≥1,183 mg/kg/day.
• **Hepatic effects:** Increases in liver weight and serum ALT activity were observed in one repeated-dose study at a dose level of 1,678 mg/kg/day.
• **Ocular effects:** Lens abnormalities were observed in one repeated-dose study at a dose level of 940 mg/kg/day.
• **Renal effects:** Indicators of renal toxicity were noted in rats and mice administered glyphosate technical in the diet for 2 years at high doses (940 and 6,069 mg/kg/day, respectively).
• **Other effects:** Neurological, hematological, immunological, and reproductive endpoints have been evaluated but do not appear to be targets of glyphosate toxicity.
• **Cancer:** Upon evaluation of available carcinogenicity studies in laboratory rodents, multiple agencies or organizations have concluded that glyphosate technical does not appear to be an animal carcinogen. In contrast, IARC considered the animal data to provide "*sufficient evidence*" of glyphosate carcinogenicity.

Table 2. US DHHS agency for toxic substances and disease registry (animals)

• **Developmental effects:** Histopathologic testicular lesions, decreased sperm production, and increased incidence of fetal skeletal malformations were reported in response to oral dosing of rat weanlings or pregnant rats with selected glyphosate formulations in the range of 5–500 mg/kg/day.
• **Endocrine effects:** Decreased serum testosterone was noted in male rat weanlings administered a glyphosate formulation orally at 5 mg/kg/day.
• **Body weight effects:** Seriously depressed body weight gain was observed in mice administered a glyphosate formulation orally at 50 mg/kg/day.
• **Renal effects:** Histopathologic kidney lesions were noted in male rats gavaged once with a glyphosate formulation at 250 mg/kg.
• **Hepatic effects:** Increased serum liver enzyme activity and histopathologic liver lesions were reported in male rats repeatedly gavaged with a glyphosate formulation at 487 mg/kg/day.
• **Hematological effects:** Decreases in red blood cells, hematocrit, and hemoglobin, and increases in mean corpuscular volume and neutrophils were reported in mice administered a glyphosate formulation orally at 500 mg/kg/day.
• **Reproductive effects:** Increased percentage of morphologically abnormal sperm was reported among rats receiving a glyphosate formulation from the drinking water for 8 days at 640 mg/kg/day.

RELEVANT AGENCIES FOR GLYPHOSATE USE INTERNATIONAL, FEDERAL, AND STATE LEVELS

Globally, glyphosate use has increased 15-fold. Over 750 products contain glyphosate, registered in 130 countries, including the United States, as approved weed control methods in over 100 crops (Valavanidis, 2018). Table 3 and Table 4 reveal that glyphosate use must comply with applicable US and international regulations and guidelines from the Environmental Protection Agency (EPA), the World Health Organization (WHO), the US Food and Drug Administration (FDA), the US Department of Health and Human Services (HSS), the International Agency for Research on Cancer (IARC), the American Council of Governmental Industrial Hygienists (ACGIH), the Occupational Safety and Health Administration (OSHA), The National Institute for Occupational Safety and Health (NIOSH), and the US Department of Energy (DOE), (Pohl et al., 2019).The US Environmental Protection Agency regulates the use of pesticides and herbicides to protect public safety. However, state and local laws prohibit glyphosate due the health risks to children, agriculture workers, and the local community (Rabine & Faber, 2025). The State of Washington has taken a more approach; finding a middle-ground to ensure the safety of the local community while protecting local agriculture from weeds and persistent pests.

Table 3. Regulations and guidelines applicable to glyphosate

Agency	Description	Information	Reference
		Air	
EPA	RfC	Not evaluated	IRIS 1989
WHO	Air quality guidelines	No data	WHO 2010
		Water & Food	
EPA	Drinking water standards and health advisories		EPA 2012d
	1-Day (10-kg child)	20 mg/L	
	10-Day (10-kg child)	20 mg/L	
	DWEL	70 mg/L	
	National primary drinking water regulations		EPA 2009b
	Maximum Contaminant Level	0.7 mg/L	
	Maximum Contaminant Level Goal	0.7 mg/L	
	RfD	1.0 mg/kg/day[a]	EPA 2017d
WHO	Drinking water quality guidelines	Not established[b]	WHO 2017
FDA	EAFUS	No data[c]	FDA 2013c
		Cancer	
HHS	Carcinogenicity classification	No data	NTP 2016
EPA	Carcinogenicity classification	Not likely to be carcinogenic to humans	EPA 2017c, 2017d, 2020
IARC	Carcinogenicity classification	Group 2A[d]	IARC 2017
		Occupational	
ACGIH	TLV	No data	ACGIH 2016
OSHA	PEL (8-hour TWA) for general industry	No data	OSHA 2016b

Table 4. Regulations and guidelines applicable to glyphosate

Agency	Description	Information	Reference
NIOSH	REL (up to 10-hour TWA)	No data	NIOSH 2016
		Emergency Criteria	
EPA	AEGLs-air	No data	EPA 2016b
DOE	PACs-air	No data	DOE 2018

THE STATE OF WASHINGTON DEPARTMENT

The Washington State Pesticide Laws and Related Regulations Handbook permits the purchase of glyphosate, however, an applicator license for commercial use is required or the user must be under the supervision of a Structural Pest Inspector (SPI) to apply for the product. Depending on the use of glyphosate, applicator license type and supervision requirement will vary. Table 5 lists WSDA applicator license types and supervision requirements (WSDA, 2019). SPI license holders must certify every five years and earn continuing education credits. A license applicator who supervises an unlicensed user is responsible for the safe use of pesticides. Although the State of Washington permits the use of glyphosate under strict supervision, some products are federally listed as restricted use pesticides (RUP) and are identified on the product label. Washington RUPs is listed in the WAC 16-228-1231 and 16-228-1235 under the Washington State General Pesticide Rules (WSDA, 2019). Fortunately, there are safer alternatives to glyphosate and other pesticides.

Table 5. WSDA supervision and application types

LICENSE TYPE	DIRECT SUPERVISION REQUIREMENTS
Private Applicator	Certified applicator is available if and when needed and does not have to be physically present for most uses. A few highly toxic restricted use pesticides require either on-site supervision or use by a certified applicator only, per label restrictions.
Commercial Applicator *(Non-Forestry)*	Certified applicator must be physically present and always within eye and earshot of the unlicensed person whenever an application occurs.
Commercial Applicator *(Forestry)*	These applications do not require constant voice and visual contact if the worker applies general use pesticides with non-power equipment. Certified applicator must be on site and readily available to directly observe the mixing and loading of the pesticide.
Public Operator	The unlicensed applicator must be supervised when applying a restricted use pesticide or any pesticide using power equipment. Certified applicator must be physically present and always within eye and earshot of the unlicensed person.
In all of the situations described above, the person who supervises the unlicensed applicator must be properly licensed to perform the application. This means maintaining a current license and holding any required license categories.	

ENVIRONMENTALLY SAFER ALTERNATIVES

The efficacy of pesticides and herbicides are clear, however, there are drawbacks. Chemicals such as glyphosate, if improperly used can be dangerous, and although effective, are strictly regulated, require special licensing and training, and continuing education (WSDA, 2019). Fortunately, there are safer alternatives to glyphosate. The Southern California Coastal Water Research Project (SCCWRP), SCCWRP Technical Report #1103, revealed that there are safer and environmentally friendly alternatives to glyphosate. A technical committee of leading scientists (Table 6), from the University of California, USA, the University of Guelph, Ontario, Canada, and the City of Irvin revealed in Table 7, four categories of safer alternatives to glyphosate (Chiotti et al., 2020).

Table 6. SCCWRP members of the technical committee

Area of Expertise	Name (Affiliation)
Integrated Pest Management	Dr Cheryl Wilen (University of California)
Weed Scientist	Dr Travis Bean (University of California)
Ecotoxicologist	Dr Dan Schlenk (University of California)
Human Toxicologist	Dr Len Ritter (University of Guelph)
Practitioner	Dennis Chiotti (City of Irvine)

Table 7. SCCWRP list of alternative methods for glyphosate

Physical	Mechanical	Biological	Chemical
Hand, Hoe	Mowing	Grazing	Post-emergent herbicides
Mulching	Flaming		Pre-emergent herbicides
Weed mat	Steaming		Organic herbicides
	Steaming with Foam		
	Tillage		

The alternatives listed in Table 7 are effective, however, two common, safer, and less labor-intensive alternatives are pre-emergent and post-emerge herbicides.

PRE-EMERGENT HERBICIDES – CORN GLUTEN MEAL (CGM)

Corn Gluten Meal is a safer alternative to glyphosate because it is an organic byproduct to corn that blocks the germination process, preventing the weed from sprouting (Hanson, 2025). CGMs form an invisible barrier in the soil that protects the crop, provides nutrients for growth but prevents weeds from sprouting. CGMs are safer, and unlike glyphosate, require no special licensing or supervision, basic personal protective equipment (PPE), and applied with a spreader, Image 1, found in many garden supply locations. The limitation of CGM compared to glyphosate is that CGMs are less potent and require multiple applications compared to glyphosate, which is a chemical, specially created to fight infestations. CGM should be applied in the spring to prevent spring germination and in the summer to prevent winter germination.

(Hanson, 2025)

BENEFITS OF A WHO-COMPATIBLE DATA-SHARING EHR SYSTEM

Whether the chemical is glyphosate or another substance, EHR systems enhanced with WHO chemical safety metadata can empower researchers to resolve debates in research data through cross-border surveillance in real-time, exposure tracking, and geospatial ANOVA comparisons. Additionally, the combination of WHO (global health), Public Health, and Medicine metadata creates opportunities for other chemical safety research.

Timely Detection

A WHO-Compatible EHR system allows global, public, and national health systems to share potential environmental health and safety hazard data across multiple states or international borders and make life-saving policy changes and decisions in a timely manner. An international study found that by the year 2020, over 880 tons of glyphosate and 4,090 tones enters rivers across the globe (Zhang et al., 2024). When the pollution began is not clear, however, when considering the 880 tons discovered in 2020, how many locals, people that depend on the rivers, were infected? What, if any, correlations, or causations, are there between sicknesses such as cancer and glyphosate? Mostly importantly, how would a WHO-compatible, data-sharing EHR system, have benefited national public health systems within the nations along the river?

Water Safety Plans and International Data-Sharing

Water Safety Plans (WSPs) are WHO recommended management and risk assessments to ensure water safety (String & Lantagne, 2016). In the event of correlations and causations between glyphosate and illnesses, for a care provider treating a patient, WHO metadata is vital to toxic substance detection. WHO metadata sharing with national toxic substance databases and local EHRs, allows deep learning to help providers in nations along the river to diagnose the sicknesses, determine the origin of the sickness, implement policy changes, prevent food infections such as fish or other consumables impacted by the rivers through health alerts and food recalls. The WHO has recommended Water Safety Plans (WSP) to integrated into public health systems since 2004 (Setty & Ferrero, 2021).

Transborder Cooperation

A WHO-Compatible EHR system, powered by AI, would significantly support a WSP to protect water resources between the states of Washington, Oregon, and Idaho from glyphosate. The three states share:

- The Columbia River, the largest river in the Pacific Northwest (PNW)
- The Snake River, which flows through Oregon, Washington, Idaho, and Wyoming
- Tributaries to the Snake Rivers such as the Salmon and Clearwater Rivers
- Grande Ronde and Imnaha Rivers, which flows from Oregon into the Snake River

The rivers are part of an intricate and critical network that supports agriculture, hydroelectric power, public water works, and fisheries (Whitehead, 1994). An integrated WSP supported by transborder data benefits all states in the region.

CONCLUSION

Globalization and population growth will increase global demand for food resources. Glyphosate and other pesticides are effective, but there is debate in the literature as to its safety. Environmentally friendly alternatives, as listed in Table 7, offer an opportunity to protect food resources, the environment, and human safety. A WHO-Compatible multinational data-sharing public health EHR system promotes environmental safety research, supports WSPs, and protects water resources.

REFERENCES

Carter, S. K. (2024). Using Electronic Health Records (EHR) For Disease Surveillance (EHR-DS) To Support UN Sdgs. In *Computational Convergence And Interoperability In Electronic Health Records (EHR)* (Pp. 137-152). IGI Global.

Chiotti, D., Leonard, R., Schlenk, D., Wilen, C., & Schiff, K. (2020). Alternatives To Glyphosate For Vegetation Management. In *Los Angeles County; Technical Committee Report*. Southern California Coastal Water Research Project.

De Morais Valentim, J. M. B., Coradi, C., Viana, N. P., Fagundes, T. R., Micheletti, P. L., Gaboardi, S. C., Fadel, B., Pizzatti, L., Candiotto, L. Z. P., & Panis, C. (2024). Glyphosate As A Food Contaminant: Main Sources, Detection Levels, And Implications For Human And Public Health. *Foods*, *13*(11). Https://Doi.Org/10.3390/Foods13111697 PMID: 38890925

Hanson, K. (2025). When Should You Apply Pre-Emergent To Your Lawn? *Southern Living*. Https://Www.Southernliving.Com/When-To-Apply-Pre-Emergent-11679145?Utm_Source=Chatgpt.Com

Mccloskey, D. N. (2023, September 12). *Globalization Creates A Global Neighborhood, Benefiting All*. Cato.Org. Https://Www.Cato.Org/Publications/Globalization-Isnt-Going-Anywhere

Pohl, H. R., Wohlers, D., Chou, C.-H., Citra, M. J., Fay, M., Coley, C., Harper, C., Ingerman, L., Buser, M. C., & Ingber, S. Z. (2019). Toxicological Profile For Glyphosate: Draft For Public Comment.

Rabine, A., & Faber, S. (2025). *Trump EPA May Threaten State And Local Use Of Toxic Weekkiller Glyphosate*. Https://Www.Ewg.Org/News-Insights/News/2025/02/Trump-Epa-May-Threaten-State-And-Local-Bans-Toxic-Weedkiller-Glyphosate?Utm_Source=Chatgpt.Com

Setty, K., & Ferrero, G. (2021). Water Safety Plans. In *Oxford Research Encyclopedia Of Global Public Health*.

String, G., & Lantagne, D. (2016). A Systematic Review Of Outcomes And Lessons Learned From General, Rural, And Country-Specific Water Safety Plan Implementations. *Water Science and Technology: Water Supply*, *16*(6), 1580–1594.

Valavanidis, A. (2018). Glyphosate, The Most Widely Used Herbicide. *Scientific Review (Singapore)*.

WGU. (2020b). *Lesson 2:1 Environmental Toxicology [MOOC]*. Https://Apps.Cgp-Oex.Wgu.Edu/Wgulearning/Course/Course-V1:Wgux+OEX0355+V01/Block-V1:Wgux+OEX0355+V01+Type@Sequential+Block@662276f3ef464de1ac3982501619e38b/Block-V1:Wgux+OEX0355+V01+Type@Vertical+Block@0c7456123f3e41cdb15dde01f8e15ea6

Whitehead, R. (1994). *Ground Water Atlas Of The United States: Segment 7, Idaho, Oregon, Washington* (060776757X).

Winslett, G. (2023). Digital Trade. In *Services: Globalization's Exciting New Frontier*. Globalization.

WSDA. (2019). Washington Pesticide Laws And Related Regulations Handbook. In W. S. D. O. A. P. M. Division (Ed.).

Zhang, Q., Li, Y., Kroeze, C., Xu, W., Gai, L., Vitsas, M., Ma, L., Zhang, F., & Strokal, M. (2024). A Global Assessment Of Glyphosate And AMPA Inputs Into Rivers: Over Half Of The Pollutants Are From Corn And Soybean Production. *Water Research*, *261*, 121986. PMID: 38924948

APPENDIX

Chapter 6 Study Questions

1. What are WSPs and why are they important?
2. How would an EHR system that shares metadata between the WHO, public and national health systems enhance WSP efficacy?
3. There is debate within the data on glyphosate safety, how would a WHO-Compatible data-sharing EHR system improve glyphosate safety research?
4. Based off what you have learned, how could the State of Washington and its surrounding states of Oregon and Idaho benefit from a WSP?
5. How could a WHO-Compatible EHR system prevent chemical contamination in water sources?
6. What is the US DHHS Agency for Toxic Substances and Disease Registry and why is it important?
7. Natural alternatives to glyphosate are often used in states or nations with more stringent environmental safety requirements, based on what you have learned, as a leader in a government organization, how would you use a WHO-Compatible EHR system to promote the use of natural alternatives.
8. How can governments and public health organizations use the WHO-Compatible EHR system to prevent events such as the 880 tons of glyphosate contamination in the future?
9. What is the Dose-Response Relationship to Glyphosate and why is it important?
10. How can a WHO-Compatible EHR system promote the use of natural alternatives to glyphosate?

Chapter 7
Public Health Functions From a Multinational Perspective

ABSTRACT

This chapter, titled "Public Health Functions from a Multinational Perspective," maps core public health functions—surveillance, outbreak response, health promotion, and policy development—onto a multinational framework. It explores how interoperable EHR systems can enhance coordination across borders, especially during pandemics and humanitarian crises. Drawing on examples from regional blocs such as the African Union and ASEAN, the chapter identifies both technical and diplomatic challenges to multinational public health integration.

INTRODUCTION

The threat of disease outbreaks increasingly plagues international cities, endangering millions of lives and strangulating domestic and global economies and public health agency resources. The first U.S. travel-associated cases of Ebola in Dallas, TX, in 2014, and COVID-19 in Seattle, WA, in 2020 highlight the importance of epidemic preparedness in large urban settings. Although globally, the disease has taken more lives than all the world's wars combined (Norrie, 2016), large international cities are particularly vulnerable to outbreaks as they are essential to globalization and hubs to international trade with transcontinental logistics operations, business travelers, tourism, and immigration and asylum seekers, escaping poverty and seeking a better life (Carter, 2024). In 2020, during the COVID-19 pandemic, urban areas (large cities) experienced more loss of life, 97.7 per 100,00, as shown in Figure 1, than rural areas (Curtin & Heron, 2022). The earth consists of 8.2 billion

DOI: 10.4018/979-8-3693-2027-3.ch007

people within 195 countries, of which the United Nations recognize 193, sharing human and natural resources, goods, and services across 510 million kilometers (197 million miles) (Carter, 2024). Most of the world's population resides in urban areas, and large cities directly and indirectly impact human health (Kadakia & Galea, 2023). However, increased urbanization and the accompanying challenges are not a temporary trend; they will increase.

Figure 1. Age-adjusted COVID-19 death rates by urbanicity of county residence: United States 2020

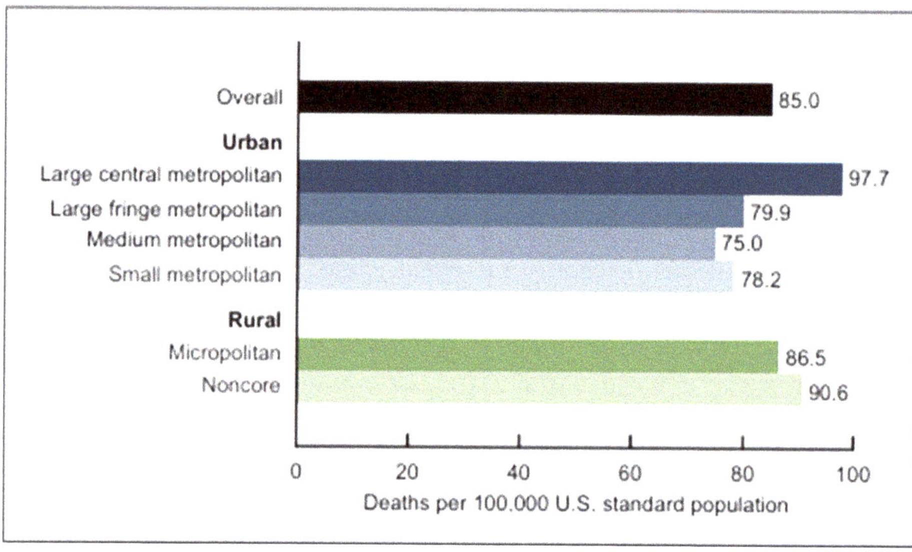

In 2018, the global population was 4.2 billion, of which 55% lived in large cities. By 2050, 68% of the global population will live in densely populated metropolitan areas where infectious diseases originate or propagate (Lee et al., 2020). Globalization and its impact on large cities offer businesses in Low-to-Middle Income Countries (LMIC) access to international markets to share resources, goods, and services. Globalization and its impact on large cities also provide immense opportunities to those seeking better employment and escape poverty (Follett, 2023). There are, however, significant risks to increased human mobilization (Carter, 2024). Protecting large towns from the dangers of globalization, such as outbreaks, is essential to urban populations and those who travel to and from them. Although the Ebola outbreak and Covid-19 pandemic originated on foreign soil, they traveled to the United States, making global health a challenge to population health and public health systems.

POPULATION HEALTH AND PUBLIC HEALTH

Population health addresses threats and targets efforts on interventions in specific groups within a population. Cities and populations are interlinked (Lai et al., 2020). Public health is a multidisciplinary science requiring a convergence of data-driven resources to develop an effective outbreak prevention and response system. In a more simplistic and supplemental context, public health prevents disease, promotes health, and protects populations (Caron, 2022). The primary objective of public health is to prevent and reduce the impact of a public health event (Nassar, 2024). Public health agencies endeavor to develop and maintain organized, proactive initiatives within multiple disciplines to protect the health and well-being of communities such as large cities, respond to public health emergencies, and extrapolate and monitor relevant data to predict and prepare for future public health threats. The tenets of public health are pathology and toxicology, internal medicine and epidemiology, environmental health, and health education and behavioral science (Birkhead et al., 2020). Epidemiology is indispensable to outbreak preparedness and measures the cause, migration, and impacts of disease in populations (Turnock et al., 2022). A timely and effective response is critical during an outbreak in a large city. Epidemiology is an evidence-based science that studies the cause or determinants of disease. It proactively uses multifaceted approaches in the prevention process, such as epidemiological models and methodologies, to intervene and protect populations from outbreaks or effectively respond to outbreaks and save lives. Turnock (2022) revealed that *Primary Prevention, Secondary Prevention, and Tertiary Prevention* are common approaches in public health and disease prevention.

Primary, Secondary, and Tertiary prevention measures work in tandem with a commonly used epidemiological models such as the SIR Model. During an outbreak in a large international city, the SIR model supports and enhances primary, secondary, and tertiary prevention measures by helping public health professionals divide the population into three categories, Susceptible, Infected, and Removed.

SIR MODEL

During an outbreak in a large urban setting, public trust, access to vital materials such as personal protective equipment (PPE) and vaccines and partnering with external resources such as local public health agencies and federal agencies such as the Centers for Disease Control and Prevention (CDC) are essential. Therefore, preventative measures must include multiple local and non-local agencies operating with data-driven measures to ensure that the three preventative efforts are proportionate to the threat and directed equitably. During an outbreak in a large city, the three preventative levels and epidemiological models are robust tools to enhance data-driven intervention efforts. Commonly, epidemiological models are compartmentalized, dividing large urban populations into three groups: those who are Susceptible to infection relevant to the city's population, those who are Infected relevant to the population, and those who have recovered from the infection pertinent to the percentage to the Infected percentage, and Removed from the list of Susceptible (Milgroom, 2023). Primary, Secondary, and Tertiary preventative measures and SIR Modeling are robust tools in disease prevention and outbreak responses in large cities.

Outbreak response preparedness in large urban settings is complex and delicate, with many relevant variables, as listed in Table 1 (Lee et al., 2020). The purpose of this text is to analyze the benefits of primary, secondary, and tertiary prevention measures during an outbreak in a large international city, the utilization of SIR modeling to support prevention measures, and the Centers for Disease Control and Prevention's (CDC) critical support during an outbreak in a large urban setting.

Table 1. Challenges and opportunities for epidemic preparedness associated with characteristics of urban settings

	Challenges	Opportunities
High population density and high volume of public transportation	A larger population to be managed, ease of disease spread between humans in congested areas; difficulties in contact tracing, especially causal contact in public areas; inequalities resulting in poor housing environments that might hinder outbreak prevention and control efforts; closer encounters with wildlife via food markets or because of expansion into previously untouched ecosystems	Urban planners can consider epidemic preparedness in their designs and implementation; transport networks can be used to rapidly move supplies to outbreak epicentres; harnessing advancement in technologies for more effective contact tracing
Interface between animals and humans	Areas of poor sanitation with rodents and other animal vectors, live domestic and wild animal markets; animals raised in backyard farms or industrial agricultural facilities in close proximity to humans	Improved sanitation and rodent control around humans and animal communities, vaccination of domestic animals for common zoonotic infections; precautions at slaughter to prevent contact with blood, regulating live animal markets to phase out sale of live animals or to ensure that those for sale are raised on commercial farms and have been verified to be disease free
Governance by local authorities	Competing interests within a finite local budget; insufficient authority to institute response measures promptly; insufficient epidemic preparedness capabilities or capacities at a subnational and local level, difficulties in accessing national capacities	Leaders in cities would be better placed to develop and implement effective and contextually appropriate solutions; consolidated local surveillance data can improve sense-making at the national level; local leaders can be engaged to advocate for greater investments in local systems
Heterogeneous subpopulations	A wide range of cultural factors, including modes of social interactions and acceptable control measures; some subpopulations might be difficult to reach	Community leaders can be mobilised for targeted approaches to preparedness and response; innovative solutions can be shared and adapted across cultures
High connectivity to other urban centres (domestic and international)	High likelihood of multiple importation events; risk of rapid export of disease to other parts of the country or to other countries; fear might lead to restrictions on travel and trade	Evidence-based points of entry measures and exit screening measures can be implemented; trust can be built through strong diplomatic relations to allow for better collaboration
Centres of commerce	Greater disruption to economic activity, stability, and growth	Businesses and corporations can be engaged in business continuity plans that also prevent further spread, as part of a whole-of-society approach
Unconventional communications and interactions	Multiple information sources leading to misinformation; false information might spread quickly	Unconventional but reliable information channels and social media can be used for risk communication

Table: Challenges, and opportunities for epidemic preparedness associated with characteristics of urban settings

INTERVENTION AND PREVENTION-PRIMARY, SECONDARY, TERTIARY

Intervention is a public health terminology that describes policies, strategies, sciences, and resource utilization to impact specific public health problems (Turnock et al., 2022). Interventions are relevant to the public health problem. Disease prevention in large cities such as Seattle and Dallas is an anticipatory intervention measure intended to prevent an outbreak or limit its impact on a population. Public health outbreak response and intervention efforts rely on three intervention levels: primary, secondary, and tertiary. SIR modelling is an accompaniment to the prevention level activities.

Primary Preventions – The Susceptible – Seattle, WA

Birkhead et al. (2020) opined that primary preventions are measures to prevent disease outbreaks or public injury by reducing exposure and lowering risk factors. This is foundational to an effective prevention strategy. Primary prevention measures in large cities are supported by partnerships with local and non-local resources to coach city and local officials on best practices to implement proactive measures such as vaccination programs, reducing environmental and cultural threats that elevate risks of outbreaks, lifestyle changes such as concentrated efforts on sanitation, social-distancing, avoiding large gatherings when possible, and reducing at-risk behaviors such as unprotected sex, and informing the public with robust health education programs in schools, hospitals, clinics, billboards, radio, city websites, public service announcements (PSA), and mailers. During the COVID-19 pandemic, although Seattle, WA, announced the first infection, clarity and truth were the first casualties. Misinformation and disinformation confused the public, incited panic, and fear, contributed to under vaccination, and impeded progress; primary preventative measures, such as vaccines, masking, and social distancing, became complex and contentious topics, hindering pandemic response efforts. In the event of another outbreak in Seattle, WA, public health agencies and population health agencies must synchronize and streamline efforts to target preventative efforts to specific Susceptible populations within Seattle, WA, compared to the total population (population health) of Seattle supported by verifiable data. SIR modelling is a robust tool for prevention and intervention.

Second, to confirm the Ebola outbreak in Dallas, TX, determining at-risk or susceptible communities or groups in Dallas is critical to outbreak intervention and must be data-driven. Healthcare, including public health, must be patient-centered, timely, efficient, and equitable (Schroeder et al., 2019). Data-driven susceptibility determination prevents misinformation or disinformation fear of vaccinations, reduces panic, and increases public trust. When a large city experiences an outbreak with untimely responses, conflicting information about the infection's properties, origins, and at-risk populations, such as ethnic cultures, locations, zip codes or districts, preexisting co-morbidities, and potential outcomes, panic ensues. When coupling this perfect storm with mass lockdowns where only essential workers earn income, limited government financial support resulting in the stress of unpaid rent, future eviction notices, and sources of income or employers permanently closing, the importance of determining susceptibility is evident. Determining susceptibility allows public health agencies to execute carefully thought-out protocols, target specific groups as needed, and protect economies and resources. The Centers for Disease Control and Prevention (CDC) is a government resource best suited to disease intervention and prevention.

Primary Prevention – The Susceptible and the CDC Field Epidemiology

The US CDC is the United States' primary public health agency. Based out of Atlanta, GA, the CDC protects the nation's public health, providing guidance and, when required, federally authorized mandates to prevent and control the spread of infectious diseases (Turnock et al., 2022). What makes the CDC different from local public health agencies is that in addition to its federal authority and funding, the CDC operates offices in over 60 countries, giving the CDC broad access to data resources and disease information before the infection reaches the United States, and best practices deployed in other nations. CDC support is critical in an outbreak in a large city because of its international resources, data access, and ability to respond to a crisis through *field epidemiology.*

Field epidemiology is the CDC's ability to rapidly respond to a public health crisis anywhere within its 60 countries of operation (Rasmussen & Goodman, 2018). Field epidemiology aims to select and initiate interventions to prevent or limit the impact of an outbreak. During the 1976 Legionnaire's Disease outbreak in Philadelphia, PA, a large international city, public health officials reported the disease to the CDC, and the CDC responded immediately, deploying resources hundreds of miles away. CDC solutions are data-driven, which is essential to supporting primary prevention efforts.

A large city or population's pandemic preparedness plan must be data-driven. A data-driven plan supports goal setting, promotes accuracy, prevents stigmatization of the innocent, and measures progress. The COVID-19 outbreak, which began in Seattle, WA, revealed shortfalls in decision-making and policies due to a lack of information and data or disinformation and data. The data shortfall resulted in stigmatization and discriminatory policies against demographics and nations, hurting economies and trade as many nations experienced under the 1969 version of the IHR (Carter, 2024). The CDC adopted a Public Health Data Strategy (PHDS), Figure 1, which is an effective strategy for large cities to ensure accurate disease data collection, provide correct information, and empower public health agencies to respond to outbreaks effectively(CDC, 2024). The PHDS consists of four public health goals:

- *Strengthening the core of public health*
- *Accelerate access to analytic and automated solutions to support public health investigations and advance health quality*
- *Visualize and share insights to inform public health action*
- *Advance more open and interoperable public health data*

During an outbreak, large cities like Philadelphia, Dallas, and Seattle work with population and public health agencies at the state and federal agencies. Therefore, adopting a pandemic preparedness plan or mirroring state and federal agencies is essential to save time, eliminate wasted resources, and maximize efficiency. Community-based efforts are vital (Nassar, 2024). Primary preventions are proactive, effective measures to prevent infection. However, once a population is infected, the susceptible population becomes infected, and secondary prevention measures are necessary.

Secondary Prevention – The Infected and the CDC

Early detection is vital during an outbreak in a large city such as Dallas, TX and Seattle, WA, if primary preventions are ineffective. It helps the population and public health agencies detect and prevent the spread of the disease (Turnock et al., 2022). Secondary prevention promotes identifying disease while the infected are asymptomatic with measures such as targeted screenings and early diagnosis to enhance the chances of desired outcomes in infected groups within a population. Pre-identified Susceptible groups with data-driven confirmed cases in verifiable areas allow health officials to target prevention efforts when and where needed to prevent the virus from spreading. Understanding the virus' reproduction rate among the Infected is essential to secondary prevention efforts such as machine learning, data mining, and information-sharing with the public, population health officials, state public health officials, and federal agencies. A virus' reproduction rate, the R(0), is the projected number of secondary cases by an infected patient (Yadav et al., 2021). The Infected calculation of the SIR Model is the number of people in a population currently infected from the time of outbreak confirmation to the time of the most recent reading. It is divided into the total population and the number of susceptible people within the population. However, the R_0 is the projected reproduction rate from one person to another. It is disease-specific and is based on how long the infection is contagious after infection, the possibility of infection between the infected and the Susceptible, and the contact rate (β). It is critical to understand the R_0, the contact rate (β), the average number of contacts between the Susceptible and the infected, and the Susceptible number to implement an effective Secondary prevention measure.

In a large city, in addition to individuals, local public transportation systems, airports, grocery stores or other venues for large gatherings are susceptible to outbreaks. Contact-tracing and contact rates are essential for tracking the infected. Foot traffic is a measurement used to determine the number of people entering an area over time. The Centers for Disease Control and Prevention (CDC) and its experts and resources are exponentially relevant and essential to such detailed measurements during an outbreak in a large city.

Tertiary Prevention – Measuring Removal and the CDC

Tertiary prevention occurs after an infection event (Nassar, 2024), and its purpose is to slow or block it entirely to reduce harm to the infected. It is post-diagnosis and requires timely treatment, follow-up, and patient recovery services such as rehabilitation and education (Turnock et al., 2022). During the COVID-19 pandemic, tertiary efforts in large cities were and remain essential to restoring the sick to full Recovery and protecting those with weakened immune systems from infections. The COVID-19 pandemic remains the most significant health emergency of the 21st century because, in addition to the acute COVID symptoms, tertiary prevention efforts and compiling Removal data are hindered due to post-infection longer-term symptoms and challenges, post-acute COVID (long COVID) (Koc et al., 2022). Koc et al., (2022) revealed in Figure 2 that after the Infectious state, trackable with the SIR Model, if the patients survive between the infectious and Recovery phases, the convalescence phase, the patient will recover, and public and population health officials can Remove the retrieved from the roster of infected. However, some infected with acute COVID experience post-acute symptoms such as pulmonary function impairment, neurological damage, cognitive impairment, dysbiosis and compromised integrity, metabolic disorder, and kidney injury phase, putting their Recovery into question. Therefore, a tertiary prevention plan in a large city must be prepared for post-acute or long-term residual symptoms. Collaboration and synergized efforts between local state public health officials, population health agencies, and the CDC are vital to tertiary prevention efforts in the event of an outbreak in a large city to not only treat acute symptoms of an infection in large populations but to diagnose, monitor, and care for the those infected with post-diagnosis impairments.

Figure 2. Long COVID and its management

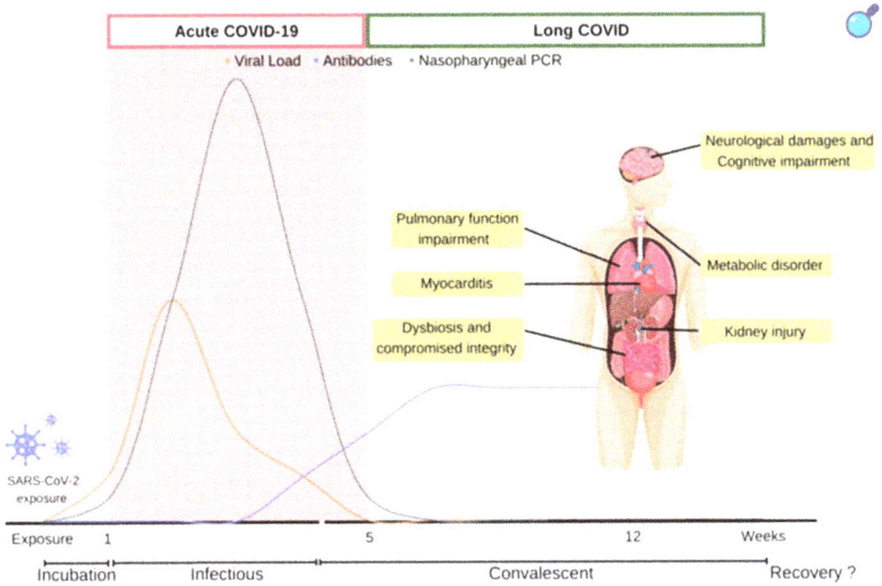

Note. Created Figure 2 from Long COVID and its Management. Int J Biol

KEY INSIGHTS

The three levels of prevention are essential to pandemic response planning. They are especially critical to responding to an outbreak in a large urban area, such as Seattle, WA, and Dallas, TX. While large cities benefit from current processes and prevention levels before, during, and after an event (Nassar, 2024), current processes and systems are not interoperable across nations and verticals, nor do they share data across the methods a virus travels.

Globalization will continue to expand (Lincicome, 2023). The projections for urban population growth and increased human mobility associated with globalization put large cities at risk and susceptible to outbreaks (Kadakia, 2023). Global health security begins with robust public health processes (Carter, 2024). Therefore, because outbreaks in large cities are multinational, public health officials must include the three levels of prevention but apply them from a multinational perspective, understanding the positive and negative elements of the prevention strategies.

Primary Prevention – Positives

During a disease outbreak, primary prevention measures are proactive actions taken to prevent diseases from occurring (Turnock et al., 2022). Population analysis with SIR modeling provides public health officials with data to identify Susceptible (at-risk) groups within a population over a period of time. Identifying susceptible groups rely on data. The data highlights leading indicators to potential outbreaks of known infection, and public health emergencies may be averted through vaccinations, public health education, and lifestyle changes. However, misinformation, disinformation, and a lack of leadership buy-in will stifle the most comprehensive primary prevention efforts.

Primary Prevention – Negatives

During the COVID-19 pandemic, the first casualties were transparency, accurate data, leadership buy-in, and public trust. Political polarizations opportunistically promoting one conspiracy theory after another relevant to the origins of the virus, the fear of a publicly unknown virus, lack of vaccine access, and ambiguous answers from local and global health organizations to prevent panic created fear and eroded public trust. While the efficacy of primary prevention is apparent, the only vaccines for misinformation, fear, and poor leadership are data-driven truths and transparency. However, due to supply chain shortages, truths, facts, and clarity were limited in quantities.

Secondary Prevention – Positives

During a disease outbreak such as COVID-19 in Seattle, WA, secondary preventions occur during an event, and the number of infections within a group of susceptible populations is measured over time and treated promptly. Secondary preventions rely on screenings and early diagnosis in targeted groups to initiate rapid responses and interventions to limit the impact of infection and preserve life. The process relies on data such as the R(0), which is a virus' reproduction rate (Yadav et al., 2021), the contact rate (β), the average number of contacts between the Susceptible and the infected, and the Susceptible number to implement an effective Secondary prevention measure. Secondary prevention also has challenges and limitations displayed during the COVID-19 pandemic. SIR Modeling effectively divides populations into groups: Susceptible, Infected, and Recovered (Milgroom, 2023). The Infected data of the SIR Model is an effective accompaniment to secondary preventions. However, although the two processes are effective when implementing an outbreak preparedness plan, there are shortfalls to consider.

Secondary Prevention – Negatives

During a disease outbreak, early detection screening to calculate the infection is a delicate process that must be data-driven, and consider the patient's needs and rights, the uninfected, and privacy. During the recent COVID-19 pandemic, testing was a contentious and, at times, combative conversation. Nations implementing travel bans require proof of negative test results and vaccinations before boarding an aircraft or clearing customs checks. Although the processes were consistent with secondary prevention measures, they incited anger, fear, and distrust. The lack of data-driven coherent information was a contributing factor to staunch resistance.

Tertiary Prevention – Positives

Tertiary prevention measures are post-infection processes that focus on restoring the patient's health and preventing long-term effects or disability from a disease. Also, tertiary prevention provides self-help programs to empower the patient to protect family members from infections and protect themselves from recurrences. The Removal data within the SIR model helps public health officials track patients who are no longer sick and may be removed from the list of infected or susceptible but may require additional rehabilitative care.

Tertiary Prevention – Negatives

A negative aspect of tertiary care is that it is challenging to determine patient needs and treat the long-term effects of diseases like COVID-19. Although COVID-19 vaccines are available, and millions are vaccinated, currently, many suffer from post-acute COVID (long COVID) with debilitating symptoms. COVID-19 is a new virus, and so is its vaccine. Due to the severity of the crisis and lethality of COVID-19, vaccines were expeditiously approved for use without understanding their long-term effects. The relevant data on the causation or correlation of long COVID-19, whether the vaccine or the virus itself, remains under review.

SUSTAINABILITY PREVENTION LEVELS

Primary Preventions - Vaccinations

Primary prevention strategies are paramount to disease intervention planning. Vaccination programs, for example, build community (herd) immunity to viruses, reducing the number of susceptible. Lessening the number of susceptible, reduces the likelihood of being infected.

Vaccine access is a potential barrier to sustainability during an outbreak due to the lengthy approval process for a new vaccine. Also, once a vaccine is approved, supply chain shortages may make the vaccine unattainable. A strategy to overcome vaccine accessibility is to include alternative medicine experts as subject matter experts (SMEs) in the outbreak response planning process. Before modern medicine, communities relied on herbal remedies and survived horrible diseases like the Black Plague. Although millions died during the Black Plague, millions also survived.

Secondary Preventions – Surveillance

Secondary prevention measure enhances early detection through screening and surveillance of susceptible populations, crisis management, and rapid response teams. Secondary also involves data-sharing with public health organizations, and health alerts.

Tertiary Preventions - Health Education

Health education programs with data-driven information inform the public of the infection, its threat, how to protect themselves and family members, and community activities and self-help resources. Data-driven health information prevents panic and hysteria and builds and maintains public trust and cooperation.

During the COVID-19 pandemic, access to reliable health information was a barrier to sustainability. There were many heartbreaking stories of families losing a loved one due to misinformation, often information regarding masking, social distancing, or vaccinations. A strategy to overcome a health information /self-help gap is to protect oneself and keep a supply of antibacterial soap, hand sanitizer, extra cans of approved disinfectants such as Lysol, and N95 masks in the home, personal carry bags or purses, or car glove box. Surgical gloves are handy when in a public setting. If one must leave the house, one shouldn't eat a large meal or drink a lot of fluids before leaving the home to prevent public bathroom trips. Schedule non-essential face-to-face meetings via a virtual platform such as Zoom or Webex when possible.

CONCLUSION

There are many key takeaways from this text. One is that the threat of a pandemic in a large city is just as accurate, if not more so, than a military invasion by an enemy from a hostile nation because the disease has claimed more lives than all the world's wars combined. Large international cities are more susceptible to infection than rural areas. By 2050, over 68 per cent of the world will live in densely populated cities. Understanding that global health emergencies begin as domestic public health problems is the foundation for building an outbreak preparedness system. The COVID-19 and Ebola infections revealed many opportunities for improvement. Still, there must be significant policy changes at the city, county, state, and federal levels, as well as at the global level.

There must be a convergence of technologies from all industries and commitments from all global leaders to develop and form more collaborative and effective alliances to combat the spread of diseases, not ideologies (Carter, 2019). Nations invest hundreds of billions of dollars in military defense to fight a war that may never come. At the same time, an elusive and lethal enemy which has no political or geopolitical leanings, religious biases, or preferences has already killed millions and continues to kill every year on all sides.

Action Plan

Funding is often a barrier to changing initiatives, but self-analyses are free. Public health officials and pandemic response planners at all levels can create policies that begin with the lessons learned from COVID-19 and Ebola and understand that both outbreaks were transcontinental. They can form policy review committees and devote 10-20 minutes of monthly or quarterly meetings to ask questions such as what worked during the COVID-19 pandemic? What failed? Why did it fail? What could have been avoided? What are the contingency plans and protocols for the next pandemic? They can also create new policies by understanding their communities' demographics, travel habits, and when. Although a direct connection to the holiday has not been established, COVID-19 began during the Chinese New Year, so are there times of the year when the planners should exercise more caution and release more public service messages on the dangers of disease? When compared to the high price of the COVID-19 pandemic, these ideas are but a handful of many no-cost discussions on low-cost possibilities and opportunities for change.

REFERENCES

Birkhead, G. S., Morrow, C. B., & Pirani, S. (2020). *Turnock's Public Health: What It Is and How It Works: What It Is and How It Works*. Jones & Bartlett Learning.

Caron, R. M. (2022). *Population health, epidemiology, and public health: management skills for creating healthy communities*. Health Administration Press.

Carter, S. K. (2019). *The strategies global leaders need to improve interoperability of an EHR system*. Colorado Technical University.

Carter, S. K. (2024). Using Electronic Health Records (EHR) for Disease Surveillance (EHR-DS) to Support UN SDGs. In *Computational Convergence and Interoperability in Electronic Health Records (EHR)* (pp. 137-152). IGI Global.

CDC. (2024). *CDC Public Health Data Strategy: About the Public Health Data Strategy (PHDS)*. United States Centers for Disease Control and Prevention. https://www.cdc.gov/public-health-data-strategy/php/about/index.html

Curtin, S. C., & Heron, M. (2022). COVID-19 death rates in urban and rural areas: United States, 2020.

Follett, C. (2023). *Globalization and Growing Global Equality*. Globalization.

Kadakia, K. T., & Galea, S. (2023). Urbanization and the Future of Population Health. *The Milbank Quarterly*, *101*(S1), 153–175. DOI: 10.1111/1468-0009.12624 PMID: 37096620

Koc, H. C., Xiao, J., Liu, W., Li, Y., & Chen, G. (2022). Long COVID and its Management. *International Journal of Biological Sciences*, *18*(12), 4768–4780. DOI: 10.7150/ijbs.75056 PMID: 35874958

Lai, K. Y., Webster, C., Kumari, S., & Sarkar, C. (2020). The nature of cities and the Covid-19 pandemic. *Current Opinion in Environmental Sustainability*, *46*, 27–31. https://doi.org/https://doi.org/10.1016/j.cosust.2020.08.008 PMID: 32874374

Lee, V. J., Ho, M., Kai, C. W., Aguilera, X., Heymann, D., & Wilder-Smith, A. (2020). Epidemic preparedness in urban settings: New challenges and opportunities. *The Lancet. Infectious Diseases*, *20*(5), 527–529. PMID: 32224312

Lincicome, S. (2023, September 12). *Globalization isn't going anywhere*. CATO Institute. https://www.cato.org/publications/globalization-isnt-going-anywhere

Milgroom, M. G. (2023). Epidemiology and SIR Models. In Milgroom, M. G. (Ed.), *Biology of Infectious Disease: From Molecules to Ecosystems* (pp. 253–268). Springer International Publishing., DOI: 10.1007/978-3-031-38941-2_16

Nassar, A. (2024, December 19, 2024). *D617 Public Health Core Functions and Essential Services: Task 3: Public Health Strategies.* https://wgu.hosted.panopto.com/Panopto/Pages/Viewer.aspx?id=0062fa01-13a2-441b-ab7d-b1d801216963

Norrie, P. (2016). A History of Disease. In *Ancient Times More Lethal Than War.* Springer International Publishing.

Rasmussen, S. A., & Goodman, R. A. (2018). *The CDC field epidemiology manual.* Oxford University Press.

Schroeder, P., Parisi, L. L., & Foster, R. (2019). Healthcare quality improvement: Then and now. *Nursing Management*, *50*(9), 20–25. DOI: 10.1097/01.Numa.0000579004.87116.35 PMID: 31460894

Turnock, B. J., Birkhead, G. S., Morrow, C. B., & Pirani, S. (2022). *Turnock's public health: what it is and how it works.* Jones & Bartlett Learning.

Yadav, A. K., Kumar, S., Singh, G., & Kansara, N. K. (2021). Demystifying R naught: Understanding what does it hide? *Indian Journal of Community Medicine : Official Publication of Indian Association of Preventive & Social Medicine*, *46*(1), 7–14. PMID: 34035567

APPENDIX

Chapter 7 Study Questions

1. Please explain prevention and intervention levels in global health and how they protect populations from international disease migration.
2. How can multinational global health data-sharing be used to close some of the negative gaps in prevent and intervention levels?
3. Large international cities offer global career opportunities, attract immigrants seeking a new life, and increase tourism. How can a WHO-Compatible multinational interoperable EHR system reduce or prevent Indigenous populations from potentially infected travelers or immigrants?
4. What is SIR modeling and why is it important?
5. How can integrated global health data-sharing support effective SIR modeling?
6. How can global health data-sharing support post-pandemic research?
7. Is long COVID and sickness at the primary, secondary, or tertiary prevention / intervention levels, and how can an integrated global health data-sharing system be used in research and pandemic preparedness?
8. Given what you have learned, what would you recommend to a public health official for your community?
9. What is field epidemiology?
10. In your opinion, is data-sharing vital to field epidemiology?

Chapter 8

WHO-Compatible EHR Systems to Align With Health Sustainable Prevention Measures, UN Sustainable Development Goals, and the WHO Pandemic Agreement

ABSTRACT

This chapter synthesizes the technical and policy requirements for developing EHR systems that align with WHO standards, the Sustainable Development Goals (SDGs), and the WHO Pandemic Agreement. It outlines interoperability benchmarks, equity safeguards, and governance mechanisms necessary for LMICs to participate meaningfully in global health data ecosystems. The chapter concludes with a roadmap for integrating digital health infrastructure into pandemic prevention strategies, emphasizing the need for inclusive design and sustained investment.

INTRODUCTION

There is an erroneous, and often accepted belief that the needs of the nation state always supersede the needs of the global community, or global challenges, are without question more important than the needs of a sovereign nation (Waldman & Javidan, 2020). Although in some instances both ideologies are appropriate, disease

DOI: 10.4018/979-8-3693-2027-3.ch008

surveillance and pandemic preparedness, however, demand a global approach. Ebola, COVID-19, Marburg, and Nipah, are deadly viruses and make no distinctions between demographics, nationalities, religions, political leanings, or sexual orientations. The false dichotomy between globalism and nationalism has hindered progress in global health also stated that global pandemic preparedness requires a multinational approach to combating disease, and that multinational EHR interoperability increases accessibility to urgent data for disease surveillance. The shortfalls in the 2005 IHR iteration reveal gaps in equality and data-sharing between national and global health systems, which contributed to a global pandemic and the deaths of millions. Fortunately, the World Health Assembly (WHA), in partnership with nation states, now share the vision and objective of a global approach to pandemic preparedness.

On April 16, 2025, during the 78th World Health Assembly, the Intergovernmental Negotiating Body (INB) approved a draft for a proposal for a global approach to pandemic prevention, preparedness, and response (UN, 2025). The WHO Pandemic Agreement lists three chapters and 35 articles that support a global approach to pandemic preparedness. *Chapter II, Articles 4-18, The World together equitably: Achieving equity in, for and through pandemic prevention, preparedness, and response,* available at https://www.who.int/news/item/20-05-2025-world-health-assembly-adopts-historic-pandemic-agreement-to-make-the-world-more-equitable-and-safer-from-future-pandemics highlight critical tenets of the agreement that has an immediate impact on frontline healthcare professionals battling disease. Fortunately, many of the articles listed in the agreement align with UN Sustainable Development Goals (SDGs), and Sustainable Prevention and Intervention Measures commonly practiced in global and public health, and the WHA is already positioned to implement the agreement with a WHO-Compatible data-sharing system EHR system.

SDGS / PREVENTION MEASURES / WHO PANDEMIC AGREEMENT ARTICLES

1. **SDG 1 (No Poverty) - Primary Prevention Measure – WHO Pandemic Agreement, Article 4 Pg10.** Pandemic preparedness must include increased surveillance and access to global health metadata sets from remote LMICs (Carter, 2024). Impoverished nations have a greater susceptibility to disease due to poor sanitation, unclean drinking water, unsafe food, and others socioeconomic causation to disease (Worsley-Tonks et al., 2022). Poverty is a leading indicator to disease outbreaks, and poor recovery once infected due to poor infrastructure, accessibility to care, and exposures.
2. **SDG 2 (Zero Hunger) - Primary Prevention Measure – WHO Pandemic Agreement Article 4 Pg 10.** One in nine people do not have enough food; es-

pecially in Asia and Sub-Saharan Africa (Kılıç, 2022). Pandemic preparedness must include a global effort to support UN SDG 2 to prevent disease outbreaks. A health human immune system, through proper nutrition, is essential to protecting the body from disease (Munteanu & Schwartz, 2022). global health metadata on hunger in LMICs, help global health organizations to reduce hunger and support pandemic preparedness.

3. **SDG 3 (Good Health and Well-being) - Primary, Secondary, and Tertiary Prevention Measures, WHO Pandemic Agreement Article 1 Pg 1, Article 7, Pg 13.** Good health and well-being are essential to pandemic preparedness, and are Primary, Secondary, and Tertiary sustainability prevention and intervention measures (Turnock et al., 2022). Vaccinations, education, and surveillance protects populations. Transborder data-sharing promotes multinational global health collaboration in combating disease outbreaks.
4. **SDG 4 (Quality Education) - Primary Prevention Measure – WHO Pandemic Agreement Article 5 Pg 12, Article 15, Pg 24.** Multinational data-sharing supports research between hospitals, global and public health agencies, which may be used in SIR modeling. In the event of an outbreak, SIR modeling is a tool used in disease surveillance, and it measures and tracks those who are **S**usceptible to the disease, those who are **I**nfected with a disease, and those who **R**ecover from a disease (WGU, 2024). Educating a population to preventative measures such as WASH, reduces exposures to disease and promotes better hygiene.
5. **SDG 5 (Gender Equality) - Primary Prevention Measure – WHO Pandemic Agreement Article 3, Pg 9** Ensuring that women and girls have equal access to screening, vaccines, and treatments is essential to combating disease and is essential to SIR modeling (WGU, 2024). Women and girl must have the screenings, vaccines, and treatments to not only protect themselves, but their nursing babies, and family members. In many cultures, women are responsible for food preparation and taking care of children. Also, in some cultures, multigenerational families are common. If the mother is sick, the children and the family's elders are potentially exposed.
6. **SDG 6 (Clean Water and Sanitation) - Primary Prevention Measure – WHO Pandemic Agreement Article 4, Pg 10.** Clean water and sanitation are critical to good health and disease prevention. Foodborne illnesses common causes to disease (Pires et al., 2021). Water is critical to disease prevention and is vital to irrigation systems for agriculture, food preparation, or drinking. Clean water and sanitation prevent disease migration.
7. **SDG 7 (Affordable and Clean Energy) - Primary Prevention Measure – WHO Pandemic Agreement Article 6, Pg 12** Affordable clean energy is essential to disease surveillance and intervention in LMICs and was of the fail-

ures of the International Health Regulations (IHR). The IHR requires nations to report disease outbreaks to the WHO, however, LMICs often do not have the infrastructure to operate labs, surveillance equipment, diagnostics systems, and other essentials to detect diseases or treat the infected. Simply put, LMICs are at a disadvantage without clean and renewable energy (Scheifele, 2024). LMICs must have affordable and clean energy to support a pandemic preparedness initiative.

8. **SDG 8 (Decent Work and Economic Growth) - Primary Prevention Measure – WHO Pandemic Agreement Article 7, Pg 13** Economic growth is vital to fund training and education in health sciences needed to prevent disease outbreaks. Unfortunately, some LMICs remain poor due to colonizations and other oppressions; being forced to surrender excessive quantities of GDP to their oppressors, leaving next to nothing to fund infrastructure projects such as hospitals, laboratories for epidemiological research, or medical training to develop new doctors. Also, many LMICs sit on a wealth of natural resources that could make them financially independent, however, oppressions and extortions from their former colonizers make benefiting from their natural resources and general development impossible (Bertocchi & Canova, 2002). When a sovereign nation has full access and unimpeded use of is financial resources, it can implement measures to be less dependent on external resources.
9. **SDG 9 (Industry, Innovation, and Infrastructure) - Secondary Prevention Measure – WHO Pandemic Agreement Article 6, Pg 12.** United Nations Sustainable Development Goal (SDGs) align with Global Health Sustainable Prevention Measures Multinational disease surveillance requires transnational EHR infrastructure integration (Igwama et al., 2024). Multinational digital health innovations and integrations are essential to global health initiatives (UN, 2021). SDG-9 offers LMICs opportunities to produce local innovations and industries to promote disease surveillance.
10. **SDG 10 (Reduced Inequalities) - Tertiary Prevention Measure – WHO Pandemic Agreement Article 2, Pg 8, Article 3, Pg 8** Equitable access is essential to global health initiatives and UN SDGs. The IHR system has significant gaps in global health equity (Carter, 2024); and the inequalities were exacerbated during the COVID-19 Pandemic (Alevizos et al., 2023), (Stuckelberger & Urbina, 2020). Determining **S**usceptibility to disease of all populations is critical SIR modeling and pandemic preparedness.
11. **SDG 11 (Sustainable Cities and Communities) - Secondary Prevention Measure – WHO Pandemic Agreement Article 11, Pg 17.** Due to their dense multinational populations, large international cities are preferred locations for industries, tourism, and immigration. International airports such as in Dallas, Seatle, Paris, and Berlin have numerous international departures and arrivals, and

are vulnerable to disease outbreaks transmitted by a sick patient, who depending on the R_0, may not display symptoms until after arrival to their destination (Sevilla, 2018). Urban planning must ensure that cities and communities are not only sustainable, but pandemic resilient (AbouKorin et al., 2021). Large cities have international airports and support multinational populations, international organizations and business travelers, and draw millions of tourists. Large cities and airports are on the frontline of disease surveillance.

12. **SDG 12 (Responsible Consumption and Production) - Secondary Prevention Measure – WHO Pandemic Agreement Article 10, Pg 16.** The objectives of SDG-12 and Global Health Secondary Prevention measures align with a global approach to disease surveillance and prevention. Responsible waste management, strict sterilization and biosafety protocols prevent disease (Thoradeniya & Jayasinghe, 2021). SDG-12 is UN approved, when used in tandem with the health levels of prevention and intervention, the WHO has a solid foundation for the WHO Pandemic Agreement.
13. **SDG 13 (Climate Action) - Primary Prevention Measure – WHO Pandemic Agreement Annex Pg, 6.** SDG-13 and the WHO Pandemic Agreement are interconnected and interrelated Primary Preventions. UN SDG-13 and the WHO Pandemic Agreement Objectives strive to promote prevent disease, promote public health, sustainability and safety, and reduce climate disruption which contribute to disease (Thoradeniya & Jayasinghe, 2021). In addition to Primary Prevention measures, the WHO's Pandemic Agreement and UN SDGs are approved of United Nations' initiatives and have the support of all UN recognized nations, allowing for pilot programs and in-depth explorations for implementation.
14. **SDG 14 (Life Below Water) - Primary Prevention Measure – WHO Pandemic Agreement Article 4, Pg 9** Some disease are waterborne and protecting water sources is critical to Primary Prevention (Grace, 2023). Zoonotic disease can travel through water, food from contaminated water, or ingesting rodents (Rahman et al., 2020). SDG-14 is especially sensitive as it can relate to culture. Some nations, out of culture or necessity, consume rodents such as rats for protein. However, there are alternative and safer sources for protein and global health organizations can enhance SDG-14 efforts through educating populations on safer choice.
15. **SDG 15 (Life on Land) - Tertiary Prevention Measure – WHO Pandemic Agreement Article 4, Pg 9** There is a significant correlation between deforestation and Zoonotic virus spillover (transmission from animals to human) (Fedurek et al., 2024). Protecting the earth's forests prevents a zoonotic spill over and the environment. In addition to SDG15, there are several UN initiative to reduce or prevent deforestation such as the UN Decade for Ecosystem Restoration (2021-2030), UN Decade for Afforestation and Reforestation (2027-2036), UN

Strategic Plan for Forest (2017-2030), and the UN Reducing Emissions from Deforestation and Forest Degradation (REDD) program. The global health community can accelerate progress by pursuing global health initiatives such as the WHO Pandemic agreement in tandem with SDG-15, and prevention and intervention levels through multinational WHO-Compatible EHR system.

16. **SDG 16 (Peace, Justice, and Strong Institutions) - Primary Prevention, Secondary, and Tertiary Prevention Measures – WHO Pandemic Agreement Article 9, Pg 15** Carter (2024) opined that global challenges and problems require global solutions. The World Health Organization, the World Health Assembly, and multinational Public Private Partnerships from many industries offer global leaders the ability to achieve global health goals such as the WHO Pandemic Agreement.
17. **SDG 17 (Partnerships for the Goals) - Primary Prevention, Secondary, and Tertiary Prevention Measure – WHO Pandemic Agreement Article 10, Pg16** Multinational collaboration is critical to pandemic preparedness initiatives such as the WHO Pandemic Agreement (Chattu et al., 2024). Public Private Partnerships (PPP) support the initiative by partnering the private sector which has the expertise required to accomplish the objectives but limited financial resources with the public sector who has the financial means, but lacks the expertise (Carter, 2024).

REFERENCES

AbouKorin, S. A. A., Han, H., & Mahran, M. G. N. (2021). Role of urban planning characteristics in forming pandemic resilient cities–Case study of Covid-19 impacts on European cities within England, Germany and Italy. *Cities (London, England), 118*, 103324. PMID: 34539022

Alevizos, A., Michail, M., Eleftheroglou, M., & Sidiropoulos, S. (2023). COVID-19 and the Exacerbation of Existing Inequalities: Why the Lower Socioeconomic Stratums Were Influenced the Most. *HAPSc Policy Briefs Series, 4*(1), 33–41.

Bertocchi, G., & Canova, F. (2002). Did colonization matter for growth?: An empirical exploration into the historical causes of Africa's underdevelopment. *European Economic Review, 46*(10), 1851–1871.

Carter, S. K. (2024). Using Electronic Health Records (EHR) for Disease Surveillance (EHR-DS) to Support UN SDGs. In *Computational Convergence and Interoperability in Electronic Health Records (EHR)* (pp. 137-152). IGI Global.

Chattu, V. K., Mol, R., Singh, B., Reddy, K. S., & Hatefi, A. (2024). Pandemic treaty as an instrument to strengthen global health security: Global health diplomacy at its crux. *Health Promotion Perspectives, 14*(1), 9. PMID: 38623344

Fedurek, P., Asiimwe, C., Rice, G. K., Akankwasa, W. J., Reynolds, V., Hobaiter, C., & Goldberg, T. L. (2024). Selective deforestation and exposure of African wildlife to bat-borne viruses. *Communications Biology, 7*(1), 470. PMID: 38649441

Grace, D. (2023). Burden of foodborne disease in low-income and middle-income countries and opportunities for scaling food safety interventions. *Food Security, 15*(6), 1475–1488. DOI: 10.1007/s12571-023-01391-3

Igwama, G. T., Olaboye, J. A., Maha, C. C., Ajegbile, M. D., & Abdul, S. (2024). Integrating electronic health records systems across borders: Technical challenges and policy solutions. *International Medical Science Research Journal, 4*(7), 788–796.

Kılıç, R. (2022). The problem of hunger in the world and a new model proposal to solve this problem. *Balkan Sosyal Bilimler Dergisi, 11*(21), 63–68.

Munteanu, C., & Schwartz, B. (2022). The relationship between nutrition and the immune system. *Frontiers in Nutrition, 9*, 1082500. PMID: 36570149

Pires, S. M., Desta, B. N., Mughini-Gras, L., Mmbaga, B. T., Fayemi, O. E., Salvador, E. M., Gobena, T., Majowicz, S. E., Hald, T., & Hoejskov, P. S. (2021). Burden of foodborne diseases: Think global, act local. *Current Opinion in Food Science, 39*, 152–159. PMID: 34178607

Rahman, M. T., Sobur, M. A., Islam, M. S., Ievy, S., Hossain, M. J., El Zowalaty, M. E., & Ashour, H. M. (2020). Zoonotic diseases: Etiology, impact, and control. *Microorganisms, 8*(9), 1405. PMID: 32932606

Scheifele, F. (2024). *Green Industrial Policy in Renewable Energy: Insights from Developing Countries*. Technische Universitaet Berlin.

Sevilla, N. L. (2018). Germs on a plane: The transmission and risks of airplane-borne diseases. *Transportation Research Record: Journal of the Transportation Research Board, 2672*(29), 93–102. PMID: 34285452

Stuckelberger, A., & Urbina, M. (2020). WHO international health regulations (IHR) vs COVID-19 uncertainty. *Acta Biomedica, 91*(2), 113. PMID: 32420935

Thoradeniya, T., & Jayasinghe, S. (2021). COVID-19 and future pandemics: A global systems approach and relevance to SDGs. *Globalization and Health, 17*(1), 59. PMID: 34020654

Turnock, B. J., Birkhead, G. S., Morrow, C. B., & Pirani, S. (2022). *Turnock's public health: what it is and how it works*. Jones & Bartlett Learning.

UN. (2025). *Intergovernmental Negotiating Body to draft and negotiate a WHO convention, agreement or other international instrument on pandemic prevention, preparedness and response.* United Nations. Retrieved 2025 from https://www.who.int/news/item/20-05-2025-world-health-assembly-adopts-historic-pandemic-agreement-to-make-the-world-more-equitable-and-safer-from-future-pandemics

Waldman, D., & Javidan, M. (2020). *The false dichotomy between globalism and nationalism*. Harvard Business Review.

WGU. (2024). *Western Governors University: D-618 Environmental Health*. Western Governors University.

World Health Organization. (2019). Global strategy on digital health 2020-2024.

Worsley-Tonks, K. E., Bender, J. B., Deem, S. L., Ferguson, A. W., Fèvre, E. M., Martins, D. J., Muloi, D. M., Murray, S., Mutinda, M., & Ogada, D. (2022). Strengthening global health security by improving disease surveillance in remote rural areas of low-income and middle-income countries. *The Lancet. Global Health, 10*(4), e579–e584. PMID: 35303467

APPENDIX

Chapter 8 Study Question

1. What are UN SDGs?
2. Why are primary, secondary, and tertiary preventions relevant to UN SDGs?
3. What is the WHO Pandemic Agreement?
4. How important is equity to the WHO Pandemic Agreement articles?
5. Why are UN SDGs relevant to the WHO Pandemic Agreement articles?
6. What are Public Private Partnerships (PPPs)?
7. Are PPPs beneficial to the WHO Pandemic Agreement articles?
8. What organization approved the WHO Pandemic Agreement proposal?
9. What was one of the shortfalls of 2005 IHR?
10. How will the WHO Pandemic Agreement improve disease surveillance and intervention?

Chapter 9
Change Management Models for Multinational Projects

ABSTRACT

Leadership in the healthcare industry has an opportunity to improve following the outcomes of the global pandemic. This chapter explores transformational leadership and the models, frameworks, and tools to create the transformations needed to accomplish multinational electronic health records interoperability. Application of the models can be challenging at the organizational level when stakeholders are not informed or have not been prepared to embrace the new environment. In the multinational setting, the shared vision helps bridge understanding and promote collaboration. Case studies using fictitious organizations demonstrate how the models may be used to show a new way of managing the changes they will likely experience as they are implementing the proposed strategies. Sustainability of the new working environment will require stakeholders to operate as a team and distribute tasks to expedite the implementation. This chapter provides a recommendation for interdepartmental approaches within organizations and collaboration strategies for multinational proactive preparedness.

INTRODUCTION

The opportunity for leadership in healthcare has been recently highlighted by Forbes (Llopis, 2024). The title that catches the attention of the reader is, *Healthcare Leadership In Crisis: Time For Reinvention.* What would cause healthcare leaders to self-identify that healthcare leadership is in crisis? In the work environment following the pandemic, healthcare leaders are facing a fallout from working through

DOI: 10.4018/979-8-3693-2027-3.ch009

crisis situations. These situations were not business as usual and exposed problems in operational processes. The awareness leaders gained showed opportunities for change, not just for the organizations but for themselves as leaders.

The new normal as described by Kotter et al. (2021), acknowledges a growing uncertainty and complexity in organizations following the COVID-19 pandemic. In response to the situation, many leaders became aware of the need to transform or reconstruct the organization. In healthcare organizations, employees struggled to adjust to the new and consistently evolving environment. Global leaders recognize the new normal as a continually changing environment (Bloom & Cadarette, 2021). The uncertainty of the future and the complexity of the organizations stretch the skills of the leader. In both situations, leaders are presented with the task of accomplishing an unprecedented feat in leveraging the best minds to ignite a sense of urgency, establish a coalition or team, create a shared vision of the future state, communicate the shared vision with stakeholders, eliminate the barriers in the way of change, celebrate quick wins, improve on the process in an iterative way, and maintain sustainability by connecting the culture of the followers with the new approach (Kotter, 2012). The shared circumstances of the new normal provides an opportunity for global leaders to face the opportunities as a team.

In Chapter 7, we introduced The GLOBE Model, Complexity Theory, Chaos Theory, The Holonic Model, and other related theories and frameworks to support the work of implementing multinational electronic health records interoperability strategies. Global leaders are coming together to agree on a common approach to pandemic preparedness (WHO, 2025). The agreement sets the stage for establishing multinational working groups to address some of the issues with communicating across borders. Now we will explore the needs of the leaders, stakeholders, countries, companies, and organizations related to implanting multinational interoperability strategies.

For multinational interoperability of EHRs, the coalition will need to include all stakeholders or at least a representation of the stakeholders. The leaders are those representing the world's countries, companies, and organizations who are impacted by or benefit from improving EHR interoperability. Benson & Grieve (2021) describe the horizontal and vertical challenges of interoperability, acknowledging the issues of multiple organizations with multiple locations. This collaboration presents an opportunity to manage change to scale. Large-scale transformation at scale will leverage methods, models, and theories beyond individual or even organizational needs and embrace the shared needs of the multinational stakeholders. While technological advancements continue to improve, leaders must manage the resulting change.

Multiple industries have a stake in the outcome at a multinational level (Bakker et al., 2021). The discussion of shared paradigm shift is just starting. For example, governments have a stake due to international information sharing. Multinational companies' stake in the outcome could be related to employee or client needs and the business outcomes. Insurance companies may be interested in the outcome due to fluctuations in health insurance payouts. Healthcare organizations from clinics to hospitals are both creating data in doctor-patient communication, managing the data and metadata through their systems, and using the EHR data to improve patient outcomes. Additionally, other industries have a stake in disease surveillance and prevention such as logistics, hospitality, food service, manufacturing, and service.

In healthcare, seeing employees and patients as end users can be difficult. When healthcare leaders are focused on the business of healthcare, they may be seeing problems and challenges through only one side or through old paradigms. The challenge is easy to understand considering the complexities in healthcare, the duality of frontline clinical procedures, policies, and workflows and the back-office business demanding the attention of financial, operational, technical, legal, regulatory, risk management, and functional departments (Burke, 2024). Dealing with complexity requires leadership skills expertise in managing change, developing the organization, and leading people in two hierarchies.

Strategic resilience is a term used to describe learning from events that have not yet happened (Valkangas et al., 2016). Proactive activity is not a new concept, but is a way to anticipate organizational impact, multinational needs, and planned leader actions. For leaders to be proactively working toward a global solution, a shared vision is needed. The specific shared vision that will likely promote this type of strategic resilience is the WHO Pandemic Agreement (World Health Organization, 2025). This agreement, coupled with the U.N. Sustainable Development Goals, provides a foundation for leaders to prepare to meet the challenges of future crises before they happen (United Nations, 2025). In the context of interoperable EHRs, sharing information is one-way leaders come together in a proactive approach. Global leaders have an opportunity to develop strategic resilience for their followers by coming to the table prepared to communicate with other leaders and listen to collective needs.

TRANSFORMATIONAL LEADERSHIP

Transformational leadership is a leadership theory that describes how leaders accomplish the type of transformation needed for organizations and countries to embrace the need to support stakeholders and make the changes necessary for aligning efforts (Burrell, 2024). Bass (1997) presents the components of transformational leadership as charisma, followers' cognitive engagement, and consideration of individual followers. Aligning the leadership approach is one way to collaborate and learn from other successful leaders. GLOBE Project leverages implicit leadership theory and has developed a "working definition of leadership" by consensus of a diverse group of leaders representing 38 countries. The resulting definition of organizational leadership is, "the ability of an individual to influence, motivate, and enable others to contribute toward the effectiveness and success of the organizations of which they are members" (Dorfman & House, 2004, p.56).

Today, organizations face an enormous amount of change in an effort to become more effective. In this nearly universal approach to leadership, leaders use models to simplify the complex and manage multiple competing priorities. Transformational leadership embodies advocating for change and uses a process to help others accomplish change (Northouse, 2022). For the world to work together to create interoperability of systems, leaders will need to communicate in a collaborative way. This combined effort implies that the leaders work together to accomplish a shared goal while still representing the organizations or countries they lead.

When identifying a strategy for transformation, it is critical to consider the type of company and needed change. Reasons to choose one strategy over another emerge as the strategies are identified and applied in various examples. While many companies may have used a strategy in the past and achieved success in the transformation, selecting the one that is right for the company, capacity, type of change, and resources available is important for a successful outcome.

FOCUS ON QUALITY

One assessment strategy discussed by Beach (2005) that is related to quality is the Quality Improvement Strategy (QIS). The customer's perception is one factor of consideration, but the actual quality of the product or service is also important. In this strategy, the object is to recognize the differentiation from competition based on the quality of the product or service. The connection between the customer's expectations and what is received determines satisfaction. If the client can obtain a better-quality product or service from another provider, he or she will most likely seek the other source.

When an organization can assess that they are falling short of meeting the customers' needs, they can use an improvement strategy to address the quality shortfall. Continuous improvement strategies and innovation strategies are two ways to accomplish the improvement process (Paraschivescu & Cotîrlet, 2015). If the organization has the luxury of time, a gradual process such as the continuous improvement process will allow for less resistance. In an organization that conducts frequent reviews of procedures, success is likely because employees will already be in the process of change. Innovative strategies provide the same quality improvement, but with the encouragement for change participants to create some new way to address the issues.

The ultimate goal in either of these approaches is to gain a competitive advantage over companies not accustomed to change or surprised by the customer demands.

SEARCH CONFERENCES

Where change agents use focus groups to assess the issues in an organization, search conferences accomplish a similar end. The goal is to identify areas of the corporation that need to change. The process of bringing stakeholders together to create a plan for approaching the change is similar to action research (Selin et al., 2007). By allowing the group to brainstorm the process and develop a plan, there is much less resistance, because everyone has a stake in the success of the transformed organization. Including employees at this level, participation creates the engagement necessary to carry the group through the large-scale change process.

Warzynski (2004) shows the use of a search conference as action research to identify the best way to accomplish the improvement process. As groups discuss forming the future, strategies emerge, and ideas are allowed to fully form and grow. Solving problems in this way leads to increased commitment by group participants to see the outcome of the work. When employees are involved in the planning, they can contribute front-line perspective to the plan creation instead of being consulted for feedback after the fact. Valuable talent and experience may be leveraged to identify opportunities based on what employees frequently see at work, which translates into working solutions with commitment.

Since this solution takes time, it is important that the strategy is used in future-state brainstorming rather than a cleanup process. When stakes are high and there is a right answer for the outcome of the transformation, this would not be the approach to use. Creativity must be allowed to emerge and cannot be stifled by regulatory burdens or rules. The leader must be willing to allow the group to discover multiple methods and determine which one is the best solution. Very often leaders just look for an answer to the problem and neglect the critical thinking process that would prove useful in such planning. Patience will pay off when the details come together.

LEAD-LAG

Burn (1996) discovered that the needs of technology departments and needs of other areas of the business have a lead-lag or push-pull relationship. The comparison of these strategies to bottom-up and top-down strategies showed that care should be taken to determine the right strategy to fit the necessary change. With so many options to choose from, selecting the appropriate process to manage the large-scale transformation will be instrumental in setting up the change process for success.

The correlation between technology departments and organizational change is directly related to the lead-lag conceptual models (Smaczny, 2001). Making advancements in technology or other departments requires a significant transition in the company in many cases. Once the leader recognizes this fact, it is then a race to determine which should change first. Even if the company culture accepts the idea of the new technology, there may be other measures that need to change before the organization can afford to make the necessary changes for technology. If the culture is not ready for the new technology, then transformation of the culture will be required before such changes in technology can be made.

Another necessary distinction based on the lead-lag strategy is to determine whether micro-level changes are necessary before or after the macro-level changes. As explained by Spencer (2007), department or individual (micro) changes will impact the company's ability to make organization-wide (macro) changes. Ideology will need to be accepted if the transformation is big enough to change the way work is done. Individuals will be reluctant to let go of processes or policies that have worked before without the leader's message. Departures from what departments view as normal damage trust without the change in culture.

BOTTOM-UP OR TOP-DOWN

If the decisions need to be made quickly and accomplish specific outcomes, top-down leadership will address specific problems directly. It also assumes that the organization adheres to a standard when implementing incremental improvements (Thomas & McGarry, 1994). The bottom-up strategy can be equally effective but will make improvements based on the value of the experience of the workers. Employees may know the specific way to improve a product or process because they are ultra-familiar with the details of product design and what can be done to improve the process.

If the transformation can be more creative, bottom-up will provide the benefit of built-in buy-in and sustainability with little resistance. Communication and support are critical to this transformation strategy. The leader will need to share the vision and details with the employees to provide perspective on the change before proceeding (Kezar, 2013). When employees understand the boundaries, they will feel more secure during the transformation.

EXPERIMENTATION

One of the benefits of bottom-up strategies is that the organization can learn from employees. If the transformation has the luxury of time, including employees in the focus group process can implement lessons from the front line. Test and learn is one method that allows a group to make a change and record the lessons learned from the pilot to determine if future change efforts will use the same process (Scott, 2001). In open action research, the group can test a process and record findings as well as make adjustments while the research continues. In this way, the answer to the problem will surface during transformation. Creating the plan during change allows for the best outcome if the conditions are right. Experimental strategies require openness and flexibility not often utilized at the organizational level due to rigidity. The culture is the determining factor.

In the adhocracy culture (Cameron & Quinn, 2011), the innovation is naturally present and would allow for such experimentation. Employees and leaders are both accustomed to looking for new and different ways to accomplish things. Incremental improvements are part of the work environment so that this transformation strategy would be more of the same business as usual.

Selecting the right strategy to match the change needed for an organization will be best suited when the plan matches the culture and the size and scope of the change. Each situation can be assessed to determine the needs and priorities for the outcome. Transformation can be painful if the process lacks the proper fit for the organization's culture so that transforming the culture may be required as a part of the transformational change process.

The partnership of leaders representing countries, nations, and organizations looks to approach the global problems in a collaborative way (Binder, 2016). While much research is underway to establish methods of problem solving and process improvement, some methods are proven and could be leveraged to establish a model for approaching change "at scale." For example, a fictitious company we will call "PNW Global Consulting" established a method of iterative assessment and transformation to improve the work they were conducting and prepare to expand their global presence.

CASE STUDY: PNW GLOBAL CONSULTING

In the world of consulting firms, PNW Global Consulting holds a moderate position. They employ a total of 6,000 employees between consultants, sales force, project managers, facilitators, IT professionals, and support staff. Since the company began in 1985, much has changed in the industry of organizational development and change management. While they originally began as facilitators of organizational culture development for healthcare environments, more recently they have found themselves competing in the organizational development space including digital transformation and training to support companies in changing organizational culture to meet a multitude of fast-moving external forces including AI implementation (Davenport & Redman, 2025).

Headquarters for the company resides in Portland, OR but offices in San Francisco, CA and Vancouver, B.C., provide additional support. The company is looking to add three new sites in the next five years based on client demand to expand operations to Mexico, China, and LMICs nations (London, 2021). While the organization is relatively small by global comparison, the passion of the leadership team is to work toward a model of partnering consulting efforts to amplify the voices of low- to middle-income countries (LMICs) and provide consulting services to bridge the gap between what is available for a high-income country.

Annual revenue for PNW Global Consulting has grown to $520 million at the end of the fiscal year 2023. However, the profitability margins show a significant decline due to the increase in the cost of travel for employees and the advancements in the technology required for work in the organizational development space. Digital transformations are an excellent example of the cost increase over time (Sun et al. 2022). Since the ROI on these efforts is significant, clients are interested in taking advantage of the lessons learned through PNW Global Consulting's own large-scale transformation. The healthcare vertical shows a strong propensity to benefit from the lessons (Vărzaru, 2022). Most of the clients requiring large-scale transformative change need reporting and training with more advanced project platforms than the software and systems that have been used over the last decade since PNW Global Consulting's last major technological upgrade.

There has been an increase in a number of hospitals and clinics as a more specialized client type. Additional work has been required by the consulting and project management groups to understand the type of systems upgrades that are required by the new regulations surrounding the insurance industry and other digital initiatives. While PNW Global Consulting has not created a dedicated resource for this changing demographic in the client base, there are members of the sales force and consulting group who have partnered and developed customized adjustments on their own. The addition of this specialized group of consultants will improve the offerings and help expand the network to amplify the needs of LMICs nations (Jafar et al., 2024). The goal of providing a balanced voice has been a commitment of PNW Global Consulting and remains at the forefront of their approach to improving global health.

The structure of PNW Global Consulting, Inc. includes six divisions, each with an executive manager as shown in the organizational chart in Figure 1. Departments have traditionally been working together to partner for the best client result. The existing organizational culture could be categorized as a Clan culture (Cameron & Quinn, 2016) but would be better positioned as an Adhocracy culture considering the evolving needs of the industry. Continuous improvement will be necessary to stay ahead of the competition.

Figure 1. Organizational chart of PNW global consulting

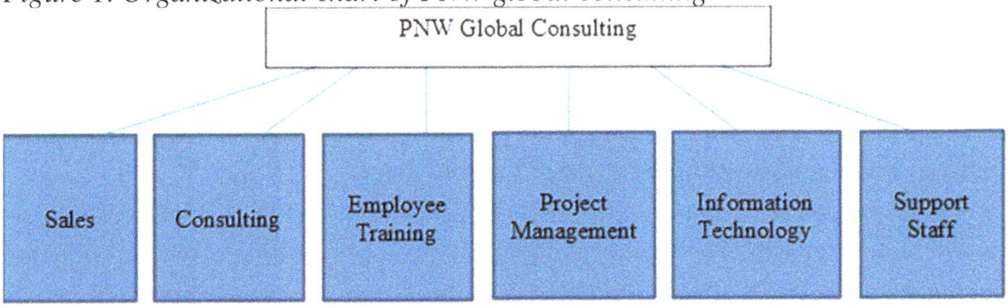

The leadership team has included various individuals and teams to solve the problem and seems to be taking a middle-out approach (Sweet, 2011) and ignoring the need for top-down decision making. While analysis is important, a more strategic approach is necessary to have a more consistent process and provide a framework for change. The philosophy and change process selection is between the Action Research Model (Powell, 2002) and the Quality Improvement Strategy (QIS) discussed by Beach (2005), which assesses the gap between what the organization provides to customers and what customers want as well as how other organizations comparatively provide goods or services to customers.

Improvements in the technology used to manage employee training have advanced and changed PNW Global Consulting's clients' needs. There is a greater demand for more accessible training in self-study and virtual classroom platforms. Companies are asking for bite-sized training and gamification in order to maintain learner attention and promote engagement during the change. PNW's existing staffing model includes 800 classroom facilitators, 300 consultants, and 450 project managers who travel to accommodate the change management processes for companies without the existing staff to support a large-scale transformational change. By moving to an online training platform, PNW Global Consulting can save money and resources that would normally be spent on paper materials and business travel.

A transformation is needed because profitability will need to improve if the company is to compete with larger consulting firms. Moving the training portion to online learning taught from hubs will require the office space to redirect the consulting and learning to a more remote process. To accommodate these changes, the expansion of offices will double the operations of the company. Projected cost savings include a reduction of travel for facilitators, project managers and consultants from $27.5 million to $2.8 million annually.

By offering an online solution to training materials, the printing costs will be reduced, which will remove the $450,000 cost of the participant materials in training courses. While consultants and the sales force will still use materials to present original consultative pricing, the addition of a client supporting platform could lower these costs as well. Future methods to generate revenue will include the growth of the business by adding new clients, which will offset the costs of the new offices. Additional financial resources will be required to improve the online learning platform and the client support platform. A cost analysis will be required to determine the best solution for these improvements.

The impact on the company culture will change the way they view themselves as the clientele increases. The assessments show that employee loyalty to the vision that guides the company is strong, but the clan culture reinforces the collaborative view where even the clients are in partnership with the consultants (Cameron & Quinn, 2011). Clients are demanding a more creative response, and the early assessments reveal that the adhocracy culture will be more creative and allow for innovation in approach to consulting and training. Internal training will be required to adjust the culture, and the implementation plan should reflect the various components of this type of culture change.

The proposed changes will also alter the approach of Human Resources (HR). Changing the way facilitators work will require new job descriptions, postings, performance review templates, and development processes. Updates will also be required for the project manager and technician roles. The speed of adoption of technical certifications will require a new department to oversee the proper maintenance of certifications and provide the AI implementation group with the support they need to improve processes using agile methodologies (Cosa & Torelli, 2024; Khang, 2023). The other supporting areas that will likely experience updates include the way reporting is managed in both the analytics and metrics teams as well as the finance group. By updating the job descriptions, a more comprehensive approach can be taken to support the various countries' requirements.

An assessment of the internal and external environments can reinforce the decision to make these changes. How the leader makes decisions and the style they use shapes the way employees see the change (Teoh Kae & Rashad, 2015). The communication plans the leader uses helps employees see the purpose of the change and keeps the ideas in front of the employees as they move through the transformation. The communication plan helps reduce the amount of resistance to change. The leader owns the change process and will be responsible for ensuring the company maintains business processes during the transformation (Arya, 2012). What the leader shares about the change is critical for the trust level employees have throughout the change process and in the new environment following the transformation.

The transformation will have an effect on all stakeholders and the leader should manage the issues that may come up (Koufteros et al., 2014). Some external stakeholders that may be impacted include suppliers and vendors, as well as investors and customers. The whole chain may experience challenges with the relationship. The leader should remember to address both individuals and groups as stakeholders (Kezar, 2013), maintaining communication and trust throughout the change process. There can be complications and added expenses when others are resistant to the change or reluctant to support the direction of the company. The whole organization, as well as internal and external groups, should be on board early in the process of strategic planning to reduce resistance.

Internally, PNW Global Consulting has had a history of clan culture, which can be seen in the trust level the employees have for the leader. Departments are accustomed to working together and can readily accept change when they understand the purpose behind it. The internal processes in existence will need to be addressed in the strategic plan for change. Proven methods have been used in other organizations (Ngcamu, 2016) to accomplish the efficiency and operational excellence PNW Global Consulting is trying to achieve.

Additional assessments are needed to determine specialty solutions for healthcare considering the trends in the contacts referred to the sales staff. There are some solutions that transcend all industry differences, but the regulations and federal mandates provide a challenging environment. Insurance mandates are also pushing clinics and hospitals to digitize processes, which send the doctors and office staff looking for additional advice in these areas.

Strategies

General systems theory lends the concept that boundaries can be created to determine what should change (Caws, 2015; Van Assche et al., 2019). The basic definition is provided as an explanation of how elements combined in a system interact with each other (McIntyre, 2016) and how systems may be integrated when merging strategies is necessary (Xu, 2012). Open and closed systems are both useful in appropriate situations. In large-scale transformation, the open systems models have a broader application with more flexibility.

Selecting a strategy that allows for all the variables to be included in the transformation analysis and then isolating those for change is necessary to accomplish large-scale transformational change. Using an open systems model can allow for the consideration of the variables and then be used in an ongoing way to support sustainable change and continue to adapt to maintain the success of the new environment. The open systems model provides a platform for considering all variables and is most effective when the feedback is received and can be used to determine next steps (Levasseur, 2004). Open systems allow for flexibility during the change but also promote continuous improvement in the new environment (Al-Haddad & Kotnour, 2015).

Organizational change models (Powell, 2002; McElyea, 2003) illustrate how the strategy can be created to include variables important to the transformation. The models have evolved over time and the use of open systems models more closely reflect what change leaders should be focused on in the existing industries and climate. The complexity of the multi-phased types of change that companies face today would be next to impossible to manage without the appropriate model. In the case of PNW Global Consulting, a change model will be needed to address the issues of location change (growth), product changes, procedural change, policy updates, employee job changes, and development changes. Since these changes are so complex, addressing them in an orderly fashion will be critical.

When the changes are combined in a strategy, it is necessary to consider the planned organizational culture change and the unintended consequences of the change. Moving the company from a predominant clan culture to more of an adhocracy culture (Cameron & Quinn, 2016) can be done using the Organizational Culture Assessment Instrument (OCAI). By walking through the assessment, the leader and other change managers may determine what actions should be taken to move to a decrease in clan behaviors and an increase in adhocracy behaviors. There is also a chance that they have misdiagnosed themselves and will need to address any disagreements in the process before gaining consensus.

Choosing the appropriate change strategy for this multi-faceted transformation can have severe impacts on the outcome of change (Srinidhi, 1998). Choosing a strategy that supports the organization's need for proper measurements, expenses, processes, and communication requires using a proven method to ensure success and sustainability. Beach (2005) recommends selecting a strategy that achieves quality improvement with the least amount of disruption and resistance.

Use of the open systems model results in new processes and outcomes (Brown, 2015). Openness is seen in varying degrees (Caws, 2015) and could provide openness in one area and maintain controls in another. Open communication is an important factor in an open system strategy (Urrestarazu, 2015) and will provide an important framework for the type of culture change that will be necessary. When the culture is accustomed to continuous change (Weick & Quinn, 1999), there will be frequent reasons to test new processes and learn from them. Scott (2001) supports this test-and-learn method of experimentation by suggesting that action research is used to explore options. As part of the sustainable processes for the new environment, pilot programs for a test and learn process will help the company be more comfortable transitioning to new behaviors.

PNW Global Consulting requires an open systems model for change (Busemeyer et al., 2020). Due to the significance of the transformation including additional locations, moving training from a classroom setting to either self-study or virtual classroom, changing the travel expectations, adjusting the job measurements, and transforming the corporate culture, it will be necessary to conduct the large–scale transformation in phases. The transformation strategy may seem complex, but the power of sustainable change is in the connections that are maintained for individuals in the process (Wilson & Daugherty, 2025). Since change will also need to be the future normal, making change a part of the regular process will need to happen to stay ahead of other potential external environmental factors.

Transformation Strategy

The chosen organizational change model for this process will be the Action Research Model. Powell (2002) describes Burke's original defined steps to use the model for change. The proposed large-scale transformation for PNW Global Consulting will benefit from the Action Research Model to apply the change in a test and learn fashion. The Burke-Litwin Model reinforces the need to follow a specific process when managing change and implementing large-scale transformation (Burke, 2024). The steps originally presented by Burke (1982) include the following process at its basic level:

1. Realizing the need for change
2. Clarifying the problem
3. Assessing needs and gathering feedback
4. Action Planning
5. Intervening
6. Evaluating
7. Adopting
8. Separating

Action research will be applied in the context of culture change supporting the other requested operational and client specific changes. Appreciative Inquiry can help the process preserve what is working while creating transformation at scale for what must change (Kumar et al., 2023). Dealing with growth is another issue that will need to be tracked as part of the transformation since it cannot wait until the changes are implemented to get started. The detailed process will provide an appropriate framework for communication and intervention as well as multiple opportunities for feedback.

In the initial steps to realize the need for change, a change leader is chosen and given charge of the action research process (Powell, 2002). The shared responsibility between the change leader and PNW Global Consulting's leadership team will define the relationship for the remainder of the change process. Critical definitions will need to be presented and spelled out in a statement of work with an appropriate level of interaction throughout the change. Once everyone knows the role they will play and the details of their responsibilities, each can carry out his or her duties to the transformation.

Clarifying the problem provides an opportunity to prepare the stakeholders through communication of the big picture plan so that the assessments in the next steps will be thorough and will give employees and related stakeholders advanced warning of the imminent change. Here leaders gain commitment (Bass & Avolio, 1993) for the purpose of the transformation and share ownership. Specific challenges will emerge in the clan culture without this step to be transparent and reinforce trust.

In the assessment and feedback step, the change leader gathers information through a series of measures. Qualitative measures (Creswell & Creswell, 2022) will provide information related to the character of the organization. Interviews and assessment of culture using the OCAI (Cameron & Quinn, 2016) will provide the change leader and decision makers with critical information concerning the culture. A process can then be identified for adjusting the culture to more closely match the desired end-state for PNW Global Consulting.

Quantitative measures (Creswell & Creswell, 2022) will need to be used in the form of a survey to assess the growth opportunities, a potential dedicated resource for healthcare, the transition from classroom-based learning to web-based or self-study, and support staff changes to finance, HR related functions, and employee development. Reporting changes and proposed changes to the HR policies may see resistance in the employee response. The resistance should be anticipated and planned for if there is feedback that points to such challenges. Likely pushback can be expected when job descriptions and pay are discussed.

Once the assessment results are gathered and analyzed, the information will be shared with the senior leadership team (Powell, 2002). Roles and responsibilities will then need to be defined as well as a timeline, cost analysis, communication plan, and implementation plan. When the team has gained consensus on the path to take and details of the needs for change, the planning process can begin.

Action planning (Creswell & Creswell, 2022) can include detailed large-scale transformation in a phased approach. For the particular customized approach in PNW Global Consulting, each phase will consist of a detailed implementation plan with identified components, milestones, communication plan, training solution, feedback process, and assessment to test and learn. Lessons learned will be discussed and applied to the next phase if applicable. Transparency will be respected and status results shared with the stakeholders for review at the end of each phase.

The intervention step (Powell, 2002) for PNW Global Consulting will be managed in phases to take advantage of the close culture of employees and deal with resistance head on. Here the strategic plan begins to be implemented and with the change process underway, midpoint milestones and feedback provide valuable interaction with the groups involved in the change. Once each of the phases is complete, the leader will communicate the status of the actions taken, lessons learned and future process. Once the phases have been implemented and evaluated, the adoption step helps the employees own the new environment. Ceremonial events can be held to bury the past processes that may be difficult to give up. The employees will have heavily invested in this future, so the leader can share how far they have come.

The implementation process that PNW Global Consulting will follow is presented in five phases and the change leader will manage each phase. Consulting contracts were completed between the executive leadership team and PNW Global Consulting before the assessments were completed. The leadership team will be communicating related to the area of the organization each represents according to the Communication Plan. The details of each phase are spelled out and are included in Table 1.

The final piece of the puzzle is for the change leader to separate from the change process (Powell, 2002). A public show of gratitude can help, but the best way is for the change leader to be reassigned. When separation happens successfully, there is no confusion about the ownership of the new environment following change. Sustainability depends on the connection between employees and their new environment (Wilson & Daugherty, 2025). While this should be an easy accomplishment, some leaders may inadvertently leave some employees out of the process. This type of resistance is easily avoided by connecting people to the outcomes. Contracting with the organization, planning the phases of change, assigning owners to each of the tasks, and managing the details as a team provides the most support to accomplish sustainable organizational change.

Table 1. Phased implementation plan for PNW global consulting transformation initiative

Phases	Implementation Plan	Action Learning
1 – Culture Change	**Components:** *All departments and processes will be included in this phase* **Milestones:** *Completed focus groups, Completed training* **Communication:** *Each department leader will be responsible for communicating according to the identified adjustments that will need to be made from the assessment* **Training:** *Culture training solutions will be designed and developed with the assessment as a guide. Training will need to be completed for every employee* **Feedback:** *Qualitative and quantitative data will be gathered* **Assessment:** *Data analysis and reporting due to senior leaders within a week of the final training class*	Actions Taken Lessons Learned Future Processes
2 – Dedicated Healthcare Solution	**Components:** *Sales force, Consultants, Project Managers, Facilitators, and IT will be included* **Milestones:** *Needs Assessment for Healthcare, Required compliance complete, New packaged solution ready for client, Pilot complete* **Communication:** *Department leaders will share information as needed with both employees and senior leadership* **Training:** *Compliance with insurance requirements and federal regulations* **Feedback:** *Pilot feedback shared with leaders, status reports shared with change leader* **Assessment:** *Data analysis and reporting will be developed and tested with pilot*	Actions Taken Lessons Learned Future Processes
3 – Technology Transition	**Components:** *IT, Consultants, Project Managers, and Facilitators will be included* **Milestones:** *Selected programs and platforms, training redesign, managed project milestones, facilitator preparation* **Communication:** *Status meetings with leadership and decision approvals at appropriate intervals* **Training:** *Systems training, Redesign of Facilitation to accommodate client request for online training* **Feedback:** *Communication through project functionality, appropriate testing results from pilots* **Assessment:** *Analysis for additional support*	Actions Taken Lessons Learned Future Processes

continued on following page

Table 1. Continued

Phases	Implementation Plan	Action Learning
4 - Growth	**Components:** *All departments* **Milestones:** *Location analysis, client analysis, purchase property, develop connections and network* **Communication:** *Status reports shared consistent with new adhocracy elements* **Training:** *Ramp up new staff hired to run each location. Assess new employee learning and conduct maintenance of materials for Phase 1 and 2 completions* **Feedback:** *Gather information about new locations once up and running* **Assessment:** *Analyze new locations and company performance measures*	Actions Taken Lessons Learned Future Processes
5 – Support Staff	**Components:** *All departments due to HR policy changes* **Milestones:** *New job descriptions, New performance review templates, new pay structure* **Communication:** *Leader owns primary communication plan and will include change leader and HR as needed* **Training:** *Classroom training to reinforce new adhocracy culture and new policies, procedures, and measures* **Feedback:** *Allow appropriate time to gather information from class group feedback and individual surveys* **Assessment:** *Analysis of all components and final review with change leader and leadership team*	Actions Taken Lessons Learned Future Processes

Summary

The expected output of the transformation strategy for PNW Consulting is that the assessed change needs have been accomplished. Each of the phases brought about a different change for the company, but all the changes are interrelated, and it is critical that they were handled in a specific order to avoid costly mistakes like growing to three new sites prior to changing expensive technology. With the action research model guiding the efforts, the plans could be made and customized as new information presented itself.

Before the change, the performance of PNW Consulting was moderate and adequate for the existing clients, but to take on more business it was necessary to improve performance. Performance improvement could have been incrementally achieved, but following a specific process with analysis and lessons learned in each phase gave the leaders confidence as they moved through the process. Incremental change will be a part of the Adhocracy environment (Cameron & Quinn, 2016).

Following the change, performance declined momentarily as expected with many changing processes. In the end, the performance doubled the business as projected (Marketing consulting services industry, 2017) and allowed for additional growth in the future based on the new performance measures including reporting developed through the IT department when training moved from classroom to online processes. The training became more easily measured by online statistics and immediate survey gathering.

Timeframes for performance improvement vary and sometimes the issues that present themselves create setbacks in the process. For the PNW Consulting change initiative, the phased approach spread changes out for 3 years. The length of time gave each phase needed analysis time and employees a chance to identify with the next big change before it arrived. Plans could be piloted and reviewed rather than implementation before testing. The power in the action research model was customization specific to PNW Global Consulting's needs. Future changes will be less challenging due to the innovative attitudes present on the teams since the culture change.

The most critical result is the strength of the growth of market share realized the second year following the transformation. By adding the healthcare solution and expanding to 3 new markets, PNW Global Consulting now has 10,000 employees and supports organizational development and employee training for a variety of clients. Revenue reported for 2 years following the final implementation phase as $478 million with an improved profitability margin of 28%.

Potential future change for the organization may include a global approach since many of the client companies are planning their own expansions. Processes continue to change, but with a new process of continuous improvement, PNW Global Consulting is up to the challenge.

Managing change at the organization level requires purposeful processes including all locations, departments, and employees. The leader of a multinational organization would need to manage details within the change process over locations across the globe. Models such as the Global Project Management Framework© provide a functional perspective to identify elements of a global project and the components to manage for successful implementation of a global change initiative (Binder, 2016). Managing the project can only happen once there is a project to manage. In the conceptual approach to the project, stakeholders need to plan an approach that assesses the issues, brings stakeholders together, and establishes a plan for accomplishing the desired outcomes. Complex organizational development models have also been used to support organizations in their approach to multinational expansion.

CHANGE MANAGEMENT MODELS

In the case study, we watched the fictitious company, PNW Global Consulting, implement a large-scale transformation leveraging Kotter's 8-Steps, Burke's steps, Action Research (AR), and Appreciative Inquiry (Dunlap, 2008; Kumar et al., 2023). The multinational approach to EHR interoperability requires multiple models to manage the complexity of assessment, planning, execution, and sustainability. Maintaining positive tones in the conversation can be challenging given the urgency to arrive at a solution. This section highlights how models may be used to make sense of the magnitude of the change and provide structure for analysis.

In healthcare settings, one of the most common methods of creating change is the Plan-Do-Study-Act (PDSA) framework (Bailey et al., 2024). In fact, this book represents the second in the series to approach the concepts of multinational EHR interoperability in a familiar way (Carter et al., 2024). This model is an effective way to change behavior at the individual and group level in clinics, but it can also be used to establish an iterative process for large-scale transformation. While we approached the concepts from the Plan step, in Multinational Electronic Health Records Interoperability Strategies, the Do step is really about identifying how to accomplish the elements in the Plan. The multiple models in this discussion provide an overview of the available methods for accomplishing the goals.

ACTION RESEARCH

Action Research can be used in the context of multinational problem-solving by creating an iterative approach to assessment, analysis, implementation, and review. The theory of action research (AR) includes multiple levels of thought existing in the same process. One definition presents both the idea of what is expected as well as some defined rules for accomplishing the outcome (Altrichter, Kemmis, McTaggart, & Zuber-Skerritt, 2002). It is important to include the concepts of self-diagnosis of what should change, how the participants feel about the change and communication to others about the reflection and observation. At the same time, the process is critical to the outcome.

The process of AR should include the researcher as a participant and provide reflection and modified action. Collaboration provides a valuable connection and opportunity to encourage the client to own the information and solution. These basic rules help solidify the definition of AR. When the client and the researcher are in the active and reflective processes of the iterations, they demonstrate the connection between scientific methodology and action research (Stephens, Barton, & Haslett, 2009). The concept of the researcher as participant has become known as *Use of Self* (Bushe & Marshak, 2014; Cooperrider et al., 2003; Jamieson & Davidson, 2019). Conceptually, each researcher should capture self-experience as data in the assessment. Once the reflection is captured it can be analyzed and provide additional context to the research.

The practice of AR is the application of these theoretical concepts. Observe and reflect are the basis of the AR methodology. Through cycles of action research over time, observations and reflections become deeper. Each iterative cycle lends a chance to see a new variable change or to validate the action that was present before. In the process of applying action research, the researcher should remember that studying the action is only one piece and is complex. The regular business should continue to operate throughout the observations (Gustavsen, 1993) and not be interrupted by the research. A delicate balance of action, observation, and reflection must be applied without disrupting the function of the organization being studied or damaging the perception of the leader.

One example of how AR generates knowledge for the system is presented by Ballantyne (2004). The idea that knowledge is created through deep thought process is further enhanced when the emotional connections are made through relationships. Trusting environments provide a better learning experience than studying alone because the conversation and reflection opportunity gives the learner a chance to review and practice. The example of contributing to theory shows knowledge can also be applied to other situations with similar outcomes. Through the process of validating the idea over multiple cycles of acting, observing, and reflecting, researchers draw conclusions and share validation of a variable simultaneously.

It is important that AR generates knowledge for the system because the factors considered in theory generation rely on the outcome of new ideologies. In AR these are tested and confirmed or refuted and can be validated over the next cycle of research (Gustavsen, 1993). The researcher can then continue the process of acting, observing, and reflecting to validate the theory (Gronhaug & Olson, 1999). Additionally, the previously accepted fact can be challenged through the scientific process. Recent studies show the elements of action research and appreciative inquiry provide the organization with an iterative approach to measuring and assessing within the process of change. Use of self is a concept that allows the researchers' observations to be considered as data and promotes sharing insights as they collaborate to implement new processes.

ASSESSMENT TOOLS

Multinational Adapted Burke-Litwin Model

Assessment tools and change management models help the change leader manage the complexity of the transformation. In a multinational approach, this may be a team of change leaders combining efforts. Conceptual coherence is vital to have a shared vision of the issues to avoid wasting time and resources in the process of implementation. The Burke-Litwin Model, as seen in Figure 2, provides a method for an organization to manage the complex details of large-scale transformational change (Burke, 2024). This model can help organizations get started in the type of transformation required to promote interoperability. Once the leaders of the organization have identified their role and the role of the organization in collaboration with other organizations, the model can help them strategically embrace EHR interoperability in a multinational context.

Figure 2. The Adapted Burke-Litwin model of organizational performance and change

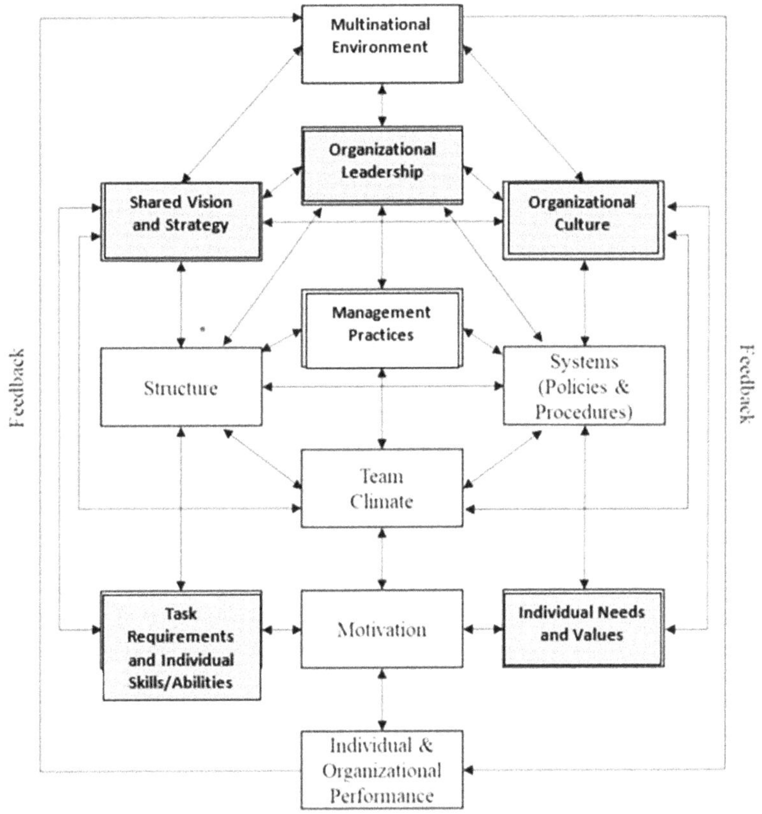

Note: Adapted from the Burke-Litwin Model of Organizational Performance and Change (Burke, 2024).

Applied SOAR Model

Some models to consider include analytical frameworks such as the SOAR Model (Watkins et al., 2011). In this model as seen in Figure 3, SOAR is an acronym for strengths, opportunities, aspirations, and results. Strategic thinking and multinational conversations can be supported by such a model. While it has been illustrated in various applications and approaches over the last few years, the conceptual approach for discussions at-scale could expand to include multiple assessments and comparisons of results.

Figure 3. The SOAR model applied to the multinational EHR interoperability analysis

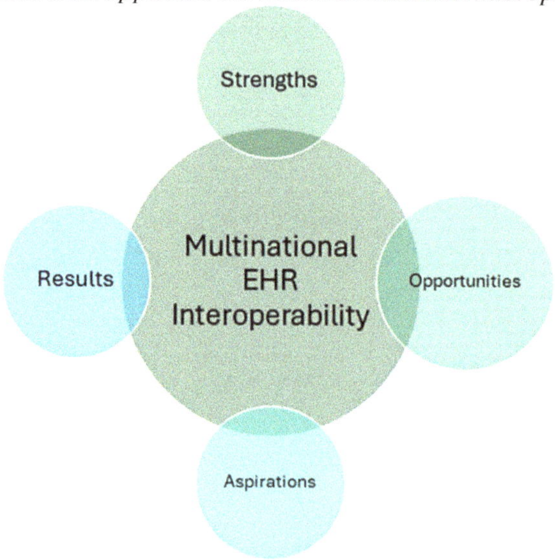

Note: Adapted to apply to the Multinational EHR Interoperability analysis

The philosophy of appreciative inquiry (AI) is that the value of research is placed in a positive approach of appreciating aspects of an organization (Bright, 2009). The SOAR model, as described by Holman, Devane, & Cady, (2007) allows the consultant the chance to ask questions from a place of discovery. The questions the consultant asks are valuable since the discovery takes place through the dialogue between the researcher and the client (Watkins, Mohr, & Kelly, 2011). To really understand the nature of what is occurring requires deriving the meaning of the events while observing the action.

Practitioners use appreciative inquiry to question the group in a positive way about the organization. An example of using appreciative inquiry (Davidson, 2014) demonstrates Strengths, Opportunities, Aspirations, and Results (SOAR) to create positive discussions. The positive approach brings out ideas that would normally remain in the minds of the individuals without contributing (Whitney & Fredrickson, 2015). Trust is high in these situations which provides the platform for individuals to feel comfortable sharing. Dialogue is an important aspect of appreciative inquiry because it lets the truth of what is working come out as a result of the process.

Aligning multinational projects is about coming together in purpose and accomplishing the work in a way that supports all stakeholders. For the change to be equitable, it will require all of us to embrace change and a conceptual understanding of the magnitude of the change. Understanding each other is critical to move forward in the combined efforts required for multinational projects at scale (Burrell, 2024). Identifying the needs of a cross-cultural community of nations continues to challenge leaders. Overwhelmingly, international discussions tend to be dominated by western voices. To create a more equitable approach to the change, dialogue must be balanced (Benatar & Brock, 2021).

One example of a multinational effort is the WHO Pandemic Agreement (WHO, 2025). The World Health Organization and the World Bank established the Global Preparedness Monitoring Board in 2018, providing a combined effort of nations to monitor health crises (Benatar & Brock, 2021). The efforts to bring global stakeholders together for positive social change have been enduring over the last several years. Several models may have helped this process of connection move more quickly.

Some tools have been used when connecting volunteers across borders. The World Café is a method that has been used worldwide to connect individuals in a brainstorming activity. Developed in 1995, The World Café has been leveraged by many diverse groups to accomplish innovation in multiple industries (theworldcafe.com, 2025). This concept could be expanded to include a virtual approach to connect multinational teams in broader discussions.

Appreciative Inquiry (Dunlap, 2008) has proven to be an effective tool in relation to evaluation processes. Just as in the Human Performance Technology example Dunlap (2008) shares, the type of evaluation necessary for process improvement and change management is more effective when the leader employs Appreciative Inquiry (AI). Using the 4D cycle (Holman, Devane, & Cady, 2007), including "Discovery, Dream, Design, and Destiny," organizes the approach to assessment in phases. What is being assessed can be described by the "Affirmative Topic Choices," which can be customized for whatever the organization needs to assess.

Action research conducted using Appreciative Inquiry shines a light on the more positive aspects of the social interactions within the organization (Calabrese & Cohen, 2013). The model can also serve as a guide through a change initiative as in the example Calabrese & Cohen (2013) share of the model in action. In this case, the objective was a cultural transformation in desperate need of positivity for an urban drug court. When a public organization struggles with pessimism, it is challenged to explore positive outcomes. Multinational interoperability provides a challenge to the stakeholders of maintaining a positive outlook when approaching those with a negative or fearful outlook.

Identifying and acknowledging the positive core helps the organization see and appreciate what is working well within the organization (Holman, Devane, & Cady,

2007). Then approaching the assessment work through positive interactions includes other stakeholders in the process of creating buy-in and minimizing resistance.

The McKinsey 7-S Framework (Bell, 2025) was developed to show how organizational factors work together. The seven factors can be used as the topics for the Appreciative Inquiry process as shown in Figure 4. The factors included in the McKinsey 7-S Framework are strategy, structure, systems, staff, style, skills, and significant values. These elements have proven to be an effective way to assess organizational components since the identified factors are interrelated.

Appreciative Inquiry Combined with 7S Model

Figure 4. Combined appreciative inquiry and McKinsey 7S model

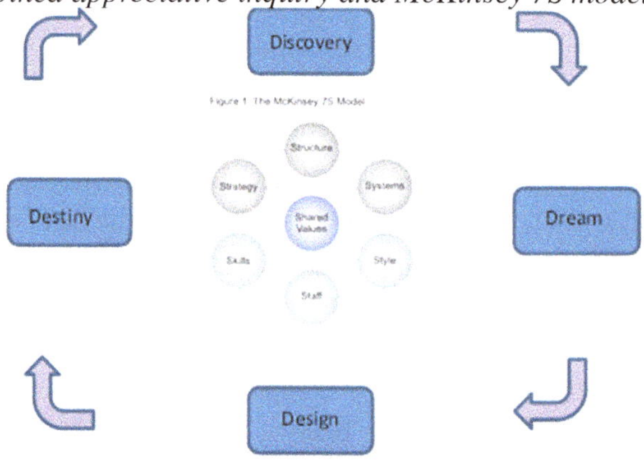

In the Discovery phase, individuals are gathered in order to assess the organization and identify aspects of the organization that work (Bertram et al., 2016). In the Discovery process using Appreciative Inquiry, maintaining the positive environment is critical to provide the right atmosphere for assessment to identify the potential for the organization. The discussion of strengths leads the way for deeper ideas about what could be improved (Browning, 2014). Success in this phase hinges on the appreciation (Bright, 2009) of what works well. The positive approach paves the way for a deeper discussion and allows people who would normally not be contributors to add their voice to the process (Whitney & Fredrickson, 2015).

Understanding the process and the added communication enhance relationships and teamwork because the individuals have a chance to interact in a way they may not have before (Whitney & Fredrickson, 2015). The discussions the individuals have in the assessment of the things that work and the things that don't serve multiple purposes in the discovery process.

The Dream phase is about creating a vision that embraces what the organization should become according to the stakeholders (Holman, Devane, & Cady, 2007). Browning (2014) shares the importance of including multiple stakeholders in the process. In the past, vision writing may have been a solo activity or one reserved just for the upper management of an organization, there are compelling reasons to bring the process to the masses. People tend to own what they create so the more interaction individuals have in the process, the more invested they feel in the outcome.

The Design phase creates the structure to support the new vision and allows the organization to come together to realize the Dream (Holman, Devane, & Cady, 2007). Designing from a place of strength adds sustainability to the organization's design because the elements of the design are things the organization already does well (Cooperrider & McQuaid, 2012). Appreciative design in higher learning has been studied including processes to design improved coursework following student feedback (Lilja & Richardsson, 2012). Whether applied to an academic environment or the potential for solving the problem of multinational interoperability, the conceptual approach to designing helps plan the outcome incorporating various aspects into managing the complexity of the global context.

The Destiny phase is where the action happens when the organization becomes what the individuals discussed and planned (Holman, Devane, & Cady, 2007). Following the identification of what should be done and the design of how it should be done is the actual doing of the activities to improve processes and achieve success (Benson & Dresdow, 2008). Done well, this phase can set the organization up for a continuous improvement process that will perpetuate additional evaluation and help make positive change a permanent part of the organization's assessment process.

In 2011, Watkins, Mohr, & Kelly presented the model in application using a 5D cycle adding the component "Define" to the beginning as seen in the adjusted model in Figure 5. Watkins et al. focused the efforts of the Definition phase on positive psychology always choosing the positive social construct. Sustainable change ignites passion in stakeholders pushing a stronger commitment to outcomes.

APPRECIATIVE INQUIRY 5-D CYCLE

Figure 5. Appreciative inquiry 5-D cycle for ED redesign

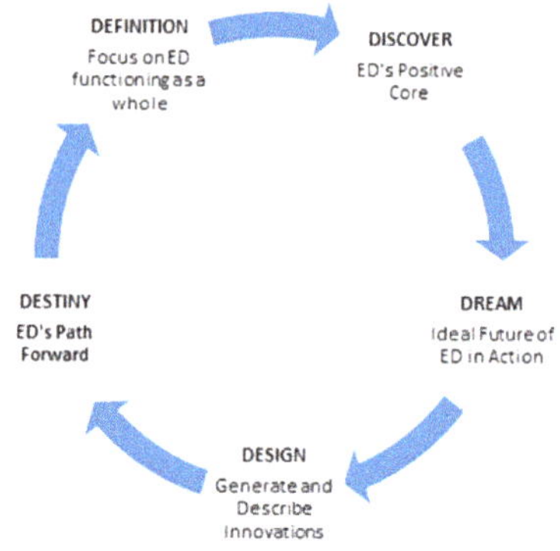

More recently, Kumar et al. (2023) presented Appreciative Inquiry as a framework for medical education due to the "positive psychology principles" present in successful change initiatives. One example of the effectiveness of the framework is the development of a second model used to assess diversity (Martens & Dehaes, 2008). The application showed positivity in the responses and effectiveness in the process improvement related to a diverse work environment.

Current research shows the value of beginning with sustainability in mind and managing an iterative process to create positive social change (Burton & Carter, 2025). The newly released book, *Sustainable Organizational Change: The Social Change Model for Systems* shows how sustainability can be enhanced through a purposeful approach to social change constructs. Burton & Carter (2025) explain how the definitions may be reframed to establish additional iterations of improvement. The Define concept was introduced in Chapter of *Multinational Electronic Health Records Interoperability Strategies* and is restated here to move the concept forward to implementation. By way of review, the model is applied to an Emergency Department's redesign and presents the application of all five phases. The Definition phase adds the meaningful opportunity to establish working definitions for the effort of expanding interoperability across borders.

Conversations about learning have been enhanced by Appreciative Inquiry and difficult conversations are made easier by beginning the discussion with open dialogue (Ohlemacher, 2015). Using a case study, Lehner & Hight (2006) demonstrate applying Appreciative Inquiry in a student environment. The positive approach allows what is normally a critical view of processes to become a more participative process. Embracing emotion can help to create a more cohesive learning environment (Naude et al., 2014). Mental, emotional, and behavioral elements were studied and determined to have a positive impact on learning. Communicating about change (Nadler & Tushman, 1997) also has a positive impact on organizational development. Application of the concepts are easily adopted in the multinational interoperability context because the various entities working on the problem should be valued for their work.

In Appreciative Inquiry, the phases clearly present a way to support change guided by the principles of human capital utilization to magnify the opportunities for growth. Including the areas of the 7S model to ensure that all the components of an organization are included in the conversation can provide peace of mind for the leader that the work will address all areas (Bell, 2025). The stakeholders for these assessment areas should all be considered part of the transformation team.

Roles and responsibilities for the process are clearly defined as the approach includes as many voices as possible. The energy of the participants (Naude et al., 2014) enhances the momentum that is gained in the dream phase. Including multiple voices creates an open and positive environment where the group members can have a voice in the organizational design process. Evaluation is a critical part of the process in order to turn the dreams into reality. The role of the evaluator is not to squelch the creativity, but rather to include all the components necessary to accomplish the dream. One example in the application is shared by Dunlap (2008) in the use of the HPT model of appreciative approach for evaluation. The detailed model shows how Appreciative Inquiry can be applied and takes into consideration many factors.

Holman, Devane, and Cady (2007) discuss principles supporting Appreciative Inquiry. The principles explain why the connection with human capital increases the value of organizational design. The following principles can be used to explore reasons for keeping some of the topics in the forefront of the change process:

- The Constructionist Principle
- The Principle of Simultaneity
- The Poetic Principle
- The Anticipatory Principle
- The Positive Principle
- The Narrative Principle
- Wholeness
- Enactment
- Free Choice

Application of the Appreciative Inquiry model creates a more positive approach to managing change (Holman, Devane, & Cady, 2007) and allows more customization than other models. Combining the SOAR analysis, which is an acronym for strengths, opportunities, aspirations, and results, adds the task of establishing a way to focus on the strengths and maintain a positive psychological approach in change management (Watkins, Mohr, & Kelly, 2011). Pryor et al (2011) provides an excellent overview of organizational theory related to systems theory and the idea that departments are interrelated and should consider multiple avenues and principles in the application of the theory to organizational design and behavior. The proposed changes to the organizational design encourage a more integrated level of thinking to combine efforts toward a central goal.

The change management model, which is both simple enough to provide a multinational process and open enough to fit the complexity of the proposed concepts, is based on Lewin's model of unfreeze, change, and refreeze (Jones, 2013). Elements of the adapted change process are illustrated in Figure 6 where the Appreciative Inquiry and McKinsey 7-S Framework serve as consultation and gap analysis components. The *Change Management Model for Successful Sustainable Change* represents the broader steps implemented in the PNW Global Consulting case study earlier in the chapter.

Change Management Model for Successful Sustainable Change

Figure 6. Change management model for successful sustainable change

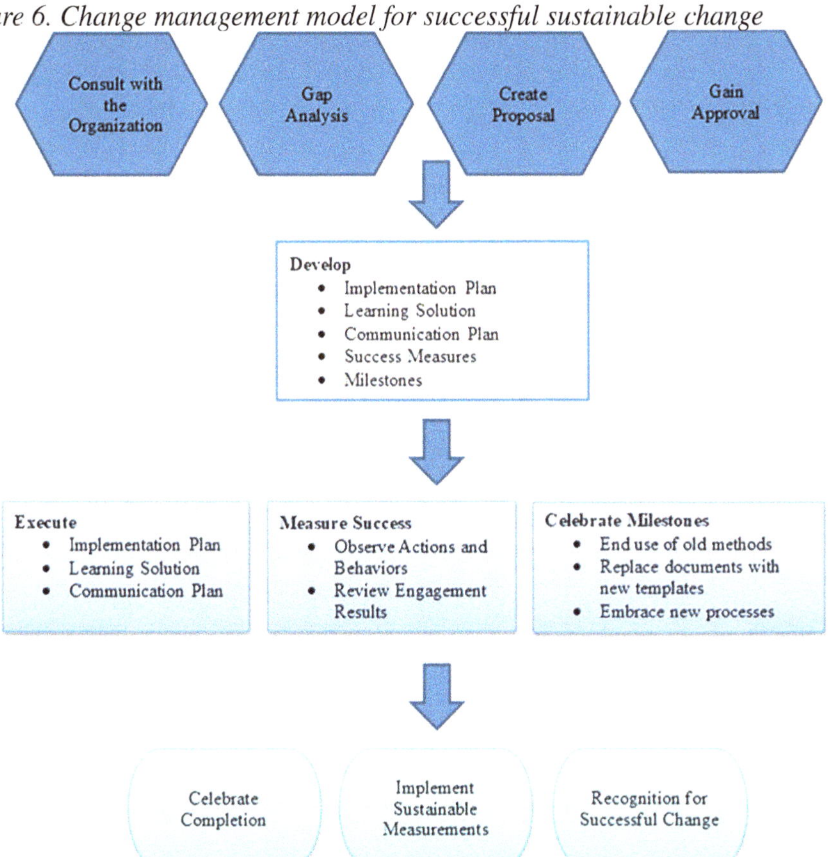

Jones (2013) shares the likelihood of resistance and the forces of change at play in relation to how a leader would implement Lewin's model. The organizational design methods including Appreciative Inquiry (Holman, Devane, and Cady, 2007) and the McKinsey 7S model will drive the major activities in the design process (Bell, 2025). Once the assessments illustrate the areas of change, a direct model such as the process of unfreeze, change, and refreeze can provide clarity in the change intervention.

Organizations adopting EHR interoperability is a significant change. The complexity such change offers can have unintended consequences such as impacts to the employees, care providers, working culture, and patients. The change model should be able to address the potential challenges and resistance while allowing for the organizational design process to unfold. Once the stakeholders are aware of the need for change, they will be more likely to support the process. Communication plans should ensure that everyone is on the same page with the change. Actions to implement the changes outlined follow the "unfreeze, change, refreeze" pattern offered by Lewin (Jones, 2013). The basic process is outlined as follows:

Unfreeze

To thaw the current components identified in the assessment process, basic pre-change processes can be used to reinforce the awareness of exactly what should be different:

- Analyze the gap between identified areas to be improved and the desired state
- Protect what should not change as a result of the initiative
- Organize the implementation into phases and create the implementation plan including a proposed statement of work with the appropriate size and scope of the change effort
- Obtain funding and approval from any required entities
- Create the design plan for related training and learning solutions
- Develop a communication plan with metrics for success and milestones to communicate progress in the change initiative
- Involve stakeholders early in the process and obtain buy-in for the change effort

Change

The actual change process sets forth in motion the plans that were part of the original assessment. Appreciative Inquiry results allow for awareness on every level of the organization since all were involved in the effort. The topics covered the McKinsey 7-S Framework, and each area was carefully considered. Components of the change process include:

- Constant communication of the change process and next steps
- Celebrate milestones as they arrive
- Implement training and learning solutions to support professors and administrative support staff during the change process and in the resulting new environment
- Re-organize the departments and hold meetings to develop team structure
- Communicate measurements and provide feedback to changing teams concerning processes and timelines

- Create guidelines and communicate new expectations

Re-Freeze

Following the change, sustainability of the new environment depends on leaders' ability to manage the change process (Jones, 2013). Purposeful activities will help support the new environment:

- Implement activities and processes that will ensure permanence
- Measure and provide feedback
- Celebrate completion of the change process elements
- Recognize success
- Revisit the Appreciative Inquiry process for continuous improvement opportunities

The lessons learned from assessing an organization that is already performing provided a view of how change models can be applied for improvement rather than repair. The organization will benefit from the changes, but a ripple effect will show stakeholders benefit when an organization makes improvements. Models dovetail nicely into each other and can work together to customize outcomes. Whether the Appreciative Inquiry model works as an organizational design model or a change model or both, other ideas may be leveraged to achieve the outcomes desired. Examples shown in the supporting literature area demonstrate that SOAR and McKinsey 7-S Framework combine with the 4-Ds or 5-Ds of Appreciative Inquiry to provide an enhanced assessment of the organization.

ORGANIZATIONAL STAKEHOLDERS

The multinational conversation rests in the hands of organizations, nations, companies, and agencies to implement. Hospitals, clinics, disease surveillance bureaus, and government entities are each potentially facing change related to the impacts of implementing an interoperable system expanding beyond borders. Looking at organizational roles and relationships can help identify those who would help with the change management initiatives.

OD and HR Collaborative Relationship

The Relationship between Organizational Development (OD) and Human Resources (HR) can be a collaborative relationship with OD reporting to an HR manager. While this is not the ideal, it will provide a framework for the relationship to continue to grow (Vogelsang et al, 2013). With a global market, we have also considered how the relationship compares to other countries' definitions. Neumann et al. (2009) describes how Organizational Development and Change has diverse applications and is interrelated to other departments and called multiple names globally. This could create confusion depending on how savvy leaders are about the different names referring to similar roles.

There are many components of OD and HR that cross-over or support the functions. The change management function seems to be a component of both departments. This idea is supported by findings presented by Worren, Ruddle, & Moore (1999), concerning the connection of change management to OD, strategic change, HR management, and project management. In each of these areas, departments work together on projects and collectively implement initiatives. The concept is further explored by odnetwork.org (2025) in the roles related to the Global OD Competency Framework™ in areas of capability including system change expertise, efficient designer including process consulting and data synthesis, business advising encompassing trust and results leadership, strategic communications collaborating across cultures, and consultancy advocating for equity as a learning practitioner. The individuals in these roles could be in a change management role, an organizational development practitioner, an HR leader, or any other number of job titles.

Organizational Design

Regardless of the role and title, some tools can help the process work more smoothly. Implementing a large-scale transformation initiative requires an organizational design. The design document governs transformational change, allows decisions to be made in a purposeful way, and provides a structure for the OD work. Kates points to building strategic capabilities as a reason for using design principles to create structure for organizational design (Rothwell, Stavros, Sullivan & Sullivan, 2010). A design creates a structure for the complex change being introduced by the OD group.

In an organization, decisions are made using documentation and a formalized process. A project plan will capture the owner of the process. Each of the areas of the company that would be included in this decisioning would have a representative with a "seat at the table" to discuss the impact to his or her part of the organization. Depending on the process owner, the change leader could be challenged in implementing without multiple discussions involving several opinions creating even more complexity. The discussions help define boundaries for the change and show potential resistance.

While the organization has design plans for implementation of most initiatives, they may or may not be accustomed to using a formal organizational design process. Each of the areas may create an independent design plan, structured as the organizational design framework discussed by Amy Kates (Rothwell, Stavros, Sullivan & Sullivan, 2010). Kates presents the concept of matching the model to the strategy and connecting the strategy with organizational development using a decision-making process.

Skills needed to create the design may not be common in the change leader who may be charged with this task within an organization (Rothwell, Stavros, Sullivan & Sullivan, 2010). A competent project manager may have background in change management, strategically creating the organizational design would involve critical skills, which Kates contends are brought by a professional with "a strategy, process or business background".

The advantages of the HR and OD collaborative relationship are illustrated in a case study by Kolachi & Akan, where they focused on "corporate thinking" as a result of the partnership between HR and OD (2014). They wanted to present a way for business students to think about the structure of the HR and OD relationship and how guidelines could be applied to other companies.

Rothwell et al. (2010) describes the relationship as a close alignment in order for HR to take the lead on change efforts like OD. The change management work could be led by both groups and name a clear leader and owner of the processes that deal with organizational change, structure, and internal processes. With one leader to address the board of directors on behalf of both functions, progress and opportunities are clearly communicated to leadership and to individual contributors.

Dave Hanna (Vogelsang, 2013) shares how important it is for HR and OD to align due to similarities as they function within an organization. One component he specifically mentions is the need for respect in their respective functions. This may be more difficult as there are fewer employees in these roles. There are multiple departments functioning with various sets of rules depending on how the HR manager embraces OD or not. What seems inevitable is the major transformational change to centralize HR in the organization and there will be fewer employees conducting the same amount of work that is needed in the current splintered groups. The hope is that the alignment of process and rules will create efficiency and effectiveness to the extent that the organization will see better processes and relationships resulting from the company-wide change efforts.

Another benefit of the relationship between HR and OD is described at length by Schein (Vogelsang, 2013). With the leadership of the HR manager which Schein refers to as "Role 4", OD can be integrated with HR, and they can coexist in a company. In the same discussion, he also acknowledges that the HR culture and OD culture are different enough to cause a question of clarity in the integration. There are many benefits to the union of HR and OD, some challenges are difficult to ignore.

DISADVANTAGED PRACTICES

The disadvantaged current OD and HR practices include cross-ownership of tasks that may not be appropriately assigned due to the nature of the transition. The company has decided to use the HR consultants and OD consultants interchangeably as if they have the same skillset. This creates several problems, one basic example being that the task could be completed by a more skilled individual or department. This example in my workplace is not the only one of it's kind. In a mixed methods study of the field of Organizational Development, researchers Wirtenberg et al. (2004) determined that as many OD practitioners are displaced as a company tries to adjust the number of OD and HR employees, work of the OD practitioner may not always be completed by an OD practitioner.

One of the major issues facing the current practices of treating HR and OD as parts of the same department with similar functions is that they are clearly not the same. Trends Schein refers to are, the creation of subcultures to deal with complexity, rapidly evolving IT impacted work processes, culturally diverse perspectives require connecting globally, cultural diversity creating more complex issues, and organizational functions realigning with social responsibility and business ethics (Vogelsang et al., 2013). These trends impact multiple organizations and transcend industry boundaries. While they affect HR and OD, they are the basis for other conflicting issues as HR and OD relate to other areas of organizations and manage large-scale change. Change managers manage change in the midst of change. This magnifies the disadvantaged practices that are currently in the way of creating the new role definitions Schein discusses.

FUTURE OF HR AND OD COLLABORATION

Organizational culture is discussed by Coghlan and Rashford (2006), who point out that there are "collective assumptions" that make up the organizational culture and become a part of the organization in the basic beliefs of individuals and teams. If HR and OD have been part of the same department within an organization, the culture may have embraced the view that they belong together. One study presents the purposeful integration of HR and OD with a strategy for how to appropriately join the two. Hawthorne (2004) synthesizes studies on the subject to make recommendations for combining efforts and creating teams of HR and OD professionals. In the article, the researcher presents ten challenges that may make integration difficult. This finding suggests that HR and OD may not be a natural fit and work should be done to determine if it is right for the company.

Determining the impact culture may have on the OD practitioner, which may be felt as a member of the occupational community of organizational development. Both OD and HR face similar duality in various capacities. They often end up self-prescribing solutions due to complex business situations. These events where the change is initiated by interdepartmental ideals may or may not fit with the vision and values of the organization. These changes enhance the culture and change the view of employees. The change influences the culture of the organization and can become a positive way to influence leadership.

The future is unknown when a major large-scale change initiative is underway. Reorganizing the company-wide HR function is likely to influence employees throughout the company. This type of transformational change will impact every employee and has been communicated and planned for the organization. New leadership may be put in place to implement the change plan and create a centralized body. Every communication should contain a reference to the timeline, which points out where the organization is in the change process and how much is yet to implement.

Based on history and how the company culture embraces change, the collaboration between HR and OD could continue to grow well past this change or may experience challenges. Examples of how the advantages and disadvantages of HR and OD relationships work or fail may be seen in multiple organizations. The future is bright for both the HR field and the OD field. With so much complexity currently facing organizations, managing internal operations and change will take an increasingly significant role in business.

APPROACH TO INTEROPERABILITY

Interoperability has been primarily focused on national efforts in most countries. In 2013, Sicilia and Balazote included the motivation to share EHR information between organizations and countries. Systems interoperability can be expensive, taking time and resources from other projects, and requiring change in procedures and workflows. Semantic approaches, interoperability, and semantic transformation of archetypes have been explored, outlining opportunities for improvement (Sicilia & Balazote, 2013). Acknowledging the complexity is critical in taking the first steps toward a shared understanding of what is needed to accomplish multinational interoperability. It is important to recognize EHR standards and how the transformation has evolved in various places with technological advancements.

Global health is impacted by technological advancements including the big data including collective EHRs and AI-powered research tools (Vayena & Ferretti, 2021). Sociotechnical theory applies in this context to approach the partnership between the human need to manage health records and the technical requirements for systems to serve these needs. One example from a healthcare setting provides a study to apply sociotechnical theory for supporting clinicians in decision-making (Jeffries et al., 2023). This element is likely to become more significant as AI is implemented in healthcare settings.

EHR systems need interoperability, but the scale that is needed for multinational interoperability is a massive scale. Change management models can be applied to systems of scale. The predictive model required to anticipate functional multinational interoperability can be created through gathering data, leveraging machine learning and developing a predictive model (Siegel, 2016). Today, increased technological capabilities have successfully created predictive models to operate at scale (Kaur, 2024). Kaur describes the power of computational intelligence to restructure the healthcare paradigm.

Health record interoperability and quality of data continue to be challenges in the healthcare industry (Khang, 2023). Even patients who have great relationships with their doctors have limited time to discuss their health situation. Doctors are also challenged to gather quality information from patients in the best circumstances. When patients are uncomfortable discussing their health situation, they may not share all the information with their doctors. The challenge is multiplied when time in the office visit is short. By creating more interoperable health records, time is saved in the office visit. Assuming the doctor accepts and adopts the integration of advanced technology, the records can be improved over time and may rely on patient validation of the EHR.

Disease surveillance incorporates predictive analytics, machine learning, and data analytics (Khang, 2023). While it may seem to be a challenge that is related to technology, the issue is also related to information provided by patients to their doctor. Predictive models can help with disease monitoring, but only if the model is updated and deep learning is allowed. The study of predictive analytics provides examples for how the process can be adopted.

POTENTIAL PREDICTIVE MODELS

At the intersection of creating change and anticipating future needs, predictive analytics provides an opportunity to move an organization and plan for future movement simultaneously. Forward-looking statements that accompany annual reports help businesses prepare for the problems that may arise in the near future but do little to provide a real vision of what is to come. Futuring in its proper form allows an organization to analyze the future using methods to fathom complexity and include all the necessary components and variables. The contributions of Peter Drucker (1998) specifically impact the role of change management. Some of the predictions for business presented by Drucker include a perspective on knowledge management that seems difficult to know 20 years ago. One begs the question, "How did he know?" There are many contributing factors to the strategy of looking forward and being able to see the writing on the wall. Futurists who consistently keep an eye on the future state of the environment are in great demand today.

The complexities present in change management are one example of how the futurist prepares an organization to take advantage of the predictions. Another example is how consulting with an expert in reading trends will add perspective to the decision-making process (Kumar, 2013). With each added level of complexity, there is a growing need to consult experts in the field. As methods improved over time, the futurist grew from a mere forecaster watching trends and extrapolating information to a more sophisticated scenario-building strategist. Once the Delphi technique was introduced in the 1980s, the study turned more to how the futuring was being done and practitioners applied the models (Okoli & Pawlowski, 2004). The Delphi technique could be leveraged in the context of multinational interoperability as a selection tool for expert stakeholders to participate in establishing interoperable electronic health records across borders.

Working together, futurists develop more intricate ideas and as experts can help others. One example is the gathering that occurred in the 1990s to address some of the world problems (Fields, 1993). The role evolved using trend analysis, forecasting, scenarios, and many other methods to create change deeply into the future (Joseph, 2007). The internet allows futurists to apply the Delphi model globally (Staykova, 2019). In both the public and private sectors, leaders need the futurist to make sense of potential future scenarios. The data needs more than reporting, complexities exist in the scenarios that cannot just be explained in a briefing. Governments and businesses alike rely on the experts to share the knowledge leaders do not have time to acquire.

Leaders expect that the forecasting they conduct will sufficiently position them for success in the industry and provide them with a competitive advantage over others who may have overlooked the details. The strength of the business' position in the market is directly impacted by how well they anticipated the problems and opportunities of the future. Businesses succeed and fail daily because they either were correct about anticipatory decisions or incorrect. Most business failures can be traced back to how the leader did not understand or neglected to prepare for what was likely to happen. Futurists have become one of the most critical roles in the survival of the organization.

The ability to compare disparate views related to a complex situation is critical and the sought-after experts are becoming indispensable to organizations due to the rate of change in many industries. Information floods into organizations faster than a person can make sense of the information and those who can make sense of the data are valuable. Many industries rely on technical advancements to grow, but the same technology that allows business to be conducted today is also helpful in envisioning the needs of the future (Al Saeed, 2011). Data is being gathered at a record pace and how leaders are able to make sense of it or not (Siegel, 2016) will often be the deciding factor in taking action in time to capitalize on the opportunities. Harnessing the data will be critical in being able to leverage the information for decision making.

Decision making is a complex process that relies on predictive analytics to create a vision of important elements related to future context (Siegel, 2016). Developing a vision that can be shared also involves critical thinking about the potential outcomes of these decisions (Millet, 2006). The details that are necessary for appropriate planning should include perspective from both a large organizational view and an individual contributor view (Lin et al., 2017). Specifically, healthcare uses electronic health records for risk profiling.

The multiple facets of the organization should all be included in a future modeling plan for the view to have the breadth and depth necessary to share a clear vision of the complex view of the future (Mack, 2005). To accomplish a critical-thinking view, it is necessary for the futurist to use a method of predictive analytics that will accommodate industry and organizational information as well as external factors that may have an impact on the outcomes.

The role of the futurists will continue to evolve as the pace and complexity of the changes increase. Impacts to business and government will likely show that the experts are more valued to the leader and the organization. As global needs change, there will be a need to know more and know it faster and those who can simplify the complexity and plan for the unknown will help usher in many new eras. Knowing what to look for and how to look at it are skills that are sharpened by continued use. Technology empowers experts to compare mounds of data in time for the information to make a difference to an organization.

Predictive analytics is a process that manages large amounts of data, organizing it so that others may leverage the information in context and make sense of the shared data (Lee, 2015). Hair (2007) points out that "predictive analytics uses confirmed relationships between explanatory and criterion variables from past occurrences to predict future outcomes" (p. 304). Decisions made using large amounts of data depend on the expertise of those managing the predictive analytics process. Organizations use predictive analytics in various ways to uncover new approaches to the customer, client, or constituent and to prevent issues and problems from occurring (Seigel, 2016). Common uses for predictive analytics are explored with examples of how organizations use the information.

COMMON USES

Seigel (2016) shares a multitude of examples encompassing the use of predictive analytics. Industries in the discussion on predictive analytics include fraud detection, healthcare, marketing, financials, safety, government, psychology, and workforce. In each of these areas, there are multiple uses for leveraging data. Some of the more common uses are outlined below, combining different applications from various organizations.

Lee (2015) discusses preventing fraud using a specific model to apply predictive analytics. Gathering and managing the data using a predictive model is best when the model is flexible enough to handle the large amounts of data being explored. Banks and government entities may use the information to manage risk and predict fraudulent behavior. Through systematic audits of the information gathered, analysis can determine potential criminal activity. Examples include law enforcement and the U.S. Department of Defense (Seigel, 2016) where predictive analytics were used to detect fraud.

Forecasting the cost of medical services (Wills, 2014) uses data to predict the cost of various medical procedures. Other healthcare-related uses of data analytics are listed by Seigel (2016) to include hospital stays, billing mistakes, drug effectiveness, and potential for infection. As fast as data is created in healthcare (Wills, 2014), using predictive analytics to sort through and discern meaning will give decision makers a way to manage the changing environment.

Trends in target marketing take information from grocery customers (Alaimo, 2015, March 23) and turn it into a way for the store to provide usable coupons that customers will value. Most shoppers carry the loyalty cards and build points while they shop in exchange for the data. In larger organizations, marketing departments work to gather information to make organizational decisions about how to position the product or service in the market to gain a competitive advantage (Zanon et al., 2013). Marketing covers many aspects of the organization's relationship with the customer and predictive analytics can be applied in various forms to most of the customer connection points (Hair, 2007). From mining data related to customer preference to analyzing the reasons a customer is complaining, the customer experience is rich with information.

Data is being used to determine the likelihood that someone will be injured at work (Using Technology to Predict Workplace Injuries, 2014). Safety concerns are greatly reduced by analyzing the data in proper context and being able to predict whether dangerous conditions will lead to injury (Seigel, 2016). Precautions can then be taken to keep workers safe and save organizations money and time.

WHY COMPANIES CHOOSE PREDICTIVE ANALYTICS

Companies are increasingly interested in the data gathered about every facet of the business. Seigel (2016) illustrates the points of interest with an outline of over 182 scenarios where organizations choose to use predictive analytics to make sense of the available information. These examples point to many reasons to use predictive analytics, but a few stand out based on appearance in other articles. Some popular reasons to use predictive analytics are to gain a competitive advantage, better meet customer expectations, make improvements, and increase market share (techadvisory.org, 2015).

Data is becoming more valuable to organizations and one way to manage the data is to use predictive analytics (Jobs et al., 2015). Companies have large amounts of information available to determine internal and external actions, but if they are unable to create a context for the data it is meaningless. Harnessing the information allows organizations to identify the next important actions to position themselves in the market.

Forecasting, as it has been viewed in the past, is not enough to compete in the current market. Joseph (2007) discusses the history of forecasting and the value of the futurist profession. While he doesn't specifically discuss predictive analytics, the premise of the points he makes emerges as a precursor to scenario planning. Halladay (2013) connects the idea of forecasting as a piece of predictive analytics encompassing various facets of analysis. Using the banking industry as an example, predictive activities such as forecasting and planning, pricing, reporting regulation compliance activity, managing risk and performance models, and determining future costs are all easier when leveraging the appropriate types of data.

FedEx determines how customers will react to changes based on an analysis of the large amounts of data at its disposal (Hair, 2007). The example is not unlike how other companies leverage the information (Seigel, 2016). Knowledge management depends on the organization's ability to use experiential learning and gathered data to create pictures of the possible future so that leadership may respond appropriately.

Informing Decisions

Gaining competitive advantage (Zanon et al., 2013) requires leaders to use predictive analytics to examine competitor information. Understanding the market conditions will help the decision maker determine the important actions that will prepare the company to compete. Predictive analytics supports leaders in making decisions by adding clarity to the data so that it can be used to evaluate business practices and make improvements to future activities (O'Flaherty & Heavin, 2015).

The context of the data can be problematic given the vast amount of data available. Wills (2014) suggests that the gathered data goes unused when decision makers are not able to identify importance in the comparison of data. Early use of analytical scenarios provides a glimpse of the power of analysis. The advice Millett (2006) gives to leaders indicates the importance of using prediction in decision making. Additional future thinking allows the leader to do more than forecast (Millett & Staley, 2009). Planning with a futurist perspective shows that the best guess about the future is not nearly good enough.

Organizational learning is one way to describe the situational use of predictive analytics to make decisions based on experiential learning (Weitzman, 2014). In a process similar to action research, cycles of reflection from the action can help with the decision making process. When a leader can see the improvements from one decision to the next based on specific information and contextual data processing, the skill is improved, and performance improves as a result. Halladay (2013) points out that getting the organized data to management within context is only part of the issue. More importantly, the leader needs to recognize the data as trustworthy. If the leader does not trust the information or the source, the decision will not likely be impacted by the real data.

Leveraging big data is important because the information represents a large cross-section of customers (Waller & Fawcett, 2013). The value is in understanding what the data represents and being able to use the information to support improvements in the organization. Since there is so much data available, it is important to find a way to distill the themes to a point where researchers can share the real meaning with leaders.

Jobs, Aukers, & Gilfoil, (2015) describe predictive analytics as a way to use the big data from online sources to improve decisions. They point out that corporate funding is being shifted from traditional methods of reaching customers to more online sources for the real-time use of big data. Sukumar, & Ferrell, (2013) take the use of the data points to a new level of significance by introducing a model and tool allowing an organization to use the data already existing in the company to identify themes and learn from experience.

Predictive analytics is only as good as the company's desire and ability to use the information. Through harnessing big data, predictive analytics provides leaders with the context needed to make decisions. Future planning and organizational improvements are informed by big data using predictive analytics provided that the organization trusts the data.

IMPLEMENTING STRATEGIES

Predictive analytics can show where the most challenging issues will be for implementation (Siegel, 2016). The opportunity to improve global health, public health, and participatory disease surveillance is magnificent when envisioning a collective approach implementing multinational information sharing (Vayena & Ferretti, 2021). The needs of individuals do not stop at the border of one nation to the next. It is time to consider the needs of the whole.

Systems thinking supports the growth of leadership in healthcare. Carr et al. (2024) studied leadership needs, collaboration, and systems thinking related to clinical scholars. Findings included a concept map highlighting the value of continuing education for the healthcare profession. Barton et al. (2009) connect open systems thinking to action research and support of the scientific method. Open systems thinking is critical as the stakeholders come together. Relationships between stakeholders should be built with the understanding of nations helping nations rather than the idea that one nation would succeed at the expense of another nation's failure.

Failure in digital transformations relates to open systems thinking and communication. Knowing why change management efforts fail can give perspective on which methods and processes are critical to change efforts. One such failed change occurred at Sample Community Bank (name changed to protect the organization). Events leading up to the change and decision making during the change created a domino effect that if not corrected, would lead to bank failure. Commonly known as the Y2K bug, organizations everywhere faced the same issue (Zhang et al., 2021). The case study follows a fictitious bank through the change process.

Until 1995, systems upgrades were affordable for Sample Community Bank, but the cost of storing paper loan documents was increasing. One solution was an upgrade to scan these documents, but in order for the documents to be admissible in court as originals once scanned there had to be no way for the documents to be changed. The technology that existed for this was expensive, but would save the bank money in storage over time once the documents were scanned. This was the start of the technology race for the bank to maintain profitability.

Other changes were needed following the upgrade to the system. Scanners were purchased and IT professionals were hired to support the effort to become paperless.

One project after another helped the bank to keep up with competition in what could be offered to customers. Profits were dwindling based on the cost of the projects in relationship to the revenue generated from the bank's loans and fee structure. Something had to change in order to afford the next upgrade on the horizon in 1999. In 1998, IT project managers and leadership met often to determine the best approach to changing mainframe systems to accommodate the year 2000 (Ettorre, 1998). Prior to this, only 2 digits were in the year field on the system. The efforts were complicated and expensive, especially if the bank expected uninterrupted customer service to maintain the 110% reputation.

THE ORGANIZATION'S INDUSTRY, ENVIRONMENT, AND COMPETITION

Banking was changing. As technology grew up, so did the need for system upgrades to remain secure and provide the necessary protection customers had come to trust. The interest rate environment was not conducive to being able to generate enough revenue by itself to accommodate these changes. Since all banks were experiencing the same issues, raising fees seemed to be the answer. The climate was able to provide some wiggle room with fees, but customers would only accept so much change before trying another bank.

The year 1999 would be a critical time for many companies because the systems issues for programmers transcended industry. Many of the qualified IT professionals were able to command salaries of significance in order to fix the mainframe problems. Since Sample Community Bank was still operating in a DOS environment, it seemed like an easy enough fix to the layperson. It was really more complicated than just changing a field. Fear was increasing among employees and customers and some thought it would be the end of the world as we knew it (Parker, 1999).

Financial Institutions alike struggled with the cost of the upgrades and related projects. Cost-cutting efforts were everywhere in the industry and beyond. Employees understood that some things were going to have to change and agreed that paper could be printed two-sided and maybe the company party could be a potluck. But when the changes came to losing jobs and co-workers, people were afraid. This fear was perpetuated by the way this change was communicated.

BACKGROUND OF THE CHANGE INITIATIVE

In order to be able to afford the looming changes, the bank was looking for ways to cut costs and grow revenue to be able to afford the real change that was coming. In preparation for those changes, the leadership knew that some self-initiated change would be necessary. What they originally thought could be transactional change with minimal impact quickly became transformational change (Anderson & Anderson, 2010). The bank was not accustomed to this type of change, so they didn't recognize the complexity of the decisions they had made to this point. Managing changes in the past had resulted in some pain for employees, but that was just the way it was to leadership.

The decision to make this change clearly was made based on external forces (Frame, 2013). It may have come as a surprise to the leaders, but underestimating the impact of the change was the first mistake of many. Since other changes had not really been sustainable, the track record for change in the company was not good. Everyone believed one change would be replaced by another in time, since that was the way things had gone in the past. This effort was a wakeup call for everyone.

From the moment the changes began in 1996, no big picture was ever shared with employees. Middle managers shared only what information was necessary and it was on a business "need to know" basis. The secrecy fostered mistrust and leaders kept making changes without measuring effectiveness. Constant change began to create issues and managers were not skilled at managing the transition. There should have been some sensitivity to the employees and the type of work environment resulting from the change (Bridges, 2017).

REVIEW OF THE FAILED CHANGE EFFORT

Orange paper at Halloween was one such insensitivity that illustrates the climate concerning the change. If the changes that were necessary for system upgrades were so important, why would the company choose to communicate the change on orange paper at Halloween? It made the change seem temporary and seasonal. The message was lost in the joke about corporate trying to scare employees. But employees kept waiting for the punchline. The punchline came in the form of layoffs at Christmas which generated more fear. Everyone had seen the lack of supplies to do regular business and now co-workers were disappearing.

Communication is critical to the change effort (Kotter, 2012) if everyone is to have a shared vision of the outcome of the change. With employees not understanding the change and lack-luster commitment, the change was doomed to fail from the beginning. The were some efforts to communicate, but the middle managers failed to reinforce the true purpose of the change, thereby reducing the chance of commitment and enhancing the resistance to the change.

In addition to the issues with communication, the strategy behind the change was flawed. The upgrade and related cost containment could have been handled in a phased strategy with an initial assessment of the potential impacts and management strategies for components that could create the unintended consequences. Without a change management consultant and little knowledge of these types of strategies, leadership maintained the top down approach that had worked for them in the past. No measures were put in place to ensure sustainability of the cost containment or take advantage of the talent and knowledge that was present in human capital.

Brown and Eisenhardt (1997) conducted a study of continuous change. Comparing six organizations related to computer changes. William Bridges book Managing Transitions was available originally in 1991 and many other authors (Bridges, 2009; Kotter, 2012) had written about such change and methods for accomplishing the effort with minimal impact. If leadership had taken advice from any of these experts, the change may have had a chance.

Other strategies had been successful for other organizations. For the leadership to be so blind or arrogant or ignorant not to take advantage of participative management at the very least kept them in the dark. Dervitsiotis (1998) studied emerging methods such as learning organizations, re-engineering, and total quality management. These methods of improvement had been successful for other organizations, why did it seem that Sample Community Bank's leadership was unaware of what was going on around them?

Banks had traditionally been able to remain behind the times due to the serious nature of the business. Trendiness had not been proven over years of testing. The attitude of wait and see may have been instrumental in the inability to manage change. They were unprepared for the resistance from employees (Folger and Skarlicki, 1999). In the past, no employees would dare to sabotage the efforts of a change initiated by management. This was uncharted territory.

Change had been continuous since the adoption of computers in banking. Although some leaders of competitors had seen methods of managing change in this way, Sample Community Bank remained unaware of the studies that had been going on at the time. Weick and Quinn (1999) studied the difference between methods of managing change if it is seen as unrelated events versus managing continuous change. Advice from experts was available, but unsolicited.

CONCLUSION

Other difficulties cascaded from the initial communication mistake. Customers felt the loss of employees they had built relationships with and chose to do business with another bank as a result. Vendors saw that the contracts were smaller and not as lucrative, so the vendors bid other contracts and things became more expensive for the bank. With the loss of employees also came loss of customers and impact to vendor relationships. This doomed the 110% reputation and soon shareholders began to question the profitability of the bank. The impacts were seen in the stock price and soon after the changes were implemented, ABC Community Bank was ripe for acquisition.

Failed change efforts in this case have the potential to derail future needed transformation based on the way this change was handled. Frame (2013) presents potential disruptors that are all present in this failed effort. With the potential sabotage from unhappy employees, improper execution from the implementers, and employees and customers rejecting the outcome, this change is unsustainable in the current environment. The future of the organization is at risk as a result. Without a successful transformation that reengages stakeholders including employees, the cost savings will be overshadowed by the expense of replacing employees that leave as an unintended consequence of layoffs in other areas.

Managing change requires the use of communication and strategy at a much higher level than in normal leadership situations. Managing change is a process of creating a new normal environment (Sullivan, Rothwell, & Balasi, 2013). Leaders need change management skills and processes to accomplish the change. Implementation strategies must include the leaders' skills and processes but also the togetherness of a shared vision. The WHO Pandemic Agreement in partnership with the United Nation's Sustainable Development Goals provide the vision of a future state (United Nations, 2025; WHO, 2025). Stakeholders uniting to continue the important conversation will need open systems thinking and a collaborative approach.

The challenge of implementation, particularly for LMICs, is quality data collection and affording advanced technology. If healthcare providers are lacking resources and training due to financial constraints, they may not be able to implement the strategies for interoperable EHRs (Vayena & Ferretti, 2021).

Electronic health records interoperability has been an example of proactive activity. The extensive discussion of potential assessment tools and models to manage complex concepts provides a foundation for the vast amount of work that is needed to approach a multinational effort. Now, let's return to the discussion of *The Global Project Management Framework©* (Binder, 2016). Earlier in this chapter, we discussed the approach to project management in the context of the broader applications for change management. While project management models deal primarily with a specific project, when it involves the stakeholders as a body and includes the assessment models within the framework it can be relied on to reduce complexity and provide a scaffolding for larger discussions.

Addressing the potential for virtual teams of stakeholders is a much broader subject (Binder, 2016; Hardin et al., 2025). In the next chapter, we will examine the possibilities of involving teams of teams to have a larger conversation (McChrystal et al., 2015). The concept of bringing stakeholders together virtually and in a

Teams-of-Teams format is reminiscent of the Holonic Model discussed in Chapter 7 (Bakos & Dumitrascu, 2017).

REFERENCES

Al-Haddad, S., & Kotnour, T. (2015). Integrating the organizational change literature: A model for successful change. *Journal of Organizational Change Management, 28*(2), 234.

Al Saeed, I. (2011). Importance of emerging technologies in society for futuring & innovation. *Journal of Applied Global Research, 4*(11), 12–22.

Alaimo, D. (2015, March 23). Technology: Future tense. *Progressive Grocer India*. Progressivegrocer.com https://progressivegrocer.com/future-tense?

Altrichter, H., Kemmis, S., McTaggart, R., & Zuber-Skerritt, O. (2002). The concept of action research. *The Learning Organization, 9*(3/4), 125.

Anderson, D., & Anderson, L. A. (2010). *Beyond change management: How to achieve breakthrough results through conscious change leadership* (2nd ed.). Pfeiffer.

Arya, D. K. (2012). So, you want to lead a transformational change! *Asia Pacific Journal of Health Management, 7*(2), 8–14.

Bailey, P., Cooper, K., Stevens, M. P., Bearman, G., & Doll, M. (2024). Contact precautions as a barrier to hand hygiene: The Plan–Do–Study–Act (PDSA) framework to improve compliance with gloved hand hygiene. *Infection Control and Hospital Epidemiology, 45*(6), 788–789. DOI: 10.1017/ice.2024.24

Bakker, I., Gill, S., & Wamsley, D. (2021). *Global health: Ethical challenges* (Benatar, S., & Brock, G., Eds.; 2nd ed.). Cambridge University Press.

Bakos, L., & Dumitra cu, D. (2017). Holonic crisis handling model for corporate sustainability. *Sustainability, 9*(12), 2266. DOI: 10.3390/su9122266

Ballantyne, D. (2004). Action research reviewed: A market-oriented approach. *European Journal of Marketing, 38*(3/4), 321–337.

Barton, J., Stephens, J., & Haslett, T. (2009). Action research: Its foundations in open systems thinking and relationship to the scientific method. *Systemic Practice and Action Research, 22*, 475–488. DOI: 10.1007/s11213-009-9148-6

Bass, B. M. (1997). Does the transactional-transformational leadership paradigm transcend organizational and national boundaries? *The American Psychologist, 52*(2), 130–139.

Bass, B. M., & Avolio, B. J. (1993). Transformational leadership and organizational culture. *Public Administration Quarterly, 17*(1), 112.

Beach, L. R. (2005). Leadership and the art of change: A practical guide to organizational transformation. *Sage (Atlanta, Ga.).*

Bell, S. (2025). *The McKinsey 7-S Framework: Making every part of your organization work in harmony.* Mindtools.com. https://www.mindtools.com/aicks4s/the-mckinsey-7-s-framework

Benatar, S., & Brock, G. (2021). *Global health: Ethical challenges* (2nd ed.). Cambridge University Press.

Benson, J., & Dresdow, S. (2008). Teaching AI to enhance students' understanding of organizational behavior. *International Journal Of Learning, 15*(2), 195-1NULL.

Bertram, R., Gilbert, W., & Culver, D. (2016). Using appreciative inquiry to create high-impact coach learning: Insights from a decade of applied research. *AI Practitioner, 18*(2), 59–65. DOI: 10.12781/978-1-907549-27-4-9

Binder, J. (2016). *Global project management: Communication, collaboration and management across borders.* Routledge.

Bloom, D. E., & Cadarette, D. (2021). Strengthening the global response to infectious disease threats in the twenty-first century, with a COVID-19 epilogue. In Benatar, S., & Brock, G. (Eds.), *Global health: Ethical challenges* (2nd ed.). Cambridge University Press.

Bridges, W. (2017). *Managing transitions (25th anniversary edition): Making the most of change.* Hachette Books.

Bright, D. S. (2009). Appreciative inquiry and positive organizational scholarship: A philosophy of practice for turbulent times. *OD Practitioner, 41*(3), 2–7.

Brown, R. S. (2015). Equifinality in open systems: Explaining the phenomenon of hard money mortgages. *Academy of Accounting & Financial Studies Journal, 19*(1), 120–132.

Brown, S. L., & Eisenhardt, K. M. (1997). The art of continuous change: Linking complexity theory and time-paced evolution in relentlessly shifting organizations. *Administrative Science Quarterly, 42*(1), 1–34.

Browning, M. (2014). Appreciative inquiry as a model for assessing the value of business school education. *Journal of Business and Educational Leadership, 5*(1), 64–70.

Burke, W. W. (2024). *Organizational change: Theory and practice* (6th ed.). Sage.

Burn, J. M. (1996). IS innovation and organizational alignment - a professional juggling act. *Journal of Information Technology, 11*(1), 3–12.

Burrell, D. N. (2024). *Change dynamics in healthcare, technological innovations, and complex scenarios*. IGI Global Scientific Publishing.

Burton, J., & Carter, B. (2025). *Sustainable organizational change: The Social Change Model for Systems*. Routledge.

Busemeyer, J., Zhang, Q., Balakrishnan, S. N., & Wang, Z. (2020). Application of Quantum-Markov open system models to human cognition and decision. *Entropy (Basel, Switzerland), 22*(9), 990. DOI: 10.3390/e22090990

Bushe, G. R., & Marshak, R. J. (2014). The dialogic mindset in organization development. *Research in Organizational Change and Development, 22*, 55–97.

Calabrese, R., & Cohen, E. (2013). An appreciative inquiry into an urban drug court: Cultural transformation. *The Qualitative Report, 18*(1), 1–14. https://files.eric.ed.gov/fulltext/EJ1004996.pdf

Cameron, K. S., & Quinn, R. E. (2011). *Diagnosing and changing organizational culture: Based on the Competing Values Framework* (3rd ed.). Jossey-Bass.

Carr, T., Rosas, S., Noble, C., Song, M., Fernandez, C. S. P., Brandert, K., Donnald, K., Corbie, G., & Dave, G. (2024). Strengthening healthcare providers' leadership capabilities, interprofessional collaboration, and systems thinking: A conceptualization of the clinical scholars program impact. *BMC Medical Education, 24*(1), 1277–11. DOI: 10.1186/s12909-024-06240-1

Carter, S. K., Anastasia, C., & Carter, B. M. (2024). *Multinational electronic health records interoperability strategies*. IGI Global Scientific Publishing.

Caws, P. (2015). General systems theory: Its past and potential. *Systems Research and Behavioral Science, 32*(5), 514–521. DOI: 10.1002/sres.2353

Coghlan, D., & Rashford, N. S. (2006). *Organizational change and strategy*. Routledge.

Cooperrider, D. L., & McQuaid, M. (2012). The positive arc of systemic strengths: How appreciative inquiry and sustainable designing can bring out the best in human systems. *Journal of Corporate Citizenship*, (46), 71–102. https://proxy.cecybrary.com/login?url=https://search.proquest.com/docview/1446323232?accountid=144789

Cooperrider, D. L., Zhexembayeva, N., Trosten-Bloom, A., & Whitney, D. (2003). Business as agent of world benefit: A worldwide action research project using appreciative inquiry. Eds. Vogelsang, J., Townsend, M., Minahan, M., Jamieson, D., Vogel, J. Viets, A., Royal, C., & Valek, L. (2013). In *Handbook for Strategic HR: Best practices in organizational development from the OD Network*. 582-589. AMACOM.

Creswell, J. W., & Creswell, J. D. (2022). *Research design: Qualitative, quantitative, and mixed methods approaches* (6th ed.). Sage.

Davenport, T. H., & Redman, T. C. (2025, January-February). How to marry process management and AI: Make sure your people and technology work well together. *Harvard Business Review*, *103*(1), 39–44.

Davidson, S. (2014). Appreciative inquiry helps a new college leader create a team environment - fast! *AI Practitioner*, *16*(2), 72–77. DOI: 10.12781/978-1-907549-19-9-12

Dervitsiotis, K. N. (1998). The challenge of managing organizational change: Exploring the relationship of re-engineering, developing learning organizations and total quality management. *Total Quality Management*, *9*(1), 109–122.

Dorfman, P. W., & House, R. J. (2004). Cultural influence on organizational leadership: Literature review, theoretical rationale, and GLOBE project goals. In House, R. J., Hanges, P. J., Javidan, M., Dorfman, P. W., & Gupta, V. (Eds.), *Culture, Leadership, and Organizations: The GLOBE Study of 62 Societies* (pp. 51–73). Sage.

Drucker, P. (1998). The future that has already happened. *The Futurist*, *32*(8), 16–18.

Dunlap, C. A. (2008). Effective evaluation through appreciative inquiry. *Performance Improvement*, *47*(2), 23–29.

Ettorre, B. (1998). Y2K and beyond. *Management Review*, *87*(6), 27.

Fields, D. M. (1993). Institutions for the 21st century. *The Futurist*, *27*(1), 33.

Folger, R., & Skarlicki, D. P. (1999). Unfairness and resistance to change: Hardship as mistreatment. *Journal of Organizational Change Management*, *12*(1), 35–50. DOI: 10.1108/09534819910255306

Frame, D. J. (2013). *Framing decisions: Decision making that accounts for irrationality, people, and constraints*. Jossey-Bass.

Gronhaug, K., & Olson, O. (1999). Action research and knowledge creation: Merits and challenges. *Qualitative Market Research*, *2*(1), 6–14.

Gustavsen, B. (1993). Action research and the generation of knowledge. *Human Relations*, *46*(11), 1361.

Hair, J. F.Jr. (2007). Knowledge creation in marketing: The role of predictive analytics. *European Business Review*, *19*(4), 303–315. DOI: 10.1108/09555340710760134

Halladay, S. D. (2013). Using predictive analytics to improve decision making. *The Journal of Equipment Lease Financing (Online)*, *31*(2), B1–B6.

Hawthorne, P. (2004). Redesigning library human resources: Integrating human resources management and organizational development. *Library Trends*, *53*(1), 172–186.

Holman, P., Devane, T., & Cady, S. (2007). *The change handbook: The definitive resource on today's best methods for engaging whole systems* (2nd ed.). Berrett-Koehler Publishers.

Jafar, A. J. N., Patel, S., Mitchell, R., & Redmond, A. (2024). Redefining global health and shifting the balance: The ARC-H principle. *BMJ Global Health*, *9*(2), 1–4. DOI: 10.1136/bmjgh-2023-014487

Jamieson, D. W., & Davidson, J. E. (2019). Advancing thinking and practice on use of self. *Organization Development Journal*, *37*(1), 39–53.

Jeffries, M., Salema, N., Laing, L., Shamsuddin, A., Sheikh, A., Avery, T., Chuter, A., Waring, J., & Keers, R. N. (2023). Using sociotechnical theory to understand medication safety work in primary care and prescribers' use of clinical decision support: A qualitative study. *BMJ Open*, *13*(4), e068798–e068798. DOI: 10.1136/bmjopen-2022-068798

Jobs, C. G., Aukers, S. M., & Gilfoil, D. M. (2015). The impact of big data on your firms marketing communications: A framework for understanding the emerging marketing analytics industry. *Academy of Marketing Studies Journal*, *19*(2), 81–92.

Jones, G. R. (2013). *Organizational theory, design, and change*. Pearson.

Joseph, E. C. (2007). Discovering the anticipatory sciences. *Futurics*, *31*(3/4), 2–20.

Kaur, J. (2024). Smart solutions for health: Computational intelligence reshaping the Industry 4.0 healthcare paradigm. In Shah, I. A., & Sial, Q. (Eds.), *Advances in computational intelligence for the healthcare Industry 4.0*. IGI Global Scientific Publishing.

Kezar, A. (2013). Understanding sensemaking/sensegiving in transformational change processes from the bottom up. *Higher Education*, *65*(6), 761–780. DOI: 10.1007/s10734-012-9575-7

Khang, A. (2023). *AI and IoT-based technologies for precision medicine*. IGI Global Scientific Publishing.

Kolachi, N., & Akan, O. (2014). HRD role in organizational development (a case of corporate thinking at ETISALAT, UAE). *International Business Research*, *7*(8), 160–167.

Kotter, J. P. (2012). *Leading change*. Harvard Business Review Press.

Kotter, J. P., Akhtar, V., & Gupta, G. (2021). *Change: How organizations achieve hard-to-imagine results in uncertain and volatile times*. John Wiley & Sons, Inc.

Koufteros, X., Peng, X., Lu, G., & Peters, R. (2014). The impact of organizational structure on internal and external integration. *Journal of Organization Design*, *3*(2), 1–17. DOI: 10.7146/jod.7386

Kumar, B., Suneja, M., & Swee, M. (2023). When I say… appreciative inquiry. *Medical Education*, *57*(11), 1006–1007. DOI: 10.1111/medu.15140

Kumar, V. (2013). *101 design methods: A structured approach for driving innovation in your organization*. Wiley.

Lee, A. J. P. (2015). Predictive analytics: The new tool to combat fraud, waste, and abuse. *Journal of Government Financial Management*, *64*(2), 12–16.

Lehner, R., & Hight, D. L. (2006). Appreciative inquiry and student affairs: A positive approach to change. *College Student Affairs Journal, 25*(2), 141-151,135.

Levasseur, R. E. (2004). Open system theory and organizations. *Futurics*, *28*(1/2), 79–85.

Lilja, J., & Richardsson, D. (2012). Putting appreciative design into practice. *International Journal of Quality and Service Sciences*, *4*(1), 4–15. DOI: 10.1108/17566691211219698

Lin, Y., Chen, H., Brown, R. A., Li, S., & Yang, H. University of Arizona, Southern Arizona VA Health Care System, National Taiwan University, Florida State University, & Stanford University. (2017). Healthcare predictive analytics for risk profiling in chronic care: A Bayesian multitask learning approach. *MIS Quarterly, 41*(2), 473-496. https://doi.org/DOI: 10.25300/MISQ/2017/41.2.07

Llopis, G. (2024, July 2). *Healthcare leadership in crisis: Time for reinvention*. Forbes.com. https://www.forbes.com/sites/glennllopis/2024/07/02/healthcare-leadership-in-crisis-time-for-reinvention/

London, A. J. (2021). Justice and research in developing countries. In Benatar, S., & Brock, G. (Eds.), *Global health: Ethical challenges* (2nd ed.). Cambridge University Press.

Mack, T. C. (2005). Profits and nonprofits: Looking for and finding value in the future. *Futures Research Quarterly*, *21*(4), 55–61.

Marketing consulting services industry (NAICS 541613). (2017). *United States Marketing Consulting Services Industry Report*, 1-195.

Martens, H., & Dehaes, R. (2008). Integrating diversity management into the management of the organisation: Multiple case study with the 7s-instrument. *The International Journal of Diversity in Organisations, Communities and Nations*, *8*(4), 161–169.

McChrystal, S., Collins, T., Silverman, D., & Fussell, C. (2015). *Teams of teams: New rules of engagement for a complex world*. Portfolio/Penguin.

McElyea, B. E. (2003). Organizational change models. *Futurics*, *27*(1/2), 57.

McIntyre, P. (2016). General Systems Theory and creativity. In *The Creative System in Action* (pp. 13-26). Palgrave Macmillan UK.

Millett, S. M. (2006). Futuring and visioning: Complementary approaches to strategic decision making. *Strategy and Leadership*, *34*(3), 43–50. DOI: 10.1108/10878570610660591

Millett, S. M., & Staley, D. J. (2009). Does future thinking need a philosophy? [World Future Society]. *World Futures Review*, *1*(5), 23–30.

Nadler, D., & Tushman, M. (1997). *Competing by design*. Oxford University Press.

Naude, L., van den Bergh, T. J., & Kruger, I. S. (2014). Learning to like learning: An appreciative inquiry into emotions in education. *Social Psychology of Education*, *17*(2), 211–228. DOI: 10.1007/s11218-014-9247-9

Neumann, J. E., Lau, C. M., & Worley, C. G. (2009). Ready for consideration: International organizational development and change as an emerging field of practice. *The Journal of Applied Behavioral Science*, *45*(2), 171–185. DOI: 10.1177/0021886309335429

Ngcamu, B. S. (2016). Conceptualizing transformation in the post-merger and incorporation environment era. *The International Journal of Sociology and Social Policy*, *36*(5/6), 270–288.

Northouse, P. (2022). *Leadership: Theory and practice* (9th ed.). Sage.

O'Flaherty, B., & Heavin, C. (2015). Positioning predictive analytics for customer retention. *Journal of Decision Systems*, *24*(1), 3–18.

ODnetwork.org. (2025). *Global OD Competency Framework*. https://www.odnetwork.org/page/global-framework

Ohlemacher, J. (2015). Fostering meaningful dialogue can improve success in learning. *Assessment Update*, *27*(2), 5–13.

Okoli, C., & Pawlowski, S. D. (2004, March 27). The Delphi method as a research tool: An example, design considerations and applications. *Information & Management*, *42*, 15–29. https://snazlan.wordpress.com/wp-content/uploads/2015/11/the-delphi-method-as-a-research-tool-an-example-design-considerations-and-applications.pdf

Paraschivescu, A. O., & Cotîrlet, P. C. (2015). Quality continuous improvement strategies Kaizen strategy — comparative analysis. *Economy Transdisciplinarity Cognition*, *18*(1), 12–21.

Parker, D. J. (1999). Y2K-OK? *EMedia*, *12*(12), 80.

Powell, W. R. (2002). Organizational change models. *Futurics*, *26*(3/4), 20–45.

Pryor, M., Humphreys, J. H., Oyler, J., Taneja, S., & Toombs, L. A. (2011). The legitimacy and efficacy of current organizational theory: An analysis. *International Journal of Management*, *28*(4), 209–228.

Rothwell, W. J., Stavros, J. M., & Sullivan, R. L. (eds), Sullivan, A. (2010). *Practicing organization development: A guide for leading change* (3rd ed.). Pfeiffer.

Scott, G. (2001). 'Seeing the Forest for the Trees': Towards a framework for effective change research in education. *Innovations in Education and Teaching International*, *38*(1), 86–92.

Selin, S. W., Pierskalla, C., Smaldone, D., & Robinson, K. (2007). Social learning and building trust through a participatory design for natural resource planning. *Journal of Forestry*, *105*(8), 421–425.

Sicilia, M.-A., & Balazote, P. S. (2013). *Interoperability in healthcare information systems: Standards, management, and techology*. IGI Global Scientific Publishing.

Siegel, E. (2016). *Predictive analytics: The power to predict who will click, buy, lie, or die*. Wiley.

Siegel, E. (2016). *Predictive Analytics: the Power to Predict Who Will click, buy, lie, or Die*. Wiley. (Original work published 2013)

Smaczny, T. (2001). Is an alignment between business and information technology the appropriate paradigm to manage IT in today's organisations? *Management Decision*, *39*(10), 797–802.

Srinidhi, B. (1998). Strategic quality management. *International Journal of Quality Science*, *3*(1), 38–70. http://search.proquest.com.proxy.cecybrary.com/docview/211982714?accountid=26967

Staykova, M. P. (2019). Rediscovering the Delphi technique: A review of the literature. *Advances in Social Sciences Research Journal*, *6*(1), 218–229. DOI: 10.14738/assrj.61.5959

Stephens, J., Barton, J., & Haslett, T. (2009). Action research: Its history and relationship to scientific methodology. *Systemic Practice and Action Research*, *22*(6), 463–474. DOI: 10.1007/s11213-009-9147-7

Sukumar, S. R., & Ferrell, R. K. (2013). Big Data collaboration: Exploring, recording and sharing enterprise knowledge. *Information Services & Use*, *33*(3/4), 257–270. DOI: 10.3233/ISU-130712

Sullivan, R. L., Rothwell, W. J., & Balasi, M. J. B. (2013). Organization development (OD) and change management (CM): Whole system transformation. *Development and Learning in Organizations*, *27*(6), 18–23. DOI: 10.1108/DLO-08-2013-0060

Sun, C., Zhang, Z., Vochozka, M., & Vozňáková, I. (2022). Enterprise digital transformation and debt financing cost in China's A-share listed companies. *Oeconomia Copernicana*, *13*(3), 783–829. DOI: 10.24136/oc.2022.023

Sweet, S. (2011). Which is Best for Us? Top Down, Bottoms Up, or Middle Out. Retrieved from http://www.i4process.com/publications/which-is-best-for-us-top-down-bottoms-up-or-middle-out/

TechAdvisory.org. (2015). *Why use predictive analytics?* TechAdvisory.org. https://www.techadvisory.org/2014/05/why-use-predictive-analytics/

Teoh Kae, N., & Rashad, Y. (2015). The general review of how different leadership styles cause the transformational change efforts to be successful. *International Journal of Management. Accounting & Economics*, *2*(9), 1130–1140.

The World Café. (2025, June 25). History. Theworldcafe.com. https://theworldcafe.com/about-us/history/

Thomas, M., & McGarry, F. (1994). Top-down vs. bottom-up process improvement. *IEEE Software*, *11*(4), 12–13. DOI: 10.1109/52.300121

United Nations. (2025, June 22). *Sustainable Development Goals*. UN.org. https://unosd.un.org/content/sustainable-development-goals-sdgs

Urrestarazu, H. (2015). Towards a consistent constructivist general systems theory. *Constructivist Foundations, 10*(2), 180–183.

Using Technology to Predict Workplace Injuries. (2014).. . *Professional Safety, 59*(6), 18. https://ehsworks1.blogspot.com/2014/02/using-technology-to-predict-workplace.html

Van Assche, K., Verschraegen, G., Valentinov, V., & Gruezmacher, M. (2019). The social, the ecological, and the adaptive. von bertalanffy's general systems theory and the adaptive governance of social-ecological systems. *Systems Research and Behavioral Science, 36*(3), 308–321. DOI: 10.1002/sres.2587

Vărzaru, A. A. (2022). Assessing digital transformation of cost accounting tools in healthcare. *International Journal of Environmental Research and Public Health, 19*(23), 15572. DOI: 10.3390/ijerph192315572

Vayena, E., & Ferretti, A. (2021). Big data and artifical intelligence for global health. In Benatar, S., & Brock, G. (Eds.), *Global health: Ethical challenges* (2nd ed., pp. 429–439). Cambridge University Press.

Vogelsang, J., Townsend, M., Minahan, M., Jamieson, D., Vogel, J., Viets, A., Royal, C., & Valek, L. (2013). *Handbook for strategic HR: Best practices in organization development from the OD network*. OD Network. AMACOM.

Waller, M. A., & Fawcett, S. E. (2013). Click here for a data scientist: Big Data, Predictive Analytics, and Theory Development in the era of a Maker Movement Supply Chain. *Journal of Business Logistics, 34*(4), 249–252. DOI: 10.1111/jbl.12024

Warzynski, C. C. (2004). Future-search conferences at Cornell University. *New Directions for Institutional Research, 2004*(123), 105–112.

Watkins, J. M., Mohr, B., & Kelly, R. (2011). *Appreciative inquiry: Change at the speed of imagination* (2nd ed.). Pfeiffer.

Weick, K. E., & Quinn, R. E. (1999). Organizational change and development. *Annual Review of Psychology, 50*, 361–386.

Weitzman, F. (2014). Organizational longevity as a predictor of organizational learning, organizational identity, organizational innovation, and fiscal conservatism. (3624405 Ph.D.), Colorado State University, Ann Arbor. ProQuest Dissertations & Theses Global database.

Whitney, D., & Fredrickson, B. L. (2015). Appreciative inquiry meets positive psychology. *AI Practitioner*, *17*(3), 18–26. DOI: 10.12781/978-1-907549-24-3-3

Wills, M. J. (2014). Decisions through data: Analytics in healthcare. *Journal of Healthcare Management*, *59*(4), 254–262.

Wilson, H. J., & Daugherty, P. R. (2025, January-February). The secret to successful AI-driven process redesign: Strong leaders put business transformation in the hands of all employees. *Harvard Business Review*, *103*(1), 45–51.

Wirtenberg, J., Abrams, L., & Ott, C. (2004). Assessing the field of organization development. *The Journal of Applied Behavioral Science*, *40*(4), 465–479. DOI: 10.1177/0021886304270246

World Health Organization. (2025, May 20). *World Health Assembly adopts historic Pandemic Agreement to make the world more equitable and safer from future pandemics* [News Release]. Geneva. https://www.who.int/news/item/20-05-2025-world-health-assembly-adopts-historic-pandemic-agreement-to-make-the-world-more-equitable-and-safer-from-future-pandemics

Worren, N. A. M., Ruddle, K., & Moore, K. (1999). From organizational development to change management: The emergence of a new profession. *The Journal of Applied Behavioral Science*, *35*(3), 273–286. DOI: 10.1177/0021886399353002

Xu, P. (2012). Architectural and landscape design: A new synthesis major proposed with interdisciplinary and general models. *The International Journal of the Arts in Society*, *5*(6), 369–388.

Zanon, C. J., Alves, F. A. G., Chiappetta, J. C. J., & Lopes de Sousa, J. A. B. (2013). Alignment of operations strategy: Exploring the marketing interface. *Industrial Management & Data Systems*, *113*(2), 207–233. DOI: 10.1108/02635571311303541

Zhang, L., Miranskyy, A., & Rjaibi, W. (2021). Quantum advantage and the Y2K bug: A comparison. *IEEE Software*, *38*(2), 80–87. DOI: 10.1109/MS.2020.2985321

APPENDIX

Chapter 9 Study Questions

1. What are the phases of Appreciative Inquiry?
2. What is the benefit of using the SOAR Model for analysis?
3. What is the relationship between Action Research and Appreciative Inquiry?
4. What is the value of systems thinking when implementing strategies?
5. How does Transformational Leadership help a leader manage change?
6. What is the benefit of using a change model to manage the change process?

Chapter 10
Multinational Teams of Teams

ABSTRACT

Chapter 10 explores the challenge of approaching the problem of multinational EHR interoperability using teams of teams. The opportunity to leverage agile methodologies and a small group approach to large-scale transformation employs the holonic model. Sustainability is a critical quality measure of the outcome and requires stakeholders to manage the details of this type of approach. With an emphasis on innovation and a shared vision, leaders will need to keep adopting future technologies into the approach and move forward at the speed of technological advancements. Utilizing existing methods, leaders can continue to implement these advancements into the iterative approach to the outcome.

INTRODUCTION

A multinational approach to interoperability will require us to work as a team. Nations, organizations, agencies, companies, and systems may already be working on elements of the problem of interoperability. The concept of *Teams of Teams* provides a framework to discuss collaborative problem-solving efforts equitably representing all stakeholders. In this chapter, the discussion approaches visualization of the outcomes, collaborative approaches to innovation, planning in various forms, sustainability through stakeholder involvement, and combining efforts through a process inspired by *Teams of Teams* (McChrystal et al., 2015; mcchrystalgroup.com).

DOI: 10.4018/979-8-3693-2027-3.ch010

SEE THE END FROM THE BEGINNING

Years ago, Stephen R. Covey (1989) encouraged readers to "Begin with the end in mind" (p. 97). This habit of highly effective people speaks to the power of visualization, which is the beginning of innovation. Combine the concept of visualization with synergy and now we look at the power of a shared vision and working together to accomplish more than each team could do alone. Shukla et al., (2025) took the concept of synergy by leveraging advancements in financial technology with advancements in healthcare technology. They acknowledge the complexity of the systems involved in each industry and promote protection through leveraging blockchain technologies.

The potential resistance to adopting more advanced technologies is in the fear of bad actors misusing technology. In our research, we have heard participants voice the fear of health information falling into the wrong hands, information being added to health records that isn't correct, or the challenge of the healthcare providers' time to put enough information in the record. Others thought that the lessons of COVID-19 already created some huge advancements, so it is no longer something to be concerned over. The truth is that we need more research, more collaborative discussion, and more collective action to take advantage of this technological opportunity.

Some research has been done following the lessons of the COVID-19 pandemic. For example, Wong et al. (2023) propose using the START tool in preparation to implement technological advancements using the Plan-Do-Study-Act (PDSA) cycles. The START acronym stands for Sharing benefits and failures, Tailoring planning with staff partners, Acknowledging staff concerns, Recruiting opinion leaders early, and Targeting residents' needs.

Advancements in technology in healthcare have grown to the level of industry including naming the industry for Health IT as HealthTech (Madir, 2020). Madir defined HealthTech including electronic health (eHealth), mobile health (mHealth), MedTech, telemedicine, and other related technologies as examples of how technology is improving the "delivery and consumption of healthcare." Wachter (2015) presented a vision for the future of Health Information Technology. The potential future described in his 2015 book *The Digital Doctor* is quickly becoming the current state complete with the use of natural language processing replacing the typed EHR of the past. Patients are completing their own digital records in preparation of a telehealth visit.

INNOVATION

The concept of innovation is becoming a differentiator among organizations and can determine whether a company exists or fails (Shukla, 2017). One way to determine the importance of innovation to organizations is to review history and discover how organizations relate to innovation. Organizational innovation responsibilities are discussed as well as the impact a leader has on the outcomes of innovation. More recently, Shukla et al. (2025) continues the conversation on advancements in healthcare through a combination of healthtech and fintech.

Overview

Innovation begins where the creative approach meets the productive approach (Steiber & Alänge, 2015; Dodge et al., 2017). Individuals and organizations have been looking for better ways to accomplish things. Some examples include inventions such as the printing press, the compass, and paper money, which changed literacy, exploration, and purchasing power as discussed in the live chat. The inventions in this list are examples of innovations since they have created lasting change for industries and entire populations. Another example provided by Valikangas, Gibbert, Nair, Paukku, and Peixoto (2016), cites Johann Sebastian Bach's *The Well-Tempered Clavier* as such an invention that was ahead of its time. While Bach wrote the musical piece for the instrument known as the clavier in about 1720 (Schwarm, 2013), the invention of the piano in 1700 provided a better way to play the piece. Many artists have played the piece of music on the piano rather than the clavier. While it didn't promote literacy for an entire population, it was pivotal in advancing musical talent for its time.

Early ideas about implementing innovation in business became popular with the introduction of organizational development in the 1960s by Wendell French (Natemeyer & Hersey, 2011). Continuous improvement moves an organization toward the innovative activities that improve products and processes. In an example of implemented innovation, Holmes, Nelson, & Stump (1993) discuss how innovation was necessary for Eastman Chemical Company in the 1980s when they faced a scenario that required them to improve or fail. Eric Von Hippel (1982) recommended that businesses should innovate by listening to their customers about product improvement ideas.

Strategic innovation is when an organization creates something that changes an industry or redefines the purpose of the product (Valikangas et al., 2016). Finding new ways to accomplish a process or create a product gives an organization a competitive advantage. In the healthcare industry, new research shows ways to implement health technology while assessing the opportunity to improve patient experience

(Aytekin et al., 2025). Innovation has evolved to include more than just the notion of doing things differently. The strategy to have continuous improvement at the center of the organizational culture can be the difference for how organizations maintain a competitive advantage (Fareed, Noor, Isa, & Salleh, 2016). A leader who can instill a culture of continuous improvement benefits from the human capital of the people working for the organization.

For context, innovation history could be industry related or product specific. Kumar (2013) gives the example of progress in how an automobile is powered as providing context to the potential for innovations. If one considers the historical significance of steam, gasoline, and electricity as power sources for the vehicles, the next innovation could build from the context of historical evolution.

Responsibility

The responsibility for innovation is everyone's job. Corporate culture determines whether it is possible or not for everyone to innovate since the actions of individuals are limited to what is allowed in the company. The shared organizational values empower employees to learn and share knowledge with the organization (Jayanti, 2013). Employees want to contribute when they feel that their contributions will be valued. Nouri, Ghorbani, & Soltani (2017) discuss the importance of individual learning within a firm to promote an innovative environment. The company is better able to take advantage of the contributed ideas of the employees if the organization can manage the knowledge on an organizational level. The knowledge management requires training courses and learning opportunities to share new processes and better ways to accomplish the goals of the organization.

Morente & Ferras (2017) suggest that managing innovation comes from an internal source other than leadership. In the context of internal operations, the study found individuals who managed innovation possessed the quality of openness and that the person was not typically a formal leader, but a project manager or similar role. Cottam, Ensor, & Band (2001) suggest that the formal leader may lack the skills to engage employees in innovation. In a study by Cottam, Ensor, & Band (2001), the findings indicate that in many cases there is no innovation leader, but that a department manages innovation. Where there was a formal innovation leader, the person was a middle manager with duties to organize innovation activities. Deploying activities in a small area of the organization is not the same as building an organizational culture.

Some employees may have difficulty letting meaningful things end. Innovation requires that the old pass away so the new can arrive. Weitzman (2014) connects the idea of creative destruction as the process that will let the past fall away as part of the innovation process. Individuals who embrace continuous improvement operate in a way that abandons old processes in favor of new ones.

Leadership Style

The leader is ultimately responsible for the culture of the organization (Dodge, Dwyer, Witzeman, Neylon, & Taylor, 2017). Leadership style (Teoh Kae & Rashad, 2015) could have a great deal to do with whether the employees feel that they have a voice in the organization. Leaders demonstrate the value of activities and share the vision through the way they communicate. Without empowerment, creativity can be stifled, and the organization will not experience as much innovation as a result.

Leaders should know what to innovate about, and the culture of innovation needs to be securely in place for this to happen. In organizations where high-performance levels are valued, innovation is likely (Brasfield, 2015). One requirement for creating an innovative environment is for the leader to have systems thinking (Kumar, 2013). The leader develops opportunities for improvement from the gathered information. If leaders use systems thinking, they can have perspective about the complexity of the organization that sees patterns in the data gathered, develops models from the patterns, and in turn find the opportunity for improvement.

Dodge, Dwyer, Witzeman, Neylon, & Taylor (2017) found that employees believe that their leaders should provide encouragement, a supportive work environment, and assign meaningful work to establish a culture of innovation. Miranda Silva, Gomes, Filipe Lages, & Lopes Pereira, (2014) share the idea that leaders who use Total Quality Management are more innovative because of the principles of continuous improvement, performance measures, and openness. A logical leadership style, as described by Teoh Kae & Rashad (2015), supports innovation through the leader's ability to place the focus of the work on improvement and share progress with the employees.

One study finds that the adhocracy type of organizational culture instilled by a leader is more likely to encourage innovation than hierarchical culture (Sanz-Valle, Naranjo-Valencia, Jiménez-Jiménez, & Perez-Caballero, 2011). However, the type of organizational culture is only one factor contributing to the ability to innovate and a leader can change the organizational culture by implementing transformational change for the organization (Fareed et al., 2016). Jurik & Cavender (2016) found that the leader's ability to create a stable work environment impacted the innovativeness.

Innovative leaders believe that they influence future events through today's activities (Pesut, 2013). A specific innovative process using modes of innovation is introduced by Kumar (2013) and involves seven modes including "sense intent, know context, know people, frame insights, explore concepts, frame solutions, and realize offerings" (pp. 10-13). Using the process Kumar introduced, a leader can implement innovation and inspire the culture to be more creative. The process will allow a leader to minimize the complexity of the improvements.

While anyone in the organization can innovate, the leader creates an environment where it can happen. A recent study shows that transformational leadership is a preferred method for leading innovation based on a case study of innovation-driven leadership in the UAE (Al-Maazmi, & Hashmi, 2024). Creating an innovative culture may involve transformational change if the organizational type is a closed environment. Open leadership styles and participative management skills encourage employees to be creative and innovate. The history of innovation illustrates that what used to be a way to improve processes and products to gain market share has now become the way to survive as an organization.

Preparing for the future requires organizations to continue to support the innovative culture within the work environments. By envisioning the future of the healthcare industry, countries and organizations can continue to collaborate to take advantage of this opportunity to improve the implementation of technological synergies and quality of patient experience using HealthTech. Trust in the system teeters on the edge of belief daily. Casey and Vigna (2018) propose protecting the trust by leveraging blockchain technology to both improve healthcare technology by protecting electronic health records and establish a "self-sovereign identity."

CONTINGENCY PLANNING VERSUS SCENARIO PLANNING

Contingency planning and scenario planning are terms that are sometimes incorrectly used interchangeably. The definition of contingency planning compared to scenario planning will illustrate the difference as well as the connection between the two. Also included is a discussion on the scenario planning process with the steps as outlined by Wade (2012) and the importance of the components of the process related to organizational decision making.

Contingency Planning

Leaders use contingency planning to manage risk by dealing with potential crisis situations (Hall et al., 2012). Hall, Skipper, Hazen, and Hanna (2012) continue to define contingency planning in several ways. They describe it as a way to assess areas of the organization that are not strong and prepare for potential challenges in those areas. It is critical for a company to be able to plan for scenarios where there could be an interruption to business such as transporting raw materials into the organization or getting the product to market in a timely fashion. What the organization is really trying to do in the uncertain situation is to prepare in a way that limits negative impact.

Contingency planning can be split into two categories, business continuity planning and uncertainty planning (Simpkins, 2009). Business continuity planning helps leaders in an organization prepare for uncertain events that would disrupt business. Uncertainty planning is more about a potential interruption of a strategic plan and the possibility of impact. Either way, the company needs to have a plan for the unknown factors that could cause disruption. Detailed plans help the leaders of the organization feel confident in the direction the company is headed because they have had conversations about what would happen if the organization experienced the worst case scenario.

In a case study example, Wade (2012) suggests that one benefit of scenario planning is the ability to create contingency plans to preplan what will happen following uncertain events. As in the example of Scotland's tourism plans, preparations give the leaders some confidence in knowing that they have thought about the potential outlier events and planned a way to deal with the potential consequences. The likelihood of the event also plays a role.

Steil & Gibbons-Carr (2005) define scenario planning as "a strategic planning tool for developing multiple views of the future." Wade (2012) pushes the subject past forecasting to anticipate potential solutions for future events. Leaders use the information from scenario planning to make decisions about what should be done if the unlikely event happens. The process for discovering potential scenarios is thorough when it is done correctly. Since organizations work to find ways to prepare for the future, having a process to rely on will give the organization better success.

Using scenario planning to build a strategy allows for leaders to create contingency plans based on the scenarios (Sawka, 2007). It is important to include preparations for the unexpected in the strategy in order to preserve the hard work that has been done. Companies that are able to anticipate potential future events and prepare to deal with the circumstances have an advantage over the competition that lacks the same preparation. Preparing for the potential challenges should include multiple scenarios (Masch, 2013) so that the contingency plans are able to counteract the negative impact of the situation based on several possible outcomes.

The key difference between contingency planning and scenario planning is that scenario planning leads the organization to plan for specific scenarios, while contingency planning bases decisions on multiple scenarios (Prakash, Jha, & Rajendra, 2012) to anticipate negative impacts. While the different methods of planning work together to influence decision making, ultimately what matters is the survival of the organization and sustainability of the changes. Just the conversation about the potential for negative scenarios can help a company be ready to respond (Mason, 2003) using a contingency plan.

Overview of Process

The process of scenario planning, as shared by Wade (2012), introduces a logical flow using specific steps including "framing the challenge, gathering information, identifying driving forces, defining the future's critical 'either/or' uncertainties, generating the scenarios, fleshing them out and creating story lines." The leader facilitating the process can use the meeting to develop scenarios and take action by following the extra steps to analyze and implement scenario planning outcomes in decision making.

For the scenarios to be of value, they need to be usable. To really use them, Wade (2012) suggests four additional steps including "validating the scenarios and identifying further research needed, assessing their implications and defining possible responses, identifying signposts, and monitoring and updating the scenarios as time goes on." Each of these additional steps provides a way for the scenario to last through the potential future events, so they may be used when the situation arises.

The context of the situation needs to be considered so that the scenario appropriately matches the real issue the organization faces. Presenting the group with the importance surrounding the challenge will give the group an idea of the type of scenario that should be built. One example explores the use of scenario planning related to regional leadership (Boo et al., 2013). The next step involves the level of information included in the scenario building process. The group should gather and consider appropriate levels of information or data related to the issue (Wade, 2012). When enough data has been gathered, it is easier to be creative in developing the story.

Driving forces are critical to having a strong scenario (Boo et al., 2013) and are a pivotal part of the process. Using a PEST analysis (Wade, 2012) is one way to ensure that the group discovers the factors with the potential to impact the organization. Combining PESTLE and SWOT, as seen in Figure 1 expands the concept to combine the efforts of the team (Nickols, 2020). The scenarios need to be realistic for the organization specific to the culture, individuals, and leadership. When the scenario is fleshed out (Wade, 2012), it takes on a more realistic picture and the group can better discuss the details.

Figure 1. SWOT/PESTLE

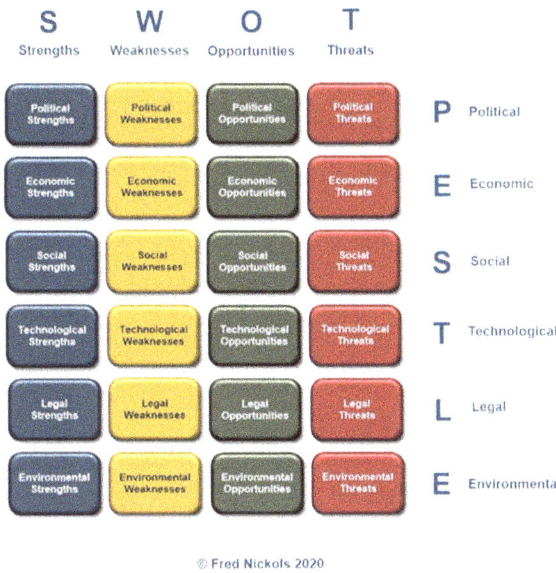

Note: Copyright Fred Nickols. (2020). SWOT/PESTLE. Odnetwork.org.

Additionally, being clear about the uncertainties facing the organization will help maintain the scope of discussion. Recognizing how significantly a factor may influence the situation can be measured against how the future of that factor is uncertain (Wade, 2012). If it is a critical component, it may need to play more prominently in the scenario. The level of detail in the process aids in the development of the scenario.

Including a variety of individuals adds a level of credibility to the meeting. Discussions should include individuals from various areas and multiple levels of the organization. Participants who are appreciated for their contributions and capable of communicating within the process elevate the discussion (Wade, 2012). Maggs and Chelin (2013) share an example of roles and responsibilities in scenario planning. A top-down approach helps the communication plan because leaders who have an advanced overview become better participants and communicators in the process and individuals included in the process develop an attachment to the outcomes.

It is important to double-check the scenario for viability. Assessing the potential for the scenario to happen and including the details gives the group a chance to review the creative work and clarify anything that may have been left out. Walking through the scenarios as if they were real, provides a way to test the ideas. Recognizing when the event is actually happening is also critical to the plans. How will the organization know when to use the plan? Outlining the signs of what to look for will add value to the plan. Following the process to completion, watching the signs, and determining when to update the plans will also be important. If there is a regular review of the process, checking the scenario for flaws should be part of the evaluation.

In an example using a dental conference (Steil & Gibbons-Carr, 2005), the group developed four scenarios leading to a strategy as an outcome of the process. Several demonstrations of the scenario planning process follow Wade's (2012) introduction of the process steps. Examples show how the process plays out in different situations.

Importance of the Process

Nyuur (2015) discusses the importance of scenario planning as it relates to the uncertainty within the global arena. Complexities of multiple cultural differences in addition to the speed of change for organizations require the thoughtful approach to anticipated events. As the steps of the process come together, it is clear that each step creates a foundation for the next and the building blocks develop the scenario into a story that can be compared to other stories.

If the information gathering process is detailed, presenting the data in a scenario can help decision makers (Halladay, 2013) envision the outcome and make better decisions. The steps of the process of forecasting presented by Joseph (2007) can be compared to Wade's (2012) steps to see how important the process is and how it has evolved. Decision trees (Seigel, 2016) are an example of the relevance of data to applicable models. The process and tools chosen to develop scenarios are an important part of the decision making about the planned response. If the tool or model used is too remote or overused the process may lose energy for participants. Keeping the group engaged in the creativity of the process produces a better outcome.

It is dangerous to think there is only one way to view the future. Using multiple tools and processes expands the way a visionary assesses and communicates the vision of the information. As learned through the shared experience of the COVID-19 pandemic, the new normal allows organizations to improve as they acknowledge the uncertain future, complex nature of organizations, volatile global events, and ambiguous details (Kotter et al., 2021). Through detailed scenarios, discussions may approach more detailed analysis, which encourages more detailed solutions. The more prepared an organization is the better able they are to manage uncertain events.

SUSTAINABILITY STAKEHOLDERS

The organization's ability to maintain successfully changed environments requires a constant focus on sustainability. The organizational environment and individuals working in the organization are connected to the outcome of change. It is critical then for the change to have a strategy to sustain the effort to gain productivity improvements, innovation, competitive advantages and other planned benefits from the change. The organization's approach to growth and innovation helps them remain effective in business and develop consistent improvements over time.

Strategies

Strategic Human Resource Management (SHRM) is one strategy that supports the idea that developing people encourages effectiveness and sustainability in the change process (Fareed et al., 2016). Change at the individual level supports change at the organizational level, so identifying ways to develop the employees will positively impact the individual and the organization (Jurik & Cavender, 2016). Employees' attitudes toward change and innovation impact the culture of the company and dictate the speed the organization can change. Culture change can be extraordinarily slow when elements of resistance are present. Leaders' efforts to employ strategies for sustainability will fail if the organization's culture does not support a rapidly changing environment (Brasfield, 2015). The leader's ability to develop people is the first link to effectiveness in the sustainability strategy.

The strategy of socio-technical work systems as presented by Fischer and Zink (2012) provides support for the connection between people and technology. When systems change, the company must provide a way for employees to learn the systems. Technological advances are constant in today's workplace. The minute employees are comfortable working with the technology that is available; new technology replaces the comfort zone. The socio-technical strategy allows for leaders and organizations to acknowledge this truth and prepare for the advancements before the need becomes dire. Socio-technical work systems add effectiveness to sustainability by addressing issues with either training programs or communication from the leader.

Talent development is one way that the two strategies can be optimized together. Identifying the skills and knowledge necessary for an employee to be productive and positive about the environment is the focus of effectiveness. Strategic human resources management and socio-technical work systems are powerful together in recognizing the needed development areas and providing the development opportunity for the individual to be successful (Fareed et al., 2016; Fischer & Zink, 2012). Purposeful development of a workforce can prepare the organization for external changes that are constantly on the horizon. When the changes are coming fast enough, continuous improvement processes can be effective as the norm within the organizational culture.

Sustainable work systems are a strategy for effectiveness long-term (Jurik & Cavender, 2016). A leader who supports the work system supports the whole organization. Stable leadership gives employees dependable communication and a trusting environment. When employees trust where the organization is going, they will have less resistance to immediate change. Complexity provides an interesting challenge for leaders (Lawler III et al., 2011). Managing all the components during change gives the sustainable environment a chance to survive, but identifying the complex components can be difficult if they are not already in the implementation plan.

Priorities

An organization is sustainably effective when people, planet, and profit are at the center of work activities (Lawler III, 2012). Sustainability should be a priority for organizations because the way a company does business is just as important as making money. Sustainability ranks as a top priority for organizations to be successful (Lawler III 2011). Performance results from the necessity of redesigning the organization to become sustainable. Customers care about how the organization makes money and will vote with their dollars. The company competes in the market for the customers' attention and must demonstrate that they are about more than the profit.

Alignment with operational strategies (Zanon, 2013) is one way to tell if a company is sincere in the approach to being sustainably effective. Everything they do should reflect the values the organization holds as important. Authentic behavior demonstrates that customers, patients, clients, members, and employees can trust the organization. Behaviors that align with organizational strategies encourage more aligned behaviors from others. The measure of performance rises to the level of expectation when the leader demonstrates action in line with communication.

Challenges

Transformational change required to implement the design of a sustainable organization takes a great deal of time and resources to accomplish. Changing organizational culture tends to be transformational change and is often underestimated by leaders. Leaders with a transformational leadership style are more successful at achieving cultural change and better able to sustain the results (Brasfield, 2015). Since only a portion of leaders have a transformational leadership style, others are left looking for the necessary skills in a trusted advisor or change consultant. Those leaders with a logical leadership style are also successful in sustaining success because they share the vision of the organization (Teoh Kae & Rashad, 2015). Strong communicators will find the transformational change process easier and will be better able to adopt culture change.

The complexity of transformational change can be unappealing to organizations because it is a lot of work. Change to gain sustainable effectiveness requires a commitment of time, resources, and personnel up front. While the process is grueling, the outcome usually makes up for the process. Redesigning the vision of the organization and therefore redesigning the rest of the organization will be necessary to change a culture and to have a sustained performance following the change (Arya, 2012). The strategy becomes a sustainable process when the people have accepted their new roles, the environment supports the changes made, and the performance of the organization results in profitable growth.

Several companies have hired people to oversee sustainability, but having the burden of transformation on one person's shoulders is a lot to bear (Strand, 2014). Many leaders and organizations found that it was not an effective way to accomplish the change. The leader of the organization is ultimately in charge of communication during the change process for employees to trust that it is not just a temporary change (Teoh Kae & Rashad, 2015). While one person may lead an effort to ensure that the organization balances the elements of sustainability, everyone in the organization has a role in making effectiveness sustainable.

MULTINATIONAL APPROACH TO TEAMS OF TEAMS

McChrystal et al. (2015) present the concept that small teams accomplish more. Leaders who possess Emotional Intelligence also accomplish more (Gianakos, 2019). Synergy is Covey's (1989) concept that suggests that more can be achieved when we pull the load together as a team. The learning opportunity is easier to manage as a group than alone. Each of these statements helps leaders stay in touch with how they lead groups.

Taking a closer look at group behavior with a focus on teamwork, collaboration, consensus decision-making, and individuals in the workplace who are members of formal and informal groups (Robbins & Judge, 2023). Teams are unique in their approach to decision-making as a group. Each team has a culture and climate influencing the process and outcome of the decision.

The topic of group decision-making is not new to organizations. While there are many different methods that could be used to help the group decide, some are better at maintaining relationships and group trust. The nominal group technique is closely related to brainstorming and consensus-building (Robbins & Judge, 2023). Building consensus requires facilitation and a methodical approach (Gupta, 2018). This activity can create conflict in a team.

Whether the group is working through a Kaizen, deciding how they will handle a digital transformation, or ordering lunch, trust and team cohesiveness may be at risk. In a 2019 study, the themes that came out of participant responses didn't point directly to trust, but rather addressed elements that lead to trust. The group activities in high-stakes decision making provide opportunities for communication, collaboration, flexibility, and authenticity (Carter, 2019).

In a healthcare environment, conducting change can be even more divisive than in other industries (Carter et al., 2024). Processes exist for helping groups work together but sometimes convincing a team to use a unique process is challenging. When lives are at stake, it is important that leaders move more quickly to a result. If there is a luxury of time, just the activity of group decision-making can be a team-building event (McClernon & Swanson, 1995). While this is a classical perspective, it is also still effective.

Hierarchical agent architecture demonstrates the concept of teams of teams, but for systems (LangChain, 2024). In Chapter 7, we introduced the holonic model as a way to illustrate a recommended collaborative partnership for multinational EHR interoperability. To further define this recommended collaboration, consider the way autonomous teams might share information with other teams working toward a common goal. In Figure 2, we show how the concept of teams of teams might apply to countries or organizations participating in the problem-solving activities.

Figure 2. Representation of teams of teams as a holonic model

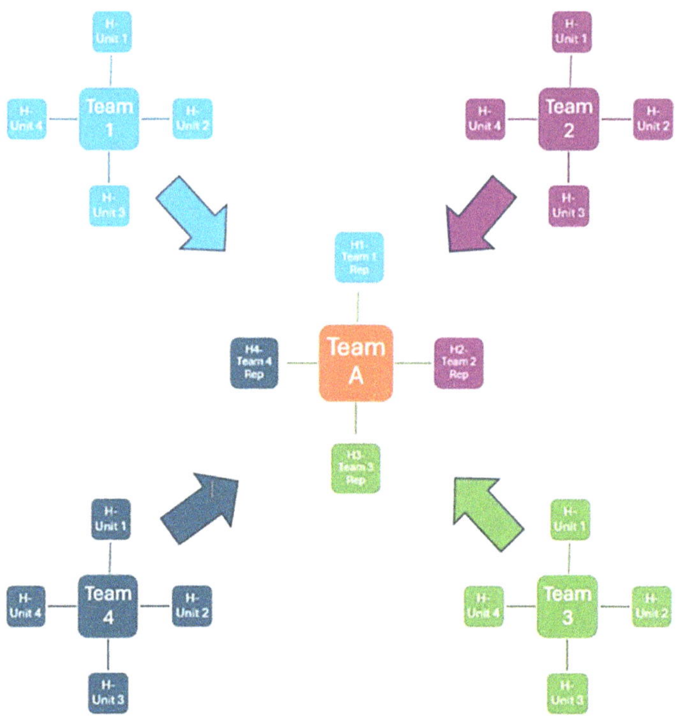

In an analogy, consider how the holonic model works for multi-agent systems (Koestler, 1978; Bakos, & Dumitra cu, 2017). The holonic model was introduced in

Chapter 7, but here we revisit the concept in terms of crisis management and scenario planning. When gathering stakeholders to brainstorm actions to either manage a crisis or plan for future crises situations, the holonic model can help the group envision the connection with the broader group and help individuals manage their own role. The evolution of complexity as described in Bakos, & Dumitra cu's (2017) work, provides a way for leaders to identify with corporate sustainability and risk management. Multi-agent planning (MAP) is a common concept explaining how a network of agents in a multi-agent system plans to achieve common objectives or goals (Dehimi et al., 2023).

Agile Leadership

One proposed method for managing an iterative process of implementing a new approach to multinational EHR interoperability is to leverage agile leadership. The challenge with the complexity of multinational approaches to anything is the sheer magnitude of the undertaking. When planning to scale, the conversation must include the stakeholders from multiple countries with an equitable approach. Individuals must be represented as peers without the stigma of being from a high-income country (HIC) or a LMIC low- to middle- income country (Al-Maazmi & Hashmi, 2024). In *Strategic Doing*, Morrison et al. (2019) promote leveraging skills to lead the type of agile methodology or iterative approach needed to both work and improve simultaneously. In a study of applying agile methods to innovation, Hannola et al. (2013) found significant guidelines for leaders and participants in the process. This type of approach is needed to move the teams forward. Once the commitment is made to establish equity among participating countries and organizations, agile methods of organizing the work promotes rapid adoption of ideas.

External alignment is a critical element of establishing the multinational approach to interoperability. For the collaboration to manifest and be a sustainable answer, the diverse group of stakeholders should collectively embrace the shared vision (van Tulder, & van Mil, 2023). This continuous conversation must demonstrate a peer relationship to maintain the trust of all stakeholders. In an agile approach, the innovation process gains efficiency when the teams are able to move forward by embracing shorter iterations and limiting documentation in exchange for bite-sized user stories (Hannola et al., 2013). Lessons from other large-scale transformations can inform how the teams are coming together.

Many organizations have moved from managing projects using a waterfall approach to embracing the agile methodology. In an action research study, Natarajan and Pichai (2024) explored the transition from waterfall to agile. Leveraging lessons from those who have been involved in the type of large-scale transformation required is helpful. The type of agile leadership needed to accomplish this change is a commitment to keeping groups small and approaching them as units of a larger whole (Morrison et al., 2019). For many organizations this may require an organizational culture change.

CONCLUSION

The topic of resistance to change and methods for managing that resistance holds significance in conducting change where the participants within the organization are lacking agreement with the change. Regardless of the type of change, employees may be sensitive to change and act in ways that prevent the change from running smoothly or happening at all. As studied by Agboola and Salawu (2011), these behaviors may be managed by employing several methods including motivation, communication, facilitation, and education. One example of communication to help improve digital innovation in healthcare is in the way organizations promote the multichannel process as a proactive way for individuals to own the experience (Allen, 2025). The future of the HealthTech approach to care relies on the patient to trust the process and accept the benefits available when the advancements are embraced. In 2025, changes to digital processes are happening so quickly that the complexities are on the brink of being fully handled by systems.

The effects of resistance to change can be devastating to a company. It appears to be a result of poor communication about the change or damaged relationships between the manager and employees attempting to carry out a change. Implementation by upper management can result in resistance when the middle manager is not in agreement with the planned change. The results are difficult to manage and painful to observe. Factors impacting resistance are observable (Raza & Standing, 2011) by including the right individuals in the discussion as stakeholders, individuals who might have an issue with some of the components of the change will not resist altogether if they have sufficient time to be involved in the conversation early and have time to prepare for the change.

In implementing change initiatives, the manager may be searching for a way to overcome the employees' desire to maintain the status quo. For example, during mergers and acquisitions, implementation strategies help experienced employees assimilate and adopt the culture of the acquiring organization. Even when the change would bring an improved environment for the employees, changing the way work is accomplished impacts habits and behaviors on the part of the employee. These changes, if complex enough, are difficult for employees to adopt for many reasons. To manage the change means leaders may need to employ several methods depending on the situation or type of resistance present. Leaders promote psychological safety by adopting the philosophy of using small groups to promote participation

(Morrison et al., 2019). Teams of teams concepts combined with this philosophy of promoting participation through safe spaces will provide a way to value contributions and reduce resistance at the same time.

When resistance to change impacts implementation, the corporate culture, including the working environment may experience disruption in the midst of improvement strategies. Carter, B. (2019) studied leadership strategies and participants suggested this phenomenon is related to motivation and engagement. Even if an employee believes that the change is good for them and the company, they still may object to putting forth the effort to change if they are not motivated to accomplish the work and are not engaged in the company's vision or purpose for the change. This creates a problem for managers implementing change initiatives. If the behaviors are allowed to continue, many other employees may be impacted. The environment is also at risk because the change has been deemed necessary and managers are implementing the change as a solution to a current problem.

This organizational behavior, where managers are working to implement solutions and employees are resisting, is nothing new (Avey et al., 2008). Leaders are consistently looking for ways to reduce resistance while managing organizational change initiatives during implementation in the organization, based on the type of anticipated resistance. If the resistance is predictable and if there is additional information on the environment or culture, the resistance could be caused by the way the change is being implemented or what the individual is actually losing.

Some questions bubbled to the surface in researching leadership practices of successful change leaders. First, what elements or components of the change process cause employees to resist the changes implemented by management? Second, if employee resistance can be predicted, would it be possible to determine which methods for managing change will be most effective in managing the change initiative? Findings from the study showed how leaders communicate, who they involve in the change process, and what actions they take make a difference in how individuals experience the change (Carter, B., 2019). Neurolinguistic programming is also a method leaders revealed worked well. By managing the word choice in communicating the required change, individuals were more willing to participate in the change initiative.

REFERENCES

Agboola, A. A., & Salawu, R. O. (2011). Managing deviant behavior and resistance to change. *International Journal of Business and Management*, *6*(1), 235–242.

Al-Maazmi, S., & Hashmi, M. A. (2024). The role of innovation-driven leadership in public-sector innovation: The case in emerging economies. *The Journal of Applied Business and Economics*, *26*(2), 85–105.

Allen, R. W. (2025, March/April). Twelve considerations for the future of healthcare. *Journal of Healthcare Management*, *70*(2), 87–92. DOI: 10.1097/JHM-D-25-00012 PMID: 40059201

Arya, D. K. (2012). So, you want to lead a transformational change! *Asia Pacific Journal of Health Management*, *7*(2), 8–14.

Avey, J. B., Wernsing, T. S., & Luthans, F. (2008). Can positive employees help positive organizational change? Impact of psychological capital and emotions on relevant attitudes and behaviors. *The Journal of Applied Behavioral Science*, *44*(1), 48–70. DOI: 10.1177/0021886307311470

Aytekin, A., Hale, A., Demirel, H., Onur, N., Yalman, A., Livberber, T., & Yiğit-Açıkgöz, F. (2025). Digital health technologies in patient experience literature: A scoping review and future outlook for sustainable digital health interventions. *Sustainability*, *17*(2), 456. DOI: 10.3390/su17020456

Bakos, L., & Dumitra cu, D. (2017). Holonic crisis handling model for corporate sustainability. *Sustainability*, *9*(12), 2266. DOI: 10.3390/su9122266

Boo, E., Abouzeedan, A., Hedner, T., Maack, K., & Lundqvist, M. (2013). Using scenario planning in regional development context: The challenges and opportunities. *World Journal of Science. Technology and Sustainable Development*, *10*(2), 103–122. DOI: 10.1108/20425941311323118

Brasfield, D. A. (2015). The effects of leadership traits in change management on operational excellence. (3684960 D.B.A.), Capella University, Ann Arbor. ProQuest Dissertations & Theses Global database.

Carter, B. M. (2019). *The leadership practices female ODC managers use to improve change initiatives* (Order No. 22621998). Available from ProQuest Dissertations & Theses Global. (2320955766).

Carter, S., Anastasia, C., & Carter, B. (2024). *Multinational Electronic Health Record Interoperability Strategies*. IGI Global., DOI: 10.4018/978-1-7998-8989-2

Cottam, A., Ensor, J., & Band, C. (2001). A benchmark study of strategic commitment to innovation. *European Journal of Innovation Management*, *4*(2), 88–94.

Covey, S. R. (1989). *The 7 habits of highly effective people*. Simon & Schuster.

Dehimi, N. E. H., Galland, S., Tolba, Z., Allaoua, N., & Ferkani, M. (2023). Distributed, dynamic and recursive planning for holonic multi-agent systems: A behavioural model-based approach. *Electronics (Basel)*, *12*(4797), 1–35. DOI: 10.3390/electronics12234749

Dodge, R., Dwyer, J., Witzeman, S., Neylon, S., & Taylor, S. (2017). The role of leadership in innovation. *Research Technology Management*, *60*(3), 22–28. DOI: 10.1080/08956308.2017.1301000

Fareed, M., Noor, W. S. W. M., Isa, M. F. M., & Salleh, S. S. M. M. (2016). Developing human capital for sustainable competitive advantage: The roles of organizational culture and high performance work system. *International Journal of Economic Perspectives*, *10*(4), 655–673. https://www.researchgate.net/publication/319304634

Fischer, K., & Zink, K. J. (2012). Defining elements of sustainable work systems - a system-oriented approach. *Work (Reading, Mass.)*, *41*, 3900–3905. PMID: 22317318

Gianakos, D. (2019). Emotional intelligence: Build by reading poetry. *Physician Leadership Journal*, *6*(4), 74–75.

Gupta, M. (2018). Consensus building process in group decision making-an adaptive procedure based on group dynamics. *IEEE Transactions on Fuzzy Systems*, *26*(4), 1923–1933. DOI: 10.1109/TFUZZ.2017.2755581

Hall, D. J., Skipper, J. B., Hazen, B. T., & Hanna, J. B. (2012). Inter-organizational IT use, cooperative attitude, and inter-organizational collaboration as antecedents to contingency planning effectiveness. *International Journal of Logistics Management*, *23*(1), 50–76. DOI: 10.1108/09574091211226920

Halladay, S. D. (2013). Using predictive analytics to improve decisionmaking. *The Journal of Equipment Lease Financing*, *31*(2), B1–B6.

Holmes, J. D., Nelson, G. O., & Stump, D. C. (1993). Improving the innovation process at Eastman Chemical. *Research Technology Management*, *36*(3), 27. https://www.jstor.org/stable/24128245

Jayanti, E. B. (2013). *An investigation of the internal corporate factors of organizational learning and innovation.* (3600937 Ph.D.), ProQuest Dissertations & Theses Global database.

Joseph, E. C. (2007). Discovering the anticipatory sciences. *Futurics*, *31*(3/4), 2–20.

Jurik, N. C., & Cavender, G. (2016). Sustainable workplaces as innovation. *The Journal of Applied Management and Entrepreneurship*, *21*(1), 53–71. DOI: 10.9774/GLEAF.3709.2016.ja.00006

Koestler, A. (1978). *Janus: A summing up*. Random House.

Kotter, J., Akhtar, V., & Gupta, G. (2021). *Change: How organizations achieve hard-to-imagine results in uncertain and volatile times*. Wiley.

Kumar, V. (2013). *101 design methods: A structured approach for driving innovation in your organization*. John Wiley & Sons.

LangChain. (2024, October 16). Conceptual guide: Multi agent architecture [Video]. YouTube. https://www.youtube.com/watch?v=4nZl32FwU-o

Lawler, E. E., III. (2011). *Sustainability must be a top priority*. Retrieved from https://www.forbes.com/sites/edwardlawler/2011/10/26/sustainability-must-be-a-top-priority/#5f8b8b9312cc

Lawler, E. E., III. (2012). *Sustainability: It should be about more than the bottom line*. Retrieved from https://www.forbes.com/sites/edwardlawler/2012/03/15/sustainability-it-should-be-about-more-than-the-bottom-line/#65a1712522c8

Lawler, E. E.III, Worley, C. G., & Creelman, D. (2011). *Management reset: organizing for sustainable effectiveness*. Jossey-Bass.

Madir, J. (2020). *HealthTech: Law and regulation*. Elgar Commercial Law and Practice.

Maggs, P., & Chelin, J. (2013). Scenario planning for an uncertain future? *Library Management*, *34*(8/9), 664–676. DOI: 10.1108/LM-02-2013-0017

Masch, V. A. (2013). Extensions of stochastic multiscenario models for long-range planning under uncertainty. *Environment Systems & Decisions*, *33*(1), 43–59. DOI: 10.1007/s10669-013-9433-x

Mason, D. (2003). Tailoring scenario planning to the company culture. *Strategy and Leadership*, *31*(2), 25–28.

McChrystal, S., Collins, T., Silverman, D., & Fussell, C. (2015). *Teams of teams: New rules of engagement for a complex world*. Portfolio/Penguin.

McChrystalgroup.com. (2025). Teams of Teams®: New rules of engagement in a complex world. https://www.mcchrystalgroup.com/capabilities/team-of-teams

McClernon, T. R., & Swanson, R. A. (1995). Team building: An experimental investigation of the effects of computer-based and facilitator-based interventions on work groups. *Human Resource Development Quarterly*, *6*(1), 39–58. https://doi.org.coloradotech.idm.oclc.org/10.1002/hrdq.3920060105

Miranda Silva, G., & Gomes, J., P., Filipe Lages, L., & Lopes Pereira, Z. (2014). The role of TQM in strategic product innovation: An empirical assessment. *International Journal of Operations & Production Management*, *34*(10), 1307–1337.

Morente, F., & Ferràs, X. (2017). Innovation management from the inside: An approach from attention and everyday praxis. *Intangible Capital*, *13*(3), 640–667. DOI: 10.3926/ic.1004

Morrison, E., Hutcheson, S., Nilsen, E., Fadden, J., & Franklin, N. (2019). *Strategic doing: Ten skills for agile leadership*. Wiley.

Natarajan, T., & Pichai, S. (2024, March 27). Transition from waterfall to agile methodology: An action research study. *IEEE Access : Practical Innovations, Open Solutions*, *12*, 49341–49362. DOI: 10.1109/ACCESS.2024.3384097

Nickols, F. (2020). SWOT/PESTLE. *Odnetwork.org*. https://nickols.us/SWOTPESTLE.jpg

Nouri, B. A., Ghorbani, R., & Soltani, M. (2017). The effect of knowledge management on organizational innovation with the mediating role of organizational learning (Case study: Agricultural bank in Iran). *Journal of Applied Economics & Business Research*, *7*(3), 194–211.

Nyuur, R. B. (2015). Unlocking the potential barriers on SMEs' uptake of scenario planning. *Journal of Strategy and Management*, *8*(2), 139–154. DOI: 10.1108/JSMA-01-2014-0007

Pesut, D. J. (2013). Creativity and innovation: Thought and action. *Creative Nursing*, *19*(3), 113–121. DOI: 10.1891/1078-4535.19.3.113 PMID: 24400465

Prakash, A., Jha, S. K., & Rajendra, P. M. (2012). Scenario planning for service quality: A monte carlo simulation study. *Journal of Strategy and Management*, *5*(3), 331–352. DOI: 10.1108/17554251211247599

Raza, S. A., & Standing, C. (2011). A systemic model for managing and evaluating conflicts in organizational change. *Systemic Practice and Action Research*, *24*(3), 187–210. DOI: 10.1007/s11213-010-9186-0

Robbins, S. P., & Judge, T. A. (2023). *Organizational behavior* (19th ed.). Pearson.

Sanz-Valle, R., Naranjo-Valencia, J. C., Jiménez-Jiménez, D., & Perez-Caballero, L. (2011). Linking organizational learning with technical innovation and organizational culture. *Journal of Knowledge Management*, *15*(6), 997–1015. DOI: 10.1108/13673271111179334

Sawka, K. A. (2007). Strategic planning in volatile industry conditions. *U.S. Banker*, *117*(2), 40.

Schwarm, B. (2013, May 2). The well-tempered clavier. *Encyclopedia Britannica*. Retrieved from https://www.britannica.com/topic/The-Well-Tempered-Clavier-BWV-846-893

Shukla, A. (2017, July 2). *What is Innovation? Why Innovation is important* Retrieved from paggu: http://www.paggu.com/getting-into-roots/what-is-innovation-why-innovation-is-important/

Shukla, R., Bagotia, H., Satish, P., Kamath, H. S., Chatterjee, S., Savariah, D., Kaulgud, V., Gobburi, H., & Acharya, S. (2025). Fintech and healthtech synergism: Pioneering a digital healthcare revolution for accessible, affordable, and effective patient-centered care. *Journal of Family Medicine and Primary Care*, *14*(3), 820–824. DOI: 10.4103/jfmpc.jfmpc_999_24 PMID: 40256084

Simpkins, R. A. (2009). How great leaders avoid disaster: The value of contingency planning. *Business Strategy Series*, *10*(2), 104–108. DOI: 10.1108/17515630910942241

Steiber, A., & Alänge, S. (2015). Organizational innovation: Verifying a comprehensive model for catalyzing organizational development and change. *Triple Helix (Heidelberg)*, *2*(1), 1–28. DOI: 10.1186/s40604-015-0026-1

Steil, G.Jr, & Gibbons-Carr, M. (2005). Large group scenario planning: Scenario planning with the whole system in the room. *The Journal of Applied Behavioral Science*, *41*(1), 15–29.

Strand, R. (2014). Strategic leadership of corporate sustainability. *Journal of Business Ethics*, *123*(4), 687–706. DOI: 10.1007/s10551-013-2005-7

Teoh Kae, N., & Rashad, Y. (2015). The general review of how different leadership styles cause the transformational change efforts to be successful. *International Journal of Management. Accounting & Economics*, *2*(9), 1130–1140.

Valikangas, L., Gibbert, M., Nair, L. B., Paukku, M., & Peixoto, I. (2016). *Strategic innovation: The definitive guide to outlier strategies*. Pearson Education, Inc.

Van Tulder, R., & van Mil, E. (2023). *Principles of sustainable business: Frameworks for corporate action on the SDGs*. Routledge.

Von Hippel, E. (1982). Get new products for customers. *Harvard Business Review*, *60*(2), 117–122.

Wachter, R. (2015). *The digital doctor: Hope, hype, and harm at the dawn of medicine's computer age*. McGraw-Hill Education.

Wade, W. (2012). *Scenario planning: A field guide to the future*. John Wiley & Sons, Inc.

Weitzman, F. (2014). *Organizational longevity as a predictor of organizational learning, organizational identity, organizational innovation, and fiscal conservatism.* (3624405 Ph.D.). ProQuest Dissertations & Theses Global database.

Wong, J., Young, E., Hung, L., Mann, J., & Jackson, L. (2023). Beyond Plan-Do-Study-Act cycle – staff perceptions on facilitators and barriers to the implementation of telepresence robots in long-term care. *BMC Health Services Research*, *23*, 1–16. DOI: 10.1186/s12913-023-09741-9 PMID: 37468953

Zanon, C. J., Alceu Gomes Alves, F., Charbel Jose Chiappetta, J., & Ana Beatriz Lopes de Sousa, J. (2013). Alignment of operations strategy: Exploring the marketing interface. *Industrial Management & Data Systems*, *113*(2), 207–233. DOI: 10.1108/02635571311303541

APPENDIX

Chapter 10 Study Questions

1. How can teams of teams use the holonic model to organize their approach to working toward a shared outcome?
2. What is the value of using an agile methodology as opposed to a waterfall methodology for improving innovation?
3. What can prevent resistance in the transformation process?
4. How does a sociotechnical work system support both people and technology in an organization?
5. What can organizations and countries do to come together in problem-solving efforts?

Conclusion

The COVID-19 Pandemic and the Ebola Outbreak reveal data-sharing gaps that hindered pandemic response time and efficacy. Environmental Subsystems: a blend of social subsystems and technical subsystems allows joint optimisation and proves effective in pandemic response and disease surveillance. There are several critical factors when implementing changes in global health infrastructure and policies. The approaches presented in this text offer multiple perspectives and implementation approaches to bridge the information gaps between global health, public health systems, and medicine. The consensus from all approaches is that data sharing and integrating multinational systems have the potential to enhance disease surveillance and pandemic preparedness.

A successful system requires a committed, inclusive, and equitable global health vision, infrastructural changes, and multinational collaboration with one purpose: preventing another pandemic and saving lives. A successful integrated infrastructure must also align with the WHO Pandemic Agreement and UN SDGs, so that data governance, financing, and operational protocols are in place before the next virus claims another precious life. Without these critical components, we risk repeating the previous mistakes. Without collaboration, we lose the ability to detect and contain outbreaks before they escalate. Just as no building can stand without both concrete and rebar, no EHR system can support global health without both collaboration and justice. An equitable and inclusive foundation must be laid with intention because lives depend on it.

Appendix

SEVENTY-EIGHTH WORLD HEALTH ASSEMBLY

Agenda item 16.2
WHA78.1
20 May 2025

WHO Pandemic Agreement

The Seventy-eighth World Health Assembly,

Recalling decisions SSA2(5) (2021) and WHA77(20) (2024), which, acknowledging the need to address gaps in preventing, preparing for and responding to health emergencies, inter alia, established the Intergovernmental Negotiating Body to draft and negotiate a WHO convention, agreement or other international instrument on pandemic prevention, preparedness and response (the Intergovernmental Negotiating Body), with a view to adoption under Article 19, or under other provisions of the WHO Constitution;

Expressing appreciation for the work of the Intergovernmental Negotiating Body, including its outcome as contained in document A78/10, and acknowledging with appreciation the leadership of its Bureau;

Reaffirming the need for a legally binding international instrument on pandemic prevention, preparedness and response, in line with decisions SSA2(5) and WHA77(20);

Emphasizing the role of the International Health Regulations (2005), adopted through resolution WHA58.3 (2005), and subsequently amended through resolutions WHA67.13 (2014), WHA75.12 (2022), and WHA77.17 (2024), in pandemic prevention, preparedness and response, and the need for coherence and complementarity in the implementation of the International Health Regulations (2005) and the WHO Pandemic Agreement;

Recognizing the continuing threat of pathogens with pandemic potential which calls for enhancing pandemic prevention, preparedness and response and for refraining from taking measures that adversely affect it,

1. ADOPTS, pursuant to Article 19 of the Constitution of the World Health Organization, the WHO Pandemic Agreement as annexed to this resolution;
2. RECOGNIZES that the adoption of the WHO Pandemic Agreement by the Health Assembly does not prejudice the sovereign prerogative of each State to consider the WHO Pandemic Agreement in accordance with its constitutional processes;
3. NOTES, in accordance with Article 31 of the WHO Pandemic Agreement, that the WHO Pandemic Agreement shall be open for signature after adoption of the Annex described in Article 12 of the Agreement by the Health Assembly, at the World Health Organization headquarters in Geneva, and thereafter at United Nations Headquarters in New York, on dates to be determined by the World Health Assembly;
4. CALLS UPON all States and regional economic integration organizations entitled to do so, to consider signing, ratifying, accepting, approving, formally confirming or acceding to the WHO Pandemic Agreement at the earliest opportunity in line with Articles 31 and 32 of the Agreement, with a view to bringing the WHO Pandemic Agreement, including its Annex described in Article 12, into force as soon as possible;
5. URGES all States and regional economic integration organizations to take all appropriate measures, pending the entry into force of the WHO Pandemic Agreement, to further its objective and eventual implementation, guided by equity and the principle of solidarity with all people and countries in the context of health emergencies, to prevent, prepare for and respond to pandemic emergencies, and public health emergencies of international concern;
6. URGES all States and regional economic integration organizations, in the event a pandemic emergency is determined prior to the entry into force of the WHO Pandemic Agreement, to take measures, promptly, on a voluntary basis, in line with relevant provisions of the WHO Pandemic Agreement, noting that taking such measures is without prejudice to the position of any State or regional economic integration organization with regard to the WHO Pandemic Agreement;
7. URGES all Member States, regional economic integration organizations, observers and relevant stakeholders to support the preparatory activities referred to in this resolution and to effectively encourage prompt entry into force and implementation of the WHO Pandemic Agreement;

8. CALLS UPON the United Nations and invites other relevant international organizations to continue to provide support for strengthening pandemic prevention, preparedness and response;
9. DECIDES, in accordance with Rule 41 of its Rules of Procedure, to establish an open-ended Intergovernmental Working Group (IGWG) to:
   (1) as a priority, draft and negotiate the Annex to the WHO Pandemic Agreement described in Article 12 of the WHO Pandemic Agreement and submit the outcome to the Seventy-ninth World Health Assembly for its consideration, and subsequently facilitate, as necessary, activities related to the adoption of said Annex and the opening for signature, ratification, acceptance, approval, accession or formal confirmation of the WHO Pandemic Agreement;
   (2) following completion of the activities in paragraph (1) above, conduct preparatory work on the following issues in the WHO Pandemic Agreement for consideration, as appropriate, by the Conference of the Parties:
      (a) rules of procedure for the Conference of the Parties, and its criteria for participation of observers at its proceedings;
      (b) financial rules for the Conference of the Parties and any subsidiary bodies it may establish;
      (c) a draft budget for the first financial period;
      (d) the structure, functions and modalities of the Global Supply Chain and Logistics Network as referred to in Article 13 of the WHO Pandemic Agreement;
      (e) the information, frequency and format of the reports required under Article 21.1 on the implementation of the WHO Pandemic Agreement, including Article 11.1(a);
      (f) the mechanism referred to in WHO Pandemic Agreement Article 19.5 and 19.6 to facilitate and strengthen effective implementation of the provisions of the WHO Pandemic Agreement, including its rules of procedure/terms of reference;
   (3) develop a proposal for the terms of reference for the Coordinating Financial Mechanism and the modalities for its operationalization and governance in relation to the implementation of the WHO Pandemic Agreement as described in Article 18 of the WHO Pandemic Agreement, for consideration by the Conference of the Parties, and in this regard cooperate with the States Parties Committee for the Implementation of the International Health Regulations (2005) as referred to in Article 54 bis therein and with its preparatory process;
   (4) oversee other preparations, as necessary, for the first session of the Conference of the Parties, and report directly to it in that regard;

10. FURTHER DECIDES that the IGWG shall hold its organizational meeting no later than 15 July 2025, in order to elect six officers tasked with equal responsibility in facilitating its work, namely two co-Chairpersons and four vice-Chairpersons, one from each of the six WHO regions, with two co-Chairpersons reflecting a balance of developed and developing countries tasked with steering the process, and to agree its methods and programme of work; shall be open to all States and regional economic integration organizations as referred to in Article 32 of the WHO Pandemic Agreement; shall follow the modalities of engagement for relevant stakeholders of the Intergovernmental Negotiating Body; and shall conclude its work prior to the first session of the Conference of the Parties;
11. INVITES all States and regional economic integration organizations as referred to in Article 32 of the WHO Pandemic Agreement, to submit initial text proposals, in accordance with the provisions of Article 12 of the WHO Pandemic Agreement for the development of the draft Annex to the Pandemic Agreement described in Article 12 thereof before the second meeting of the IGWG or as decided by the IGWG at its organizational meeting, with all such proposals to be made publicly available by the Director-General, unless a proponent requests otherwise with respect to its proposal;
12. REAFFIRMS the inclusive and Member State-led nature of the process for the development of the Annex described in Article 12 of the WHO Pandemic Agreement, and further decides that experts may be requested by the IGWG to provide technical advice and inputs, as and when necessary;
13. RECOGNIZES that, for the purposes of Article 4.6 and Article 5.3 of the WHO Pandemic Agreement, "other relevant intergovernmental organizations" include, inter alia, the following: United Nations Environment Programme, Food and Agriculture Organization of the United Nations and World Organisation for Animal Health;
14. REAFFIRMS that States have sovereign rights over their own biological resources, as well as the sovereign right to legislate and implement laws, including national access and benefit-sharing legislation;
15. REQUESTS the Director-General:
    (1) to ensure the uniformity of the Arabic, Chinese, English, French, Russian and Spanish texts of the WHO Pandemic Agreement, allowing for Member State review and input on language conformity and accuracy;
    (2) to provide the IGWG with the necessary services and facilities for the performance of its work, including complete, relevant and timely information and advice;
    (3) to convene the organizational meeting of the IGWG no later than 15 July 2025;

(4) to, in order to provide the technical input and advice described in paragraph 12 above to the Member State-led IGWG process, organize technical work, engaging experts, consistent with WHO Regulations for Expert Advisory Panels and Committees, and in particular the principles set out in Article 4.2, in the areas set out in Article 12 of the WHO Pandemic Agreement, to inform and support the work of the IGWG, for the consideration of the IGWG, and to make that technical input and advice publicly available;

(5) to take appropriate steps to provide support to Member States, in particular developing countries in preparation for entry into force of the WHO Pandemic Agreement;

(6) to commence, with a view to prompt implementation of the WHO Pandemic Agreement, preparatory activities on matters which are addressed or mandated to the Secretariat of the World Health Organization in the WHO Pandemic Agreement, in a phased manner, as appropriate, subject to the availability of resources, and without prejudice to the future work of the Conference of the Parties;

(7) to keep the Health Assembly informed of progress made toward entry into force of the Agreement and of preparations under way for the first session of the Conference of the Parties, with the first report to be provided to the Eightieth World Health Assembly;

(8) to invite the Conference of the Parties to direct the Secretariat to provide a report on the outcomes of each future session of the Conference to the following session of the Health Assembly, for information purposes;

(9) to provide regular reports for information purposes to the Conference of the Parties to the WHO Pandemic Agreement on resolutions and decisions of the Health Assembly relevant to the implementation of the Agreement;

(10) to develop, working in full collaboration with all States, regional economic integration organizations, relevant stakeholders and intergovernmental organizations, as appropriate, recommendations or other non-binding advice, and organize support when needed, for policies for managing legal risks related to novel pandemic vaccines during pandemic emergencies, with particular regard to humanitarian settings and provide a report to the Eightieth World Health Assembly for consideration and guidance.

ANNEX

WHO Pandemic Agreement 20 May 2025
Contents

The Parties to the WHO Pandemic Agreement,

Recognizing that States bear the primary responsibility for the health and well-being of their peoples, and that States are fundamental to strengthening pandemic prevention, preparedness and response,

Recognizing that differences in the levels of development of Parties engender different capacities and capabilities in pandemic prevention, preparedness and response, and acknowledging that unequal development in different countries in the promotion of health and control of disease, especially communicable disease, is a common danger that requires support through international cooperation, including the support of countries with greater capacities and resources, as well as predictable, sustainable and sufficient financial, human, logistical, technological, technical and digital health resources,

Recognizing that the World Health Organization is the directing and coordinating authority on international health work, including on pandemic prevention, preparedness and response,

Recalling the Constitution of the World Health Organization, which states that the enjoyment of the highest attainable standard of health is one of the fundamental rights of every human being without distinction of race, religion, political belief, economic or social condition,

Recalling the Convention on the Elimination of All Forms of Discrimination against Women; the Convention on the Rights of the Child; the Convention on the Rights of Persons with Disabilities; and the Convention on the Prohibition of the Development, Production and Stockpiling of Bacteriological (Biological) and Toxin Weapons and on Their Destruction, as relevant to the context of pandemic prevention, preparedness and response,

Recognizing that the international spread of disease is a global threat with serious consequences for lives, livelihoods, societies and economies that calls for the widest possible international and regional collaboration, cooperation and solidarity with all people and countries, especially developing countries, and notably least developed countries and small island developing States, in order to ensure an effective, coordinated, appropriate, comprehensive and equitable international response, while reaffirming the principle of the sovereignty of States in addressing public health matters,

Deeply concerned by the inequities at national and international levels that hindered timely and equitable access to health products to address coronavirus disease (COVID-19), and recognizing the need to address the serious shortcomings at the national, regional and global levels in prevention, preparedness, response and health system recovery for public health emergencies of international concern, including pandemic emergencies,

Recognizing the need for resolute action to both strengthen pandemic prevention, preparedness and response and to improve equitable access to pandemic-related health products, as well as the importance of refraining from taking measures that adversely affect prevention,

preparedness and response, while respecting States' rights to implement health measures in accordance with their relevant national law and obligations under international law, and *recalling* World Health Assembly decision SSA2(5) of 2021,

Recognizing the critical role of whole-of-government and whole-of-society approaches at national and community levels, through broad social participation, and further recognizing the value and diversity of the culture and traditional knowledge of Indigenous Peoples as well as local

communities, including traditional medicine, in strengthening pandemic prevention, preparedness, response and health systems recovery,

Recognizing the importance of ensuring political commitment, resourcing and action through multisectoral collaborations for pandemic prevention, preparedness, response and health systems recovery,

Reaffirming the importance of multisectoral collaboration at national, regional and international levels to safeguard human health,

Recognizing the importance of rapid and unimpeded access of humanitarian relief consistent with national and international law, as applicable, including applicable international humanitarian law and international human rights law,

Reiterating the need to work towards building and strengthening resilient health systems, with adequate numbers of skilled, trained and protected health and care workers to respond to pandemics, to advance the achievement of universal health coverage, particularly through a primary health care approach; and the need to adopt an equitable approach to mitigate the risk that pandemics exacerbate existing inequities in access to health care services and health products,

Recognizing the importance of building trust and ensuring the timely sharing of information to prevent misinformation, disinformation and stigmatization,

Recognizing that intellectual property protection is important for the development of new medicines and *recognizing* the concerns about its effects on prices, and *recalling* that the World Trade Organization Agreement on Trade-Related Aspects of Intellectual Property Rights (TRIPS Agreement), does not and should not, prevent Member States from taking measures to protect public health, and which provides flexibility to protect public health, as recognized in the Doha Declaration on the TRIPS Agreement and Public Health,

Emphasizing the need to improve access to quality, safe, effective and affordable medicines and other health technologies, inter alia, through building capacity for local production, especially in developing countries, transfer of technology as mutually agreed,[1] cooperation, strengthened legal and regulatory frameworks and other initiatives,

Stressing that adequate pandemic prevention, preparedness, response and health systems recovery is part of a continuum to combat other health emergencies and achieve greater health equity through resolute action on the social, environmental, cultural, political and economic determinants of health, and

Recognizing the importance and public health impact of growing threats such as climate change, poverty and hunger, fragile and vulnerable settings, weak primary healthcare and the spread of antimicrobial resistance,

Have agreed as follows:

Chapter I. Introduction

Article 1 Use of terms

For the purposes of the WHO Pandemic Agreement:

(a) "humanitarian settings" refers to settings in which an event or series of events, such as armed conflicts, natural disasters, or other emergencies, have resulted in a critical threat to the life, health, safety, security or well-being of a community or other large group of people in need of humanitarian assistance. This is without prejudice to rights and obligations under applicable international humanitarian law;

(b) "One Health approach" for pandemic prevention, preparedness and response recognizes that the health of humans is closely linked and interdependent with the health of domestic and wild animals, as well as plants and the wider environment (including ecosystems), aiming for a sustainable balance, and uses an integrated multisectoral and transdisciplinary approach to pandemic prevention preparedness and response, which contributes to sustainable development in an equitable manner;

(c) "pandemic emergency" means a public health emergency of international concern, that is caused by a communicable disease and:

(i) has, or is at high risk of having, wide geographical spread to and within multiple States; and
(ii) is exceeding, or is at high risk of exceeding, the capacity of health systems to respond in those States; and
(iii) is causing, or is at high risk of causing, substantial social and/or economic disruption, including disruption to international traffic and trade; and
(iv) requires rapid, equitable and enhanced coordinated international action, with whole-of-government and whole-of-society approaches;[2]

(d) "pandemic-related health products" means those relevant health products[3] that may be needed for prevention, preparedness and response to pandemic emergencies;

(e) "Party" means a State or regional economic integration organization that has consented to be bound by the WHO Pandemic Agreement, in accordance with its terms, and for which this Agreement is in force;

(f) "persons in vulnerable situations" and "people in vulnerable situations" mean individuals, including persons in groups or in communities or in emergency, and/or humanitarian settings, with a disproportionate increased risk of infection, morbidity, or mortality, as well as those likely

Pursuant to the International Health Regulations (2005). The Conference of the Parties shall consider any further amendments to the International Health Regulations (2005) modifying this term, with the aim to ensure consistency in the use of terms between the International Health Regulations and the WHO Pandemic Agreement to bear a disproportionate burden owing to social determinants of health in the context of a public health emergency of international concern, including a pandemic emergency;

(g) "public health emergency of international concern" means an extraordinary event which is determined:

(i) to constitute a public health risk to other States through the international spread of disease; and
(ii) to potentially require a coordinated international response;[4]

(h) "public health risk" means a likelihood of an event that may affect adversely the health of human populations, with an emphasis on one which may spread internationally or may present a serious and direct danger;[5]

(i) "relevant stakeholders" in the context of their engagement with the World Health Organization is understood in accordance with the Constitution of the World Health Organization and applicable principles, norms and standards of the World Health Organization;

(j) "regional economic integration organization" means an organization that is composed of several sovereign States and to which its Member States have transferred competence over a range of matters, including the authority to make decisions binding on its Member States in respect of those matters;[6] and

(k) "universal health coverage" means that all people have access to the full range of quality health services they need, when and where they need them, without financial hardship. It covers the full continuum of essential health services, from health promotion to prevention, treatment, rehabilitation and palliative care across the life course.

Article 2 Objective

1. The objective of the WHO Pandemic Agreement, guided by equity and the principles further set forth herein, is to prevent, prepare for and respond to pandemics.
2. In furtherance of this objective, the provisions of the WHO Pandemic Agreement apply both during and between pandemics, unless otherwise specified.

Article 3 Principles and approaches

To achieve the objective of the WHO Pandemic Agreement and to implement its provisions, the Parties shall be guided, inter alia, by the following:

1. the sovereign right of States, in accordance with the Charter of the United Nations and the principles of international law to legislate and to implement legislation, within their jurisdiction.
2. full respect for the dignity, human rights and fundamental freedoms of all persons, including the enjoyment of the highest attainable standard of health of every human being, as well as the

Where appropriate, "national" will refer equally to regional economic integration organizations. right to development and full respect for non-discrimination, gender equality, and the protection of persons in vulnerable situations;

3. full respect for international humanitarian law as relevant to effective pandemic prevention, preparedness and response;
4. equity as a goal, principle and outcome of pandemic prevention, preparedness and response, striving in this context for the absence of unfair, avoidable or remediable differences among and between individuals, communities and countries;
5. solidarity with all people and countries in the context of health emergencies, as well as inclusivity, transparency and accountability, to achieve the common interest of a more equitable and better prepared world to prevent, respond to and recover from pandemics, recognizing different levels of capacities and capabilities, particularly of developing countries, including landlocked developing countries, as well as the special circumstances of small island developing States and of least developed countries, in relation to pandemic prevention, preparedness and response; and
6. the best available science and evidence as the basis for public health decisions for pandemic prevention, preparedness and response.

Chapter II. The world together equitably: Achieving equity in, for and through pandemic prevention, preparedness and response

Article 4 Pandemic prevention and surveillance

1. The Parties shall take steps through international collaboration, in bilateral, regional and multilateral settings, to progressively strengthen pandemic prevention and surveillance measures and capacities, consistent with the International Health Regulations (2005) and taking into account national capacities and national and regional circumstances.
2. Each Party shall progressively strengthen measures and capacities for pandemic prevention and coordinated multisectoral surveillance, taking into account its national circumstances. In this regard, each Party shall, in accordance with its national and/or domestic law and applicable international law, and subject to the availability of resources, develop or strengthen, and implement comprehensive multisectoral national pandemic prevention and surveillance plans,[7] programmes and/or other actions, that are consistent with the International Health Regulations (2005), and take into account its public health priorities and relevant international standards, and guidelines, and that cover, inter alia:
   (a) prevention of emerging and re-emerging infectious diseases, by taking measures to promote collaboration across relevant sectors to identify and address drivers of infectious disease at the human-animal-environment interface, with the aim of early prevention of pandemics;
   (b) prevention of infectious disease transmission between animals and humans, including, inter alia, zoonotic disease spill-over, by taking measures to identify and reduce pandemic risks associated with human-animal interactions, and relevant settings, as well as measures aimed at prevention at source, while recognizing the importance of safeguarding communities' livelihoods and food security;
   (c) coordinated multisectoral surveillance to detect and conduct risk assessment of emerging or re-emerging pathogens with pandemic potential, including those pathogens that may present significant risks of zoonotic spillover and those pathogens that are resistant to antimicrobial agents, as well as sharing of the outputs of relevant surveillance and risk assessments amongst relevant sectors within its territory to enhance early detection;
   (d) early detection and control measures at the community level, through strengthening mechanisms and enhancing capacities at the community level, to prevent, detect and report unusual public health events to relevant

authorities within its territory, in order to facilitate actions for early containment at the source;

(e) strengthening efforts to ensure access to safe water, sanitation and hygiene for all, including in hard-to-reach areas;

(f) measures to strengthen effective routine immunization programmes especially by increasing and/or maintaining high immunization coverage, and timely supplementary vaccination to reduce public health risks and to prevent outbreaks, promoting public awareness of the importance of immunization, and strengthening supply chains and immunization systems;

(g) infection prevention and control measures, including safe management of medical waste, in all health care facilities, and infection prevention and control measures in long-term care facilities;

(h) surveillance, risk assessment and prevention of vector-borne diseases that may lead to pandemic emergencies, including by developing, strengthening and maintaining capacities, and by taking into account social, demographic and/or environmental factors that can impact vector distribution and disease transmission;

(i) laboratory biological risk management, including through biosafety and biosecurity training and practices, and ensuring the safety and security of transportation, in accordance with applicable international and national regulations and standards; and

(j) measures to address public health risks associated with the emergence and spread of pathogens that are resistant to antimicrobial agents, facilitating affordable and equitable access to antimicrobials and promoting appropriate, prudent, and responsible use across relevant sectors

3. The Parties recognize that a range of environmental, climatic, social, anthropogenic and economic factors, including hunger and poverty, may increase the risk of pandemics, and shall endeavour to consider these factors in the development and implementation of relevant policies, strategies, plans, and/or measures, at the international, regional and national levels as appropriate, in accordance with national and/or domestic law and applicable international law.

4. The Conference of the Parties shall develop and adopt guidelines, recommendations and other non-binding measures as necessary, to promote the effective implementation of the provisions set out in paragraphs 1 and 2 of this Article, consistent with the provisions of the International Health Regulations (2005), following, as appropriate, a One Health approach, with full consideration of the national circumstances and the different capacities and capabilities of Parties, as well as the need for capacity-building and implementation support for developing country Parties.

5. The Conference of the Parties, through its work in relation to the provisions of this Article, shall address, inter alia, cooperation for implementation, in particular through technical assistance, capacity-building, research collaboration, facilitating equitable access to relevant products and tools, technology transfer as mutually agreed,[8] and financing in line with the provisions of the WHO Pandemic Agreement; and cooperation to support global, regional and national initiatives aimed at preventing public health emergencies of international concern, including pandemic emergencies, with particular consideration given to developing country Parties.
6. Technical support in implementing this Article, in particular to developing country Parties, as appropriate and upon request, shall be facilitated by the World Health Organization, in collaboration with other relevant intergovernmental organizations.

Article 5 One Health approach for Pandemic Prevention, Preparedness and Response

1. The Parties shall promote a One Health approach for pandemic prevention, preparedness and response, recognizing that the health of people is interconnected with animal health and the environment, that is coherent, integrated, coordinated and collaborative among all relevant organizations, sectors and actors, as appropriate, in accordance with national and/or domestic law, and applicable international law, and taking into account national circumstances.
2. The Parties shall take measures, as appropriate aimed at identifying and addressing, in accordance with national and/or domestic law, and applicable international law, the drivers of pandemics and the emergence and re-emergence of infectious disease at the human-animal- environment interface, through the introduction and integration of interventions into relevant pandemic prevention, preparedness and response plans subject to the availability of resources.
3. Each Party shall, in accordance with national and/or domestic law and taking into account national and regional contexts, and subject to the availability of resources, take measures that it considers appropriate, aimed at promoting human, animal and environmental health, with support, as necessary and upon request, from the World Health Organization and other relevant intergovernmental organizations, including by:
   (a) developing, implementing and reviewing relevant national policies and strategies that reflect a One Health approach as it relates to pandemic prevention, preparedness and response, including promoting engagement of communities, in accordance with Article 15.3(a); and

(b) promoting or establishing joint training and continuing education programmes for the workforce at the human-animal-environment interface to build relevant and complementary skills, capacities and capabilities, in accordance with a One Health approach.

For the purposes of the WHO Pandemic Agreement, "as mutually agreed" means willingly undertaken and on mutually agreed terms, without prejudice to the rights and obligations of the Parties under other international agreements.

Article 6 Preparedness, readiness and health system resilience

1. Each Party, within the means and resources at its disposal, shall take appropriate measures to develop, strengthen and maintain a resilient health system, particularly primary health care, for pandemic prevention, preparedness and response, taking into account the need for equity and in line with Article 17, to achieve universal health coverage.
2. Each Party, within the means and resources at its disposal, shall take appropriate measures, in accordance with its national and/or domestic law, to develop or strengthen, sustain and monitor health system functions and infrastructure for:
   (a) the timely provision of equitable access to scalable clinical care and quality routine essential health care services, while maintaining public health functions and, as appropriate, social measures during pandemics, with a focus on primary health care, mental health and psychosocial support and with particular attention to persons in vulnerable situations;
   (b) national or, as appropriate, regional capacities to adopt transparent, cost-effective procurement practices and supply chain management of pandemic-related health products;
   (c) laboratory and diagnostic capacities, through the application of relevant standards and protocols, including for laboratory biological risk management, and as appropriate, participation in regional and global networks;
   (d) promoting the use of social and behavioural sciences, risk communication and community engagement for pandemic prevention, preparedness and response; and
   (e) post-pandemic health system recovery.
3. Each Party, collaborating with the World Health Organization, shall endeavour towards developing, strengthening and maintaining national health information systems, in accordance with national and/or domestic law, subject to the availability of resources, including through use of relevant international data standards for interoperability, as appropriate, based on good data governance for preventing, detecting and responding to public health events.

4. Each Party shall monitor its preparedness capacities, and periodically assess, if needed with technical support from the Secretariat of the World Health Organization upon request, the functioning and readiness of, and gaps in, its pandemic prevention, preparedness and response capacities.

Article 7 Health and care workforce

1. Each Party, in line with its respective capacities and national circumstances, shall take the appropriate measures with the aim to develop, strengthen, protect, safeguard, retain and invest in a multidisciplinary, skilled, adequate, trained, domestic health and care workforce to prevent, prepare for and respond to health emergencies, including in humanitarian settings, while maintaining essential health care services and essential public health functions at all times and during pandemic emergencies.
2. Each Party, taking into account its national circumstances, and in accordance with its international obligations, shall take appropriate measures to ensure decent work, protect the continued safety, mental health, well-being, and strengthen capacity of its health and care workforce, including by:
   (a) facilitating priority access to pandemic-related health products during pandemic emergencies;
   (b) eliminating all forms of inequalities and discrimination and other disparities, such as unequal remuneration and barriers faced by women;
   (c) addressing harassment, violence and threats;
   (d) supporting individual and collective empowerment; and
   (e) developing policies for work-related injury, disability or death during emergency response.
3. Each Party shall endeavour to strengthen national capacities and designate or establish, as appropriate, national, subnational and/or regional level multidisciplinary emergency health teams. Building on this, the Parties shall take measures, within their capacities and capabilities, in coordination with the World Health Organization and other relevant international and regional organizations, with the aim to strengthen, sustain and mobilize a skilled, trained and multidisciplinary global health emergency workforce to support Member States, including through deployment, upon their request.
4. The Parties shall collaborate, as appropriate, and in accordance with their national and/or domestic law, through multilateral and bilateral mechanisms, to minimize the negative impact of health and care workforce migration on health systems while respecting the freedom of movement of health professionals, taking into account the World Health Organization health workforce support and safeguards list and applicable international codes and standards, including

those of a voluntary nature, such as the World Health Organization Global Code of Practice on the International Recruitment of Health Personnel.[9]

5. The Parties, taking into account national circumstances, shall take appropriate measures in order to ensure decent work and a safe and healthy environment for other essential workers who provide essential public goods and services during pandemic emergencies. The Parties, taking into account national circumstances, shall also take measures to develop and implement coordinated policies for the safety and protection of transport and supply chain workers, as appropriate, by facilitating the transit and transfer of seafarers and transport workers, among others, and their access to medical care.

Article 8 Regulatory systems strengthening

1. Each Party shall strengthen its national and, where appropriate, regional regulatory authority responsible for the authorization and approval of pandemic-related health products, including through technical assistance from, and cooperation with the World Health Organization, and other international organizations upon request and other Parties as appropriate, with the aim of ensuring the quality, safety and efficacy of such products.

Reference to the aforementioned Global Code of Practice does not alter its voluntary nature.

2. Each Party shall take steps towards ensuring that it has the technical capacity, and legal, administrative, and financial frameworks, as appropriate, in support of:
   (a) expedited regulatory review and/or emergency regulatory authorization, and oversight of pandemic-related health products, consistent with applicable law; and
   (b) effective vigilance to monitor the safety and effectiveness of pandemic-related health products.
3. Each Party shall, in accordance with applicable national and/or domestic law, as appropriate, make publicly available and keep updated:
   (a) information on national and, if applicable, regional regulatory processes for authorizing or approving the use of pandemic-related health products; and
   (b) information on the pandemic-related health products that it has authorized or approved, including relevant additional information about the authorization or approval.

4. Each Party shall endeavour, subject to applicable national and/or domestic law, to adopt, where needed, regulatory reliance mechanisms in its national and, where appropriate, regional regulatory frameworks for use during public health emergencies of international concern, including pandemic emergencies, for pandemic-related health products taking into account relevant guidelines.
5. Each Party shall, as appropriate and consistent with applicable law, encourage relevant developers and manufacturers of pandemic-related health products to diligently seek regulatory authorizations and approvals from national and/or regional regulatory authorities, including World Health Organization listed authorities, and prequalification of such products by the World Health Organization.
6. The Parties shall collaborate, as appropriate, towards improving the World Health Organization processes for Emergency Use Listing, prequalification and any other relevant World Health Organization processes for recommending the use of pandemic-related health products.
7. The Parties shall, as appropriate, monitor and strengthen rapid alert systems and take regulatory measures to respond to substandard and falsified pandemic-related health products.
8. The Parties shall endeavour to, subject to applicable law:
   (a) cooperate with a view to align, where appropriate, relevant technical and regulatory requirements in accordance with applicable international standards and guidance; and
   (b) provide support to help strengthen national regulatory authorities' and regional regulatory systems' capacity to respond to pandemic emergencies, subject to available resources.

Article 9 Research and development

1. The Parties shall cooperate, as appropriate, to build, strengthen and sustain geographically diverse capacities and institutions for research and development, particularly in developing countries, and shall promote research collaboration, access to research, and rapid sharing of research information and results, especially during public health emergencies of international concern, including pandemic emergencies.
2. To this end, the Parties shall promote, within means and resources at their disposal, and in accordance with national and/or domestic law and policy:
   (a) sustained investment and support for research institutions and networks that can rapidly adapt and respond to research and development needs in the event of a pandemic emergency, and for research and development for public health priorities, including: (i) the epidemiology of emerging infectious diseases, factors driving zoonotic disease spill-over or emergence, and

social and behavioural science; (ii) the management of pandemics, such as public health and social measures as well as their effects and socioeconomic impacts; and
(iii) pandemic-related health products, including promoting equitable access;

(b) scientific research programmes, projects and partnerships, including through technology co-creation, and joint venture initiatives, with the active participation of, and international and regional collaboration with, scientists and research institutions and centres, particularly from developing countries;
(c) generation of and equitable access to evidence synthesis, knowledge translation and evidence-based communication tools, strategies and partnerships, relating to pandemic prevention, preparedness and response;
(d) the sharing of information on research agendas, priorities, capacity-building activities, and best practices, relevant to the implementation of the WHO Pandemic Agreement, including during pandemic emergencies;
(e) capacity-building programmes, projects and partnerships, and sustained support for all phases of research and development, including basic and applied research;
(f) accelerating innovative research and development consistent with applicable biosafety and biosecurity obligations, laws, and regulations, as well as taking into account, as appropriate, relevant standards and guidance; and
(g) the participation of relevant stakeholders in accelerating research and development.

3. Each Party shall, in accordance with its national or domestic circumstances and law, and taking into account relevant national and international ethical guidelines and guidance, promote, during public health emergencies of international concern, including pandemic emergencies, the conduct of well-designed and well-implemented clinical trials in its jurisdiction, including by:

(i) promoting representative trial populations; (ii) promoting, as appropriate, sharing of pandemic- related vaccines, therapeutics and diagnostics for use as comparator products[10] in the conduct of clinical trials of pandemic-related vaccines, therapeutics and diagnostics; and (iii) promoting access to safe and effective products that result from these trials for such trial populations and for populations at risk in its communities.

4. Each Party shall, pursuant to paragraph 1 of this Article, in accordance with national and/or domestic law and policies, and taking into account relevant international standards, support the. For the purposes of this paragraph, "comparator product" means an investigational or marketed product (i.e., active control), or

placebo, used as a reference in a clinical trial. rapid and transparent publication of clinical trial protocols and other research results related to the implementation of the WHO Pandemic Agreement.

5. Each Party shall develop and implement national and/or regional policies, adapted to its domestic circumstances, regarding the inclusion of provisions in publicly funded research and development grants, contracts, and other similar funding arrangements, particularly with private entities and public-private partnerships, for the development of pandemic-related health products, that promote timely and equitable access to such products, particularly for developing countries, during public health emergencies of international concern, including pandemic emergencies, and regarding the publication of such provisions. Such provisions may include:
   (i) licensing and/or sublicensing, particularly to manufacturers of developing countries and for the benefit of developing countries, preferably on a non-exclusive basis; (ii) affordable pricing policies; (iii) provisions enabling access to technology to facilitate research and development and geographically diversified local production (iv) publication of relevant information on clinical trial protocols and relevant research results; and (v) adherence to product allocation frameworks adopted by the World Health Organization.

Article 10 Sustainable and geographically diversified local production

1. The Parties shall take measures, as appropriate, to achieve more equitable geographical distribution and rapid scale-up of the global production of pandemic-related health products and increase sustainable, timely and equitable access to such products, as well as reduce the potential gap between supply and demand during pandemic emergencies, including through the measures provided in Articles 11 and 13.
2. The Parties, in collaboration with the World Health Organization and other relevant organizations, shall, as appropriate and subject to national and/or domestic law:
   (a) take measures, to provide support for, and/or strengthen, existing or newly created production facilities of relevant health products, at national and regional levels, particularly in developing countries, with a view to promoting the sustainability of such geographically diversified production facilities, including through supporting and/or facilitating skills development, capacity-building and other initiatives for production facilities;
   (b) facilitate the continuous and sustainable operations of local and regional manufacturers, especially of developing countries, including through pro-

moting transparency of relevant information on pandemic-related health products and raw materials across the value chain that is not subject to protection under relevant domestic and international law;

(c) actively support relevant World Health Organization technology, skills and knowledge transfer and local production programmes, including those referenced in Article 11, and other relevant programmes, to facilitate sustainable, and strategically and geographically distributed, production of pandemic-related health products, particularly in developing countries;

(d) promote or incentivize public and private sector investments, purchasing arrangements, and partnerships, including public-private partnerships, aimed at creating or expanding manufacturing facilities or capacities for pandemic-related health products, including facilities with a regional operational scope in developing countries;

(e) encourage international organizations and other relevant organizations to establish arrangements, including appropriate long-term contracts for pandemic-related health products, including through procurement from facilities referenced under subparagraph 2(a) of this Article and pursuant to the objectives of Article 13, especially those produced by local and/or regional manufacturers in developing countries; and

(f) during pandemic emergencies, in cases where the capacity of facilities referred to in subparagraph 2(a) of this Article does not meet demand, take measures to identify and contract with manufacturers with the aim of rapidly scaling up the production of pandemic- related health products.

3. The World Health Organization shall, upon request of the Conference of the Parties, provide assistance to the facilities referenced under paragraph 2 of this Article, including, as appropriate, with respect to training, capacity-building, and timely support for development and production of pandemic-related products, especially in developing countries, with the aim to achieve geographically diversified production.

Article 11 Transfer of technology and cooperation on related know-how for the production of pandemic-related health products

1. Each Party shall, in order to enable the sustainable and geographically diversified production of pandemic-related health products for the attainment of the objective of the WHO Pandemic Agreement, as appropriate:

(a) promote and otherwise facilitate or incentivize, transfer of technology as mutually agreed,[11] including transfer of relevant knowledge, skills, technical expertise, and cooperation on any other related know-how for production of pandemic-related health products, in particular for the benefit of developing countries, through measures which may include, inter alia, licensing, capacity-building, relationship facilitating, incentives or conditions linked to research and development, procurement or other funding and regulatory policy measures;

(b) take measures to enhance the availability of licences for pandemic-related health technologies to which it owns the rights, on a non-exclusive, transparent and broad geographic basis and for the benefit of developing countries, where and as feasible, in accordance with national and/or domestic law, and international law and encourage private rights holders to do the same;

(c) take measures to publish, in a timely manner the terms of its licensing agreements relevant to promoting timely and equitable global access to pandemic-related health technologies, in accordance with applicable law and policies, and shall encourage private rights holders to do the same;

(d) encourage holders of relevant patents or licences for the production of pandemic- related health products to forgo or otherwise charge reasonable royalties in particular to developing country manufacturers during a pandemic emergency, with the aim to increase the availability and affordability of such products to populations in need, in particular people in vulnerable situations;

(e) promote the transfer of relevant technology as mutually agreed,[12] including transfer of relevant knowledge, skills and technical expertise, for pandemic-related health products by private rights holders, to established regional or global technology transfer hubs, coordinated by the World Health Organization, or other mechanisms or networks; and

(f) during pandemic emergencies, encourage manufacturers to share information, relevant to the production of pandemic-related health products, in accordance with national and/or domestic law and policies.

2. Each Party shall provide, as appropriate and subject to available resources and applicable law, support for capacity-building, especially to local, subregional and/or regional developing country manufacturers, for the implementation of this Article.

3. The Parties shall cooperate, as appropriate, with regard to time-bound measures to which they have agreed within the framework of relevant international and regional organizations to which they are a party, to accelerate or scale up the manufacturing of pandemic-related health products, to the extent necessary to increase the availability, accessibility and affordability of pandemic-related health products during pandemic emergencies.

4. The Parties that are World Trade Organization members reaffirm that they have the right to use, to the full, the World Trade Organization Agreement on Trade-Related Aspects of Intellectual Property Rights and the Doha Declaration on

the TRIPS Agreement and Public Health of 2001, which provide flexibility to protect public health including in future pandemics. The Parties shall respect the use of these flexibilities that is consistent with the World Trade Organization Agreement on Trade-Related Aspects of Intellectual Property Rights.

5. The Parties shall, in collaboration with the World Health Organization, identify, assess and, as appropriate, strengthen and/or develop mechanisms and initiatives that promote and facilitate the transfer of technology as mutually agreed,[13] with a view to increasing access to pandemic- related health products, particularly in developing countries, including through the pooling of intellectual property, relevant knowledge, skills and technical expertise and data and transparent, non-exclusive licensing. Such mechanisms may, where appropriate, be coordinated by the World Health Organization, in collaboration with other relevant mechanisms and organizations, enabling increased participation of manufacturers from developing countries.
6. Each Party should review and consider amending, as appropriate, its national and/or domestic legislation with a view to ensuring that it is able to implement this Article in a timely and effective manner.

Article 12 Pathogen Access and Benefit-Sharing System

1. Recognizing the sovereign right of States over their biological resources and the importance of collective action to mitigate public health risks, and underscoring the importance of promoting the rapid and timely sharing of "materials and sequence information on pathogens with pandemic potential" (hereinafter "PABS Materials and Sequence Information") and, on an equal footing, the rapid, timely, fair and equitable sharing of benefits arising from the sharing and/or utilization of PABS Materials and Sequence Information for public health purposes, the Parties hereby establish multilateral system for safe, transparent, and accountable access and benefit-sharing for PABS Materials and Sequence Information, the "WHO Pathogen Access and Benefit-Sharing System" (hereinafter the "PABS System"), to be developed pursuant to paragraph 2 of this Article.
2. The provisions governing the PABS System, including definitions of pathogens with pandemic potential and PABS Materials and Sequence Information, modalities, legal nature, terms and conditions, and operational dimensions, shall be developed and agreed in an instrument in accordance with Chapter III (hereinafter the "PABS Instrument") as an annex. The PABS Instrument shall also define the terms for the administration and coordination of the PABS System by the World Health Organization. For the purposes of the coordination and operation of the PABS System, the World Health Organization shall collaborate with

relevant international organizations[14] and relevant stakeholders. All elements of the PABS System shall come into operation simultaneously in accordance with the terms of the PABS Instrument.

3. Taking into account the differences in the use of PABS Materials and Sequence Information, the development of a safe, accountable and transparent PABS System shall address traceability measures and open access to data.
4. Having regard to Article 4.4 of the Nagoya Protocol on Access to Genetic Resources and the Fair and Equitable Sharing of Benefits arising from their utilization to the Convention on Biological Diversity (hereinafter the "Nagoya Protocol"), the PABS Instrument shall be consistent with, and not run counter to, the objectives of the Convention on Biological Diversity and the Nagoya Protocol, recognising that nothing in this paragraph creates obligations under these instruments for non-Parties thereto.
5. The PABS Instrument referred to in paragraph 2 of this Article, shall contain provisions regarding, inter alia, the following:
   (a) the rapid and timely sharing of PABS Materials and Sequence Information and, on an equal footing, the rapid, timely, fair and equitable sharing of benefits, both monetary and non-monetary, including annual monetary contributions, vaccines, therapeutics and diagnostics arising from the sharing and/or utilization of PABS Materials and Sequence Information for public health purposes;
   (b) modalities, terms and conditions on access and benefit sharing that provide legal certainty;
   (c) implementation in a manner to strengthen, facilitate and accelerate research and innovation, as well as the fair and equitable sharing and distribution of benefits;
   (d) development and implementation in a manner:
      (i) complementary to, and not duplicative of, the access and benefit sharing measures and obligations of the Pandemic Influenza Preparedness Framework and other relevant international access and benefit sharing instruments, where applicable; and

In the context of collaboration with the World Health Organization, "relevant international organizations" is understood in accordance with the Constitution of the World Health Organization.

      (ii) to ensure that each Party reviews and, as it deems appropriate, aligns its national and/or regional access and benefit sharing measures applicable to PABS Materials and Sequence Information within the scope of the PABS Instrument, so that measures that are contrary to, or inconsistent with, or duplicative of, the PABS Instrument will not be applied upon entry into operation of all elements of the PABS System.

(e) implementation consistent with applicable international law and with applicable national and/or domestic law, regulations and standards related to risk assessment, biosafety, biosecurity and export control of pathogens, and data protection; and

(f) implementation in a manner to facilitate the manufacture and export of vaccines, therapeutics and diagnostics for pathogens covered by the PABS Instrument.

6. The PABS System, as set out in the Annex referred to in paragraph 2 of this Article, shall provide, inter alia, that in the event of a pandemic emergency, as determined in accordance with Article 12 of the International Health Regulations (2005):

(a) each participating manufacturer[15] shall make available to the World Health Organization, pursuant to legally binding contracts signed with the World Health Organization, rapid access targeting 20% of their real time production of safe, quality and effective vaccines, therapeutics, and diagnostics for the pathogen causing the pandemic emergency, provided that a minimum threshold of 10% of their real time production is made available to the World Health Organization as a donation, and the remaining percentage, with flexibility based on the nature and capacity of each participating manufacturer, is reserved at affordable prices to the World Health Organization; and

(b) the distribution of these vaccines, therapeutics, and diagnostics shall be on the basis of public health risk and need, with particular attention to the needs of developing countries, and the Global Supply Chain and Logistics Network referred to in Article 13 may be used to this end.

7. The PABS Instrument shall also include benefit sharing provisions, in the event of a public health emergency of international concern as determined in accordance with Article 12 of the International Health Regulations (2005), including options regarding access to safe, quality and effective vaccines, therapeutics, and diagnostics for the pathogen causing the public health emergency of international concern, pursuant to legally binding contracts signed by participating manufacturers with the World Health Organization.

8. The PABS Instrument shall also include additional benefit sharing provisions to be set out in legally binding contracts signed with the World Health Organization, including options for:

(a) Capacity-building and technical assistance;

(b) research and development cooperation;

The term "participating manufacturer" to be defined in the PABS instrument.

(c) facilitating rapid access to available vaccines, therapeutics and diagnostics with a view to responding to public health risks and events in the context of Article 13.3 of the International Health Regulations (2005);
(d) the granting of non-exclusive licences to manufacturers in developing countries, for the effective production and delivery of vaccines, therapeutics and diagnostics; and
(e) other forms of transfer of technology as mutually agreed,[16] including transfer of relevant knowledge, skills and technical expertise.

9. This Article is without prejudice to consideration of other elements for the effective operationalization of the PABS System in a fair, transparent, accountable and equitable manner.

Article 13 Supply chain and logistics

1. The "Global Supply Chain and Logistics Network" (hereinafter the "GSCL Network") is hereby established to enhance, facilitate, and work to remove barriers and ensure equitable, timely, rapid, safe, and affordable access to pandemic-related health products for countries in need during public health emergencies of international concern, including pandemic emergencies, and for prevention of such emergencies. The GSCL Network shall be developed, coordinated and convened by the World Health Organization in full consultation with the Parties, World Health Organization Member States that are not Parties, and in partnership with relevant stakeholders, under the oversight of the Conference of the Parties. The Parties shall prioritize, as appropriate, sharing pandemic-related health products through the GSCL Network for equitable allocation based on public health risk and need, in particular during pandemic emergencies.
2. The Conference of the Parties shall, at its first meeting, define the structure, functions and modalities of the GSCL Network, with the aim of ensuring the following:
   (a) collaboration among the Parties and other relevant stakeholders during and between pandemic emergencies;
   (b) the functions of the GSCL Network are discharged by the organizations best placed to perform them;
   (c) consideration of the needs of persons in vulnerable situations, including those in fragile and humanitarian settings, and the needs of developing countries;
   (d) the equitable and timely allocation of pandemic-related health products, based on public health risk and need, including through procurement from the facilities referenced under Article 10; and

(e) accountability, transparency, and inclusiveness in the functioning and governance of the GSCL Network allowing for equitable representation of the World Health Organization Regions.

3. The functions of the GSCL Network shall include, inter alia, subject to further decision-making by the Conference of the Parties with respect to further tasks that may be assigned to the GSCL Network:
   (a) identification of pandemic-related health products and relevant raw material sources;
   (b) identification of barriers to their access;
   (c) estimation of their supply and demand;
   (d) facilitation of procurement of pandemic-related health products and relevant raw materials, including from facilities referenced under Article 10, during public health emergencies of international concern, including pandemic emergencies;
   (e) coordination of relevant procurement agencies within the GSCL Network and pre-pandemic preparatory work;
   (f) promotion of transparency across the value chain;
   (g) collaboration on stockpiling both during pandemic emergencies and inter-pandemic periods to, inter alia, promote the establishment of international and regional emergency stockpiles, strengthen existing stockpiles, facilitate effective and efficient stockpiling operations and increase equitable and timely access to pandemic-related health products;
   (h) initiation and facilitation of the rapid release from international stockpiles of relevant health products in the event of outbreaks, especially to developing countries, to prevent outbreaks from progressing into public health emergencies of international concern, including pandemic emergencies; and
   (i) facilitation of, and working to remove barriers to, timely and equitable access to pandemic-related health products, through allocation, distribution, delivery, and assistance with utilization, including for products provided to the PABS System, during public health emergencies of international concern, including pandemic emergencies, with special regard to needs in humanitarian settings.
4. The Conference of the Parties shall periodically review the functions and operations of the GSCL Network, including the support provided by the Parties, World Health Organization Member States that are not Parties to the WHO Pandemic Agreement, and relevant stakeholders, during and between pandemic emergencies and may provide further guidance related to its operations.

5. The World Health Organization, as the convener of the GSCL Network, shall report to the Conference of the Parties, at intervals to be determined by the Conference of the Parties.

Article 14 Procurement and distribution

1. Each Party shall endeavour, as appropriate, during a pandemic, in accordance with national and/or domestic law and policies, to publish the relevant terms of its purchase agreements with manufacturers for pandemic-related health products at the earliest reasonable opportunity, and to exclude confidentiality provisions that serve to limit such disclosure. The Parties shall take steps to encourage regional and global purchasing mechanisms to do the same.
2. Each Party shall, in accordance with national and/or domestic law and policies, consider including provisions in its publicly funded purchase agreements for pandemic-related health products that promote timely and equitable access especially for developing countries, such as provisions regarding donation, delivery modification, licensing and global access plans.
3. During a pandemic, each Party shall consider setting aside a portion of its total procurement of, or making other necessary arrangements for the procurement of, relevant diagnostics, therapeutics or vaccines in a timely manner for use in countries facing challenges in meeting public health needs and demand.
4. The Parties recognize the importance of ensuring that emergency trade measures designed to respond to a pandemic emergency are targeted, proportionate, transparent and temporary, and do not create unnecessary barriers to trade or disruptions in supply chains.
5. Each Party shall take measures, as appropriate, including with support of the GSCL Network, to promote rational use and reduce the waste of pandemic-related health products, in order to support and facilitate the effective global distribution, delivery, and administration of pandemic-related health products.
6. During a pandemic emergency, each Party should avoid maintaining national stockpiles of pandemic-related health products that unnecessarily exceed the quantities anticipated to be needed for domestic pandemic preparedness and response.
7. Whenever possible and appropriate, when sharing pandemic-related health products with countries, organizations or any mechanism that is facilitated by the GSCL Network, each Party shall endeavour to do the following: provide product that is unearmarked and accompanied by necessary ancillaries, has sufficient shelf life, and is in line with the needs and capacities of recipients; provide recipients with expiration dates, information about required ancillaries, and other similar information; coordinate between and among the Parties and any

access mechanism; and provide product in large volumes and in a predictable manner.

Article 15 Whole-of-government and whole-of-society approaches

1. The Parties are encouraged to apply whole-of-government and whole-of-society approaches at the national level, including, according to national circumstances, to empower and enable community ownership of, and contribution to, community readiness for and resilience to pandemic prevention, preparedness and response.
2. Each Party is urged to establish or strengthen, and maintain, a national multi-sectoral coordination mechanism for pandemic prevention, preparedness and response.
3. Each Party shall, taking into account its national circumstances:
   (a) promote and facilitate the effective and meaningful engagement of Indigenous Peoples, communities, including local communities as appropriate, and relevant stakeholders, including through social participation, as part of a whole-of-society approach in planning, decision-making, implementation, monitoring and evaluation of policies, strategies and measures, and also provide feedback opportunities; and
   (b) take appropriate measures to mitigate the socioeconomic impacts of pandemics and strengthen national public health and social policies including those for social protection, to facilitate a rapid, inclusive, resilient response to pandemics, especially for people in vulnerable situations, including by mobilizing social capital in communities for mutual support.
4. Each Party shall develop, in accordance with national and/or domestic context, comprehensive, multisectoral, and, as appropriate, regional, and national pandemic prevention, preparedness and response plan(s) that address pre-, post- and inter-pandemic periods, in a transparent and inclusive manner that promotes collaboration with relevant stakeholders.
5. Each Party shall promote and facilitate, where appropriate, and in accordance with national and/or domestic law and policy, the development and implementation of education and community engagement initiatives and programmes on pandemic and public health emergencies, with the participation of relevant stakeholders in a way that is inclusive and accessible, including to people in vulnerable situations.

Article 16 Communication and public awareness

1. Each Party shall, as appropriate, take measures to strengthen science, public health and pandemic literacy in the population, as well as access to transpar-

ent, timely, accurate, science- and evidence-based information on pandemics and their causes, impacts and drivers, as well as on the efficacy and safety of pandemic-related health products, particularly through risk communication and effective community-level engagement.

2. Each Party shall, as appropriate, conduct research and inform policies on factors that hinder or strengthen adherence to public health and social measures in a pandemic and trust in science and public health institutions, authorities and agencies.
3. In furtherance of paragraphs 1 and 2 of this Article, the World Health Organization shall, as appropriate and upon request, continue to provide technical support to Parties, especially developing countries towards communication and public awareness of pandemic-related measures.

Article 17 International cooperation and support for implementation

1. The Parties shall cooperate, directly or through relevant international organizations, subject to national and/or domestic law and available resources, to sustainably strengthen the pandemic prevention, preparedness and response capacities of all Parties, particularly developing country Parties. Such cooperation shall include, inter alia, the promotion of the transfer of technology as mutually agreed,[17] including transfer of relevant knowledge, skills, and technical expertise, and the sharing of technical, scientific and legal expertise, as well as financial assistance and support for capacity-strengthening for those Parties that lack the means and resources to implement the provisions of the WHO Pandemic Agreement, and shall be facilitated, as appropriate, by the World Health Organization in collaboration with relevant organizations upon the request of the Party, to fulfil the obligations arising from this Agreement.
2. Particular consideration shall be given to the specific needs and circumstances of developing country Parties, identifying and enabling access to sustainable and predictable means necessary to support the implementation of the provisions of the WHO Pandemic Agreement.
3. The Parties shall collaborate and cooperate for pandemic prevention, preparedness and response through strengthening and enhancing cooperation among relevant legal instruments and frameworks, and relevant organizations and stakeholders, as appropriate, in the achievement of the objective of the WHO Pandemic Agreement, while closely coordinating support with that provided under the International Health Regulations (2005).

Article 18 Sustainable financing

1. The Parties shall strengthen sustainable and predictable financing to the extent feasible, in an inclusive and transparent manner, for the implementation of the WHO Pandemic Agreement.
2. In this regard, each Party, subject to national and/or domestic law and available resources, shall:
   (a) maintain or increase domestic funding, as necessary, for pandemic prevention, preparedness and response;
   (b) work to mobilize additional financial resources to support Parties, in particular developing country Parties, in the implementation of the WHO Pandemic Agreement, including through grants;
   (c) promote, as appropriate, within relevant bilateral, regional and/or multilateral funding mechanisms, innovative financing measures, including transparent financial reprogramming plans for pandemic prevention, preparedness and response, especially for developing country Parties experiencing fiscal constraints; and
   (d) encourage inclusive and accountable governance and operating models of existing financing entities to minimize the burden on countries, offer improved efficiency and coherence at scale, enhance transparency and be responsive to the needs and national priorities of developing countries.
3. A "Coordinating Financial Mechanism" (hereinafter "the Mechanism") is hereby established to promote sustainable financing for the implementation of the WHO Pandemic Agreement, to support strengthening and expanding capacities for pandemic prevention, preparedness and response, and contribute to the prompt availability of surge financing response necessary as of day zero, particularly in developing country Parties. The Coordinating Financial Mechanism established under the International Health Regulations (2005) shall be utilized as the Mechanism to serve the implementation of the WHO Pandemic Agreement, in a manner determined by the Conference of the Parties. In this regard, and for the purposes of the implementation of the WHO Pandemic Agreement:
   (a) the Mechanism shall function under the authority and guidance of the Conference of the Parties and be accountable to it;
   (b) the Mechanism's operation may be supported by one or more international entities to be selected by the Conference of the Parties. The Conference of the Parties may adopt necessary working arrangements with other international entities; and
   (c) the Conference of the Parties shall adopt by consensus terms of reference for the Mechanism and modalities for its operationalization and governance

in relation to the implementation of the WHO Pandemic Agreement, within 12 months after entry into force of the WHO Pandemic Agreement.

4. In giving effect to paragraph 3 of this Article, the Conference of the Parties shall request the Mechanism to, inter alia:
   (a) conduct relevant needs and gaps analyses to support strategic decision-making and develop every five years a financial and implementation strategy for the WHO Pandemic Agreement, which shall be submitted to the Conference of the Parties for its consideration;
   (b) promote harmonization, coherence and coordination for financing pandemic prevention, preparedness and response and the International Health Regulations (2005)-related capacities;
   (c) identify all sources of financing that are available to serve the purposes of supporting the implementation of the WHO Pandemic Agreement, and maintain a dashboard of such sources and related information and the funds allocated to countries from these sources;
   (d) provide advice and support, upon request, to Parties in identifying and applying for financial resources for strengthening pandemic prevention, preparedness and response; and
   (e) leverage voluntary monetary contributions for organizations and other entities supporting pandemic prevention, preparedness and response, free from conflicts of interest, from relevant stakeholders, in particular those active in sectors that benefit from international work to strengthen pandemic prevention, preparedness and response.
5. The Conference of the Parties shall take appropriate measures to give effect to this Article, including the possibility of exploring additional financial resources to support the implementation of the WHO Pandemic Agreement, through all sources of funding, existing and new, including innovative sources and those beyond official development assistance.
6. The Conference of the Parties shall periodically consider, as appropriate, the financial and implementation strategy for the WHO Pandemic Agreement referred to in subparagraph 4(a) of this Article. The Parties shall endeavour to align with the aforementioned strategy, as appropriate, when providing external financial support for the strengthening of pandemic prevention, preparedness and response.

Chapter III. Institutional arrangements and final provisions

Article 19 Conference of the Parties

1. A Conference of the Parties is hereby established.

2. The Conference of the Parties shall regularly take stock of the implementation of the WHO Pandemic Agreement and review its functioning every five years, and shall take the decisions necessary to promote its effective implementation. To this end, it shall take actions, as appropriate, for the achievement of the objective of the WHO Pandemic Agreement, including by engaging with the States Parties Committee for the Implementation of the International Health Regulations (2005).
3. The first session of the Conference of the Parties shall be convened by the World Health Organization not later than one year after the entry into force of the WHO Pandemic Agreement. The Conference of the Parties will determine the venue and timing of subsequent regular sessions at its first session.
4. The Conference of the Parties may establish subsidiary bodies, and determine the terms and modalities of such bodies, as well as decide upon delegating functions to bodies established under other agreements adopted under the Constitution of the World Health Organization, as it deems appropriate.
5. The Conference of the Parties at its second meeting shall consider and approve the establishment of a mechanism to facilitate and strengthen effective implementation of the provisions of the WHO Pandemic Agreement. In doing so, the Conference of the Parties may take into account other relevant mechanisms, including those under the International Health Regulations (2005).
6. This mechanism shall:
   (a) be facilitative in nature, and function in a manner that is transparent, cooperative, non-adversarial, non-punitive and cognizant of respective national circumstances;
   (b) consider the reports referred to in Article 21.1, and make non-binding recommendations, including on support to be given to a Party to facilitate implementation;
   (c) operate under the rules of procedure/terms of reference adopted by consensus by the Conference of the Parties at its second meeting; and
   (d) report periodically to the Conference of the Parties.
7. Extraordinary sessions of the Conference of the Parties shall be held at such other times as may be deemed necessary by the Conference of the Parties or at the written request of any Party, provided that, within six months of the request being communicated in writing to the Parties by the Secretariat, it is supported by at least one third of the Parties. Such extraordinary sessions may be called at the level of heads of State or government.
8. The Conference of the Parties shall, at its first session, adopt by consensus its rules of procedure and its criteria for the participation of observers at its proceedings.

9. The Conference of the Parties shall adopt by consensus its financial rules, which shall be applied to any subsidiary bodies it may establish, and shall consider for that purpose the Financial Regulations and Rules of the World Health Organization. It shall adopt by consensus a budget for each financial period.

Article 20 Right to vote

1. Each Party to the WHO Pandemic Agreement shall have one vote, except as provided for in paragraph 2 of this Article.
2. A regional economic integration organization that is Party to the WHO Pandemic Agreement, in matters within its competence, shall exercise its right to vote with a number of votes equal to the number of its Member States that are Parties to the WHO Pandemic Agreement. Such an organization shall not exercise its right to vote if any of its Member States exercises its right to vote, and vice versa.

Article 21 Reports to the Conference of the Parties

1. Each Party shall report periodically to the Conference of the Parties, through the Secretariat, on its implementation of the WHO Pandemic Agreement. The Secretariat shall report to the Conference of the Parties on its activities with respect to the implementation of the WHO Pandemic Agreement.
2. The information required, frequency and format of the reports in paragraph 1 of this Article shall be determined by the Conference of the Parties.
3. The Conference of the Parties shall adopt appropriate measures to assist Parties, upon request, in meeting their obligations under this Article, with particular attention to the needs of developing country Parties.
4. The reporting and exchange of information by the Parties under the WHO Pandemic Agreement shall be subject to national and/or domestic law, as appropriate, regarding confidentiality and privacy. The Parties shall protect, as mutually agreed, any confidential information that is exchanged.
5. Subject to paragraph 4 of this Article, the reports submitted pursuant to this Article shall be made publicly available online by the Secretariat.

Article 22 Secretariat

1. The Secretariat of the World Health Organization shall function as the Secretariat of the WHO Pandemic Agreement and shall perform the functions assigned to it under this Agreement and such other functions as may be determined by the Conference of the Parties. In performing these functions, the Secretariat of the World Health Organization shall, under the guidance of the Conference of the

Parties, ensure the necessary coordination, as appropriate, with the competent international and regional intergovernmental organizations and other relevant bodies.

2. Nothing in the WHO Pandemic Agreement shall be interpreted as providing the Secretariat of the World Health Organization, including the Director-General of the World Health Organization, any authority to direct, order, alter or otherwise prescribe the national and/or domestic law, as appropriate, or policies of any Party, or to mandate or otherwise impose any requirements that Parties take specific actions, such as ban or accept travellers, impose vaccination mandates or therapeutic or diagnostic measures or implement lockdowns.

Article 23 Settlement of disputes

1. In the event of a dispute between two or more Parties concerning the interpretation or application of the WHO Pandemic Agreement, the Parties concerned shall seek through diplomatic channels a settlement of the dispute through negotiation or any other peaceful means of their own choice, including good offices, mediation, or conciliation. In case of failure to reach a solution by the methods mentioned above, the Parties, if they so agree in writing, may resort to arbitration in accordance with the Permanent Court of Arbitration, Arbitration Rules (2012) or its successor rules, unless the disputing Parties agree otherwise.
2. The provisions of this Article shall apply with respect to any protocol adopted under Article 29 within the scope of the WHO Pandemic Agreement as between the Parties to the protocol, unless otherwise provided therein.

Article 24 Relationship with other international agreements

1. The interpretation and application of the WHO Pandemic Agreement shall be guided by the Charter of the United Nations and the Constitution of the World Health Organization.
2. The Parties recognize that the WHO Pandemic Agreement and the International Health Regulations (2005) and other relevant international agreements should be interpreted so as to be compatible.
3. The provisions of the WHO Pandemic Agreement shall not affect the rights and obligations of any Party deriving from other international agreements and legal instruments.

Article 25 Reservations

Reservations may be made to the WHO Pandemic Agreement unless incompatible with the object and purpose of the WHO Pandemic Agreement.

Article 26 Declarations and statements

1. Article 25 does not preclude a State or regional economic integration organization, when signing, ratifying, approving, accepting or acceding to the WHO Pandemic Agreement, from making declarations or statements, however phrased or named, with a view, inter alia, to the harmonization of its laws and regulations with the provisions of the WHO Pandemic Agreement, provided that such declarations or statements do not purport to exclude or to modify the legal effect of the provisions of the WHO Pandemic Agreement in their application to that State or regional economic integration organization.
2. A declaration or statement made pursuant to this Article shall be circulated by the Depositary to all Parties to the WHO Pandemic Agreement.

Article 27 Amendments

1. Any Party may propose amendments to the WHO Pandemic Agreement, including its annexes, and such amendments shall be considered by the Conference of the Parties.
2. The Conference of the Parties may adopt amendments to the WHO Pandemic Agreement. The text of any proposed amendment to the WHO Pandemic Agreement shall be communicated to the Parties by the Secretariat at least six months before the session at which it is proposed for adoption. The Secretariat shall also communicate proposed amendments to the signatories of the WHO Pandemic Agreement and, for information, to the Depositary.
3. The Parties shall make every effort to adopt any proposed amendment to the WHO Pandemic Agreement by consensus. If all efforts at consensus have been exhausted and no agreement has been reached, the amendment may as a last resort be adopted by a three-quarters majority vote of the Parties present and voting at the session. For the purposes of this Article, Parties present and voting means Parties present and casting an affirmative or negative vote. Any adopted amendment shall be communicated by the Secretariat to the Depositary, which shall circulate it to all Parties for acceptance.
4. Instruments of acceptance in respect of an amendment shall be deposited with the Depositary. An amendment adopted in accordance with paragraph 3 of this Article shall enter into force, for those Parties having accepted it, on the ninetieth

day after the date of receipt by the Depositary of an instrument of acceptance by at least two thirds of the Parties to the WHO Pandemic Agreement at the date of the adoption of the amendment.

5. An amendment shall enter into force for any other Party on the ninetieth day after the date on which that Party deposits with the Depositary its instrument of acceptance of the said amendment.
6. For the purposes of this Article, any instrument deposited by a regional economic integration organization shall not be counted as additional to those deposited by the Member States of that organization.

Article 28 Annexes

1. Annexes to the WHO Pandemic Agreement shall form an integral part thereof and, unless otherwise expressly provided, a reference to the WHO Pandemic Agreement constitutes at the same time a reference to any annexes thereto.
2. Annexes to the WHO Pandemic Agreement proposed after its entry into force shall be proposed, adopted and shall enter into force in accordance with the procedure set forth in Article 27.
3. Notwithstanding paragraph 2 of this Article, for annexes of a procedural, scientific, technical or administrative nature, the Conference of the Parties may decide that the following procedure for acceptance and entry into force applies:
   (a) Any Party that does not accept such an annex or its amendment shall so notify the Depositary of its non-acceptance, in writing, within six months from the date of the communication of the adoption by the Depositary. The Depositary shall without delay notify all Parties of any such notification received. A Party may at any time substitute an acceptance for a previous notification of non-acceptance and the annex shall thereupon enter into force for that Party;
   (b) On the expiry of six months from the date of the communication of the adoption by the Depositary, the annex shall enter into force for all Parties which have not submitted a notification of non-acceptance in accordance with the provision of subparagraph 3(a) of this Article.
4. The same procedure shall also apply for any amendments to such annexes of a procedural, scientific, technical or administrative nature.

Article 29 Protocols

1. Any Party may propose protocols to the WHO Pandemic Agreement. Such proposals shall be considered by the Conference of the Parties.

2. The Conference of the Parties may adopt protocols to the WHO Pandemic Agreement. In adopting these protocols, the decision-making terms of Article 27.3 shall apply, *mutatis mutandis*.
3. The text of any proposed protocol shall be communicated to the Parties by the Secretariat at least six months before the session of the Conference of the Parties at which it is proposed for adoption.
4. Only Parties to the WHO Pandemic Agreement may be parties to a protocol to the WHO Pandemic Agreement.
5. Any protocol to the WHO Pandemic Agreement shall be binding only on the parties to the protocol in question. Only Parties to a protocol may take decisions on matters exclusively relating to the protocol in question.
6. Any protocol to the WHO Pandemic Agreement shall be interpreted together with the WHO Pandemic Agreement, taking into account the purpose of the WHO Pandemic Agreement and of that protocol.
7. The requirements for entry into force of any protocol, and the procedure for the amendment of any protocol, shall be established by that protocol.

Article 30 Withdrawal

1. At any time after two years from the date on which the WHO Pandemic Agreement has entered into force for a Party, that Party may withdraw from this Agreement by giving written notification to the Depositary.
2. Any such withdrawal shall take effect upon expiry of one year from the date of receipt by the Depositary of the notification of withdrawal, or on such later date as may be specified in the notification of withdrawal.
3. A Party's withdrawal shall not in any way affect the duty of any Party to fulfil any obligation embodied in the WHO Pandemic Agreement to which it would be subject under international law independently of this Agreement.
4. Any Party that withdraws from the WHO Pandemic Agreement shall be considered as also having withdrawn from any protocol to which it is a Party, unless the said protocol requires its Parties to formally withdraw in accordance with its relevant terms.

Article 31 Signature

1. The WHO Pandemic Agreement shall be open for signature by all States and by regional economic integration organizations.
2. The WHO Pandemic Agreement shall be open for signature after adoption of the Annex described in Article 12.2 of this Agreement by the Health Assembly, at the World Health Organization Headquarters in Geneva, and thereafter at the

United Nations Headquarters in New York, on dates to be determined by the Health Assembly.

Article 32 Ratification, acceptance, approval, formal confirmation or accession

1. The WHO Pandemic Agreement and any protocol thereto shall be subject to ratification, acceptance, approval or accession by all States and to formal confirmation or accession by regional economic integration organizations. The WHO Pandemic Agreement shall be open for accession from the day after the date on which this Agreement is closed for signature. Instruments of ratification, acceptance, approval, formal confirmation or accession shall be deposited with the Depositary.
2. Any regional economic integration organization that becomes a Party to the WHO Pandemic Agreement, without any of its Member States being a Party shall be bound by all the obligations under this Agreement or any protocol thereto. In the case of those regional economic integration organizations for which one or more of its Member States is a Party to the WHO Pandemic Agreement, the regional economic integration organization and its Member States shall decide on their respective responsibilities for the performance of their obligations under this Agreement. In such cases, the regional economic integration organization and its Member States shall not be entitled to exercise rights under the WHO Pandemic Agreement concurrently.
3. Regional economic integration organizations shall, in their instruments relating to formal confirmation or in their instruments of accession, declare the extent of their competence with respect to the matters governed by the WHO Pandemic Agreement and any protocol thereto. These organizations shall also inform the Depositary, who shall in turn inform the Parties, of any substantial modification in the extent of their competence.

Article 33 Entry into force

1. The WHO Pandemic Agreement shall enter into force on the thirtieth day following the date of deposit of the sixtieth instrument of ratification, acceptance, approval, formal confirmation or accession with the Depositary.
2. For each State that ratifies, accepts or approves the WHO Pandemic Agreement or accedes thereto after the conditions set forth in paragraph 1 of this Article for entry into force have been fulfilled, the WHO Pandemic Agreement shall enter into force on the thirtieth day following the date of deposit of its instrument of ratification, acceptance, approval or accession.

3. For each regional economic integration organization depositing an instrument of formal confirmation or an instrument of accession after the conditions set forth in paragraph 1 of this Article for entry into force have been fulfilled, the WHO Pandemic Agreement shall enter into force on the thirtieth day following the date of deposit of its instrument of formal confirmation or of accession.
4. For the purposes of this Article, any instrument deposited by a regional economic integration organization shall not be counted as additional to those deposited by Member States of that regional economic integration organization.

Article 34 Depositary

The Secretary-General of the United Nations shall be the Depositary of the WHO Pandemic Agreement and amendments thereto and of any protocols and annexes adopted in accordance with the terms of the WHO Pandemic Agreement.

Article 35 Authentic texts

The original of the WHO Pandemic Agreement, of which the Arabic, Chinese, English, French, Russian and Spanish texts are equally authentic, shall be deposited with the Secretary-General of the United Nations.

Third plenary meeting, 20 May 2025

A78/VR/3

Compilation of References

AbouKorin, S. A. A., Han, H., & Mahran, M. G. N. (2021). Role of urban planning characteristics in forming pandemic resilient cities–Case study of Covid-19 impacts on European cities within England, Germany and Italy. *Cities (London, England)*, *118*, 103324. PMID: 34539022

Ackoff, R. L. (1981). *Creating the corporate future*. John Wiley & Sons.

Agboola, A. A., & Salawu, R. O. (2011). Managing deviant behavior and resistance to change. *International Journal of Business and Management*, *6*(1), 235–242.

Al Saeed, I. (2011). Importance of emerging technologies in society for futuring & innovation. *Journal of Applied Global Research*, *4*(11), 12–22.

Alaimo, D. (2015, March 23). Technology: Future tense. *Progressive Grocer India*. Progressivegrocer.com https://progressivegrocer.com/future-tense?

Aleem, A., Akbar Samad, A. B., & Vaqar, S. (2023, May 8) Emerging variants of SARS-CoV-2, and novel therapeutics against Coronavirus (COVID-19). In: StatPearls [Internet]. Treasure Island (F.L.): StatPearls Publishing; 2024 Jan–. PMID: 34033342.

Alevizos, A., Michail, M., Eleftheroglou, M., & Sidiropoulos, S. (2023). COVID-19 and the Exacerbation of Existing Inequalities: Why the Lower Socioeconomic Stratums Were Influenced the Most. *HAPSc Policy Briefs Series*, *4*(1), 33–41.

Al-Haddad, S., & Kotnour, T. (2015). Integrating the organizational change literature: A model for successful change. *Journal of Organizational Change Management*, *28*(2), 234.

Allen, R. W. (2025, March/April). Twelve considerations for the future of healthcare. *Journal of Healthcare Management*, *70*(2), 87–92. DOI: 10.1097/JHM-D-25-00012 PMID: 40059201

Al-Maazmi, S., & Hashmi, M. A. (2024). The role of innovation-driven leadership in public-sector innovation: The case in emerging economies. *The Journal of Applied Business and Economics*, *26*(2), 85–105.

Altrichter, H., Kemmis, S., McTaggart, R., & Zuber-Skerritt, O. (2002). The concept of action research. *The Learning Organization*, *9*(3/4), 125.

Anderson, D., & Anderson, L. A. (2010). *Beyond change management: How to achieve breakthrough results through conscious change leadership* (2nd ed.). Pfeiffer.

Arya, D. K. (2012). So, you want to lead a transformational change! *Asia Pacific Journal of Health Management*, *7*(2), 8–14.

Aschengrau, A., & Seage, G. R.III. (2020). Essentials Of Epidemiology. In *Public Health* (4th ed.). Jones & Bartlett Learning.

Avey, J. B., Wernsing, T. S., & Luthans, F. (2008). Can positive employees help positive organizational change? Impact of psychological capital and emotions on relevant attitudes and behaviors. *The Journal of Applied Behavioral Science*, *44*(1), 48–70. DOI: 10.1177/0021886307311470

Aytekin, A., Hale, A., Demirel, H., Onur, N., Yalman, A., Livberber, T., & Yiğit-Açıkgöz, F. (2025). Digital health technologies in patient experience literature: A scoping review and future outlook for sustainable digital health interventions. *Sustainability*, *17*(2), 456. DOI: 10.3390/su17020456

Bailey, P., Cooper, K., Stevens, M. P., Bearman, G., & Doll, M. (2024). Contact precautions as a barrier to hand hygiene: The Plan–Do–Study–Act (PDSA) framework to improve compliance with gloved hand hygiene. *Infection Control and Hospital Epidemiology*, *45*(6), 788–789. DOI: 10.1017/ice.2024.24

Bakker, I., Gill, S., & Wamsley, D. (2021). *Global health: Ethical challenges* (Benatar, S., & Brock, G., Eds.; 2nd ed.). Cambridge University Press.

Bakos, L., & Dumitra cu, D. (2017). Holonic crisis handling model for corporate sustainability. *Sustainability*, *9*(12), 2266. DOI: 10.3390/su9122266

Ballantyne, D. (2004). Action research reviewed: A market-oriented approach. *European Journal of Marketing*, *38*(3/4), 321–337.

Barton, J., Stephens, J., & Haslett, T. (2009). Action research: Its foundations in open systems thinking and relationship to the scientific method. *Systemic Practice and Action Research*, *22*, 475–488. DOI: 10.1007/s11213-009-9148-6

Bass, B. M. (1997). Does the transactional-transformational leadership paradigm transcend organizational and national boundaries? *The American Psychologist, 52*(2), 130–139.

Bass, B. M., & Avolio, B. J. (1993). Transformational leadership and organizational culture. *Public Administration Quarterly*, *17*(1), 112.

Beach, L. R. (2005). Leadership and the art of change: A practical guide to organizational transformation. *Sage (Atlanta, Ga.).*

Bell, S. (2025). *The McKinsey 7-S Framework: Making every part of your organization work in harmony.* Mindtools.com. https://www.mindtools.com/aicks4s/the-mckinsey-7-s-framework

Benson, J., & Dresdow, S. (2008). Teaching AI to enhance students' understanding of organizational behavior. *International Journal Of Learning, 15*(2), 195-1NULL.

Bertocchi, G., & Canova, F. (2002). Did colonization matter for growth?: An empirical exploration into the historical causes of Africa's underdevelopment. *European Economic Review*, *46*(10), 1851–1871.

Bertram, R., Gilbert, W., & Culver, D. (2016). Using appreciative inquiry to create high-impact coach learning: Insights from a decade of applied research. *AI Practitioner*, *18*(2), 59–65. DOI: 10.12781/978-1-907549-27-4-9

Binder, J. (2016). *Global project management: Communication, collaboration and management across borders*. Routledge.

Birkhead, G. S., Morrow, C. B., & Pirani, S. (2020). *Turnock's Public Health: What It Is and How It Works: What It Is and How It Works*. Jones & Bartlett Learning.

Boo, E., Abouzeedan, A., Hedner, T., Maack, K., & Lundqvist, M. (2013). Using scenario planning in regional development context: The challenges and opportunities. *World Journal of Science. Technology and Sustainable Development*, *10*(2), 103–122. DOI: 10.1108/20425941311323118

Borghi, J., Ismail, S., Hollway, J., Kim, R. E., Sturmberg, J., Brown, G., Mechler, R., Volmink, H., Spicer, N., Chalabi, Z., Cassidy, R., Johnson, J., Foss, A., Koduah, A., Searle, C., Komendantova, N., Semwanga, A., & Moon, S. (2022). Viewing the global health system as a complex adaptive system - implications for research and practice [version1; peer review: 2 approved]. *F1000 Research*, *2022*(11), 1147. DOI: 10.12688/f1000research.126201.1 PMID: 37600221

Brasfield, D. A. (2015). The effects of leadership traits in change management on operational excellence. (3684960 D.B.A.), Capella University, Ann Arbor. ProQuest Dissertations & Theses Global database.

Bridges, W. (2017). *Managing transitions (25th anniversary edition): Making the most of change*. Hachette Books.

Bright, D. S. (2009). Appreciative inquiry and positive organizational scholarship: A philosophy of practice for turbulent times. *OD Practitioner*, *41*(3), 2–7.

Broberg, M. (2020). A critical appraisal of the World Health Organization's International Health Regulations (2005) in Times of Pandemic: It Is Time for Revision. *European Journal of Risk Regulation: EJRR*, *11*(2), 202–209. DOI: 10.1017/err.2020.26

Browning, M. (2014). Appreciative inquiry as a model for assessing the value of business school education. *Journal of Business and Educational Leadership*, *5*(1), 64–70.

Brown, R. S. (2015). Equifinality in open systems: Explaining the phenomenon of hard money mortgages. *Academy of Accounting & Financial Studies Journal*, *19*(1), 120–132.

Brown, S. L., & Eisenhardt, K. M. (1997). The art of continuous change: Linking complexity theory and time-paced evolution in relentlessly shifting organizations. *Administrative Science Quarterly*, *42*(1), 1–34.

Burke, W. W. (2024). *Organizational change: Theory and practice* (6th ed.). Sage.

Burn, J. M. (1996). IS innovation and organizational alignment - a professional juggling act. *Journal of Information Technology*, *11*(1), 3–12.

Burrell, D. N. (2024). *Change dynamics in healthcare, technological innovations, and complex scenarios*. IGI Global Scientific Publishing.

Burton, J., & Carter, B. (2025). *Sustainable organizational change: The Social Change Model for Systems*. Routledge.

Busemeyer, J., Zhang, Q., Balakrishnan, S. N., & Wang, Z. (2020). Application of Quantum-Markov open system models to human cognition and decision. *Entropy (Basel, Switzerland)*, *22*(9), 990. DOI: 10.3390/e22090990

Bushe, G. R., & Marshak, R. J. (2014). The dialogic mindset in organization development. *Research in Organizational Change and Development*, *22*, 55–97.

Bustamante-Ubilla, M., & Arenas-Torres, F. (2022). Epistemological foundations of Complexity Theory. *Sustainability*, *14*(20), 13316. DOI: 10.3390/su142013316

Calabrese, R., & Cohen, E. (2013). An appreciative inquiry into an urban drug court: Cultural transformation. *The Qualitative Report*, *18*(1), 1–14. https://files.eric.ed.gov/fulltext/EJ1004996.pdf

Cameron, K. S., & Quinn, R. E. (2011). *Diagnosing and changing organizational culture: Based on the Competing Values Framework* (3rd ed.). Jossey-Bass.

Capra, F. (1996). *The web of life: A new scientific understanding of living systems*. Anchor Books.

Caron, R. M. (2022). *Population health, epidemiology, and public health: management skills for creating healthy communities*. Health Administration Press.

Carr, T., Rosas, S., Noble, C., Song, M., Fernandez, C. S. P., Brandert, K., Donnald, K., Corbie, G., & Dave, G. (2024). Strengthening healthcare providers' leadership capabilities, interprofessional collaboration, and systems thinking: A conceptualization of the clinical scholars program impact. *BMC Medical Education*, *24*(1), 1277–11. DOI: 10.1186/s12909-024-06240-1

Carter, B. M. (2019). *The leadership practices female ODC managers use to improve change initiatives* (Order No. 22621998). Available from ProQuest Dissertations & Theses Global. (2320955766).

Carter, S. K. (2024). Using Electronic Health Records (EHR) for Disease Surveillance (EHR-DS) to Support UN SDGs. In *Computational Convergence and Interoperability in Electronic Health Records (EHR)* (pp. 137-152). IGI Global.

Carter, S. K. (2024). Using Electronic Health Records (EHR) For Disease Surveillance (EHR-DS) To Support UN Sdgs. In *Computational Convergence And Interoperability In Electronic Health Records (EHR)* (Pp. 137-152). IGI Global.

Carter, S. K. (2024). Using Electronic Health Records for Disease Surveillance (EHR-DS) to support UN SDGs. In *Computational Convergence and Interoperability in Electronic Health Records (EHR)* (pp. 137-152). IGI Global Publishing.

Carter, S. K. (2019). *The strategies global leaders need to improve interoperability of an EHR system*. Colorado Technical University.

Carter, S. K., Anastasia, C., & Carter, B. M. (2024). *Multinational Electronic Health Records Interoperability Strategies*. IGI Global Publishing.

Carter, S. K., Anastasia, C., & Carter, B. M. (2024). *Multinational electronic health records interoperability strategies*. IGI Global Scientific Publishing.

Carter, S., Anastasia, C., & Carter, B. (2024). *Multinational Electronic Health Record Interoperability Strategies*. IGI Global., DOI: 10.4018/978-1-7998-8989-2

Caws, P. (2015). General systems theory: Its past and potential. *Systems Research and Behavioral Science*, *32*(5), 514–521. DOI: 10.1002/sres.2353

CDC. (2023). Summary of Variant Surveillance Str https://covid.cdc.gov/covid-data-tracker/#variant-summary

CDC. (2024). *CDC Public Health Data Strategy: About the Public Health Data Strategy (PHDS)*. United States Centers for Disease Control and Prevention. https://www.cdc.gov/public-health-data-strategy/php/about/index.html

CDC. (2024). *CDC Public Health Data Strategy: About The Public Health Data Strategy (PHDS)*. United States Centers For Disease Control And Prevention. Https://Www.Cdc.Gov/Public-Health-Data-Strategy/Php/About/Index.Html

Chattu, V. K., Mol, R., Singh, B., Reddy, K. S., & Hatefi, A. (2024). Pandemic treaty as an instrument to strengthen global health security: Global health diplomacy at its crux. *Health Promotion Perspectives*, *14*(1), 9. PMID: 38623344

Chiotti, D., Leonard, R., Schlenk, D., Wilen, C., & Schiff, K. (2020). Alternatives To Glyphosate For Vegetation Management. In *Los Angeles County; Technical Committee Report*. Southern California Coastal Water Research Project.

Cissé, G. (2019). Food-Borne And Water-Borne Diseases Under Climate Change In Low-And Middle-Income Countries: Further Efforts Needed For Reducing Environmental Health Exposure Risks. *Acta Tropica*, *194*, 181–188. PMID: 30946811

Coghlan, D., & Rashford, N. S. (2006). *Organizational change and strategy*. Routledge.

Cooperrider, D. L., Zhexembayeva, N., Trosten-Bloom, A., & Whitney, D. (2003). Business as agent of world benefit: A worldwide action research project using appreciative inquiry. Eds. Vogelsang, J., Townsend, M., Minahan, M., Jamieson, D., Vogel, J. Viets, A., Royal, C., & Valek, L. (2013). In *Handbook for Strategic HR: Best practices in organizational development from the OD Network*. 582-589. AMACOM.

Cooperrider, D. L., & McQuaid, M. (2012). The positive arc of systemic strengths: How appreciative inquiry and sustainable designing can bring out the best in human systems. *Journal of Corporate Citizenship*, (46), 71–102. https://proxy.cecybrary.com/login?url=https://search.proquest.com/docview/1446323232?accountid=144789

Cottam, A., Ensor, J., & Band, C. (2001). A benchmark study of strategic commitment to innovation. *European Journal of Innovation Management*, *4*(2), 88–94.

Covey, S. R. (1989). *The 7 habits of highly effective people*. Simon & Schuster.

Creswell, J. W., & Creswell, J. D. (2022). *Research design: Qualitative, quantitative, and mixed methods approaches* (6th ed.). Sage.

Curtin, S. C., & Heron, M. (2022). COVID-19 death rates in urban and rural areas: United States, 2020.

Davenport, T. H., & Redman, T. C. (2025, January-February). How to marry process management and AI: Make sure your people and technology work well together. *Harvard Business Review*, *103*(1), 39–44.

Davidson, S. (2014). Appreciative inquiry helps a new college leader create a team environment - fast! *AI Practitioner*, *16*(2), 72–77. DOI: 10.12781/978-1-907549-19-9-12

De Morais Valentim, J. M. B., Coradi, C., Viana, N. P., Fagundes, T. R., Micheletti, P. L., Gaboardi, S. C., Fadel, B., Pizzatti, L., Candiotto, L. Z. P., & Panis, C. (2024). Glyphosate As A Food Contaminant: Main Sources, Detection Levels, And Implications For Human And Public Health. *Foods*, *13*(11). Https://Doi.Org/10.3390/Foods13111697 PMID: 38890925

de Souza, L. E. P. F., de Castro, M. C., Hage Carmo, E., & Polidoro, M. (2022). December 31). The global failure of facing the pandemic. *Global Health Action*, *15*(1). Advance online publication. DOI: 10.1080/16549716.2022.2124645 PMID: 36285582

Dehimi, N. E. H., Galland, S., Tolba, Z., Allaoua, N., & Ferkani, M. (2023). Distributed, dynamic and recursive planning for holonic multi-agent systems: A behavioural model-based approach. *Electronics (Basel)*, *12*(4797), 1–35. DOI: 10.3390/electronics12234749

Dervitsiotis, K. N. (1998). The challenge of managing organizational change: Exploring the relationship of re-engineering, developing learning organizations and total quality management. *Total Quality Management*, *9*(1), 109–122.

Do, A.-L. (2012). *Self-Organization in Continuous Adaptive Networks*. River Publishers. *ProQuest Ebook Central*, https://ebookcentral-proquest-com.library.capella.edu/lib/capella/detail.action?docID=3400129

Dodge, R., Dwyer, J., Witzeman, S., Neylon, S., & Taylor, S. (2017). The role of leadership in innovation. *Research Technology Management*, *60*(3), 22–28. DOI: 10.1080/08956308.2017.1301000

Drucker, P. (1998). The future that has already happened. *The Futurist*, *32*(8), 16–18.

Dunlap, C. A. (2008). Effective evaluation through appreciative inquiry. *Performance Improvement*, *47*(2), 23–29.

Egbende, L., Helldén, D., Mbunga, B., Schedwin, M., Kazenza, B., Viberg, N., Wanyenze, R., Ali, M. M., & Alfvén, T. (2023). Interactions Between Health And The Sustainable Development Goals: The Case Of The Democratic Republic Of Congo. *Sustainability*, *15*(2), 1259. Https://Www.Mdpi.Com/2071-1050/15/2/1259

Englund, R. L. (2009). Applying chaos theory in a project-based organization. Paper presented at PMI® Global Congress 2009—EMEA, Amsterdam, North Holland, The Netherlands. Newtown Square, PA: Project Management Institute.

Ettorre, B. (1998). Y2K and beyond. *Management Review*, *87*(6), 27.

Fareed, M., Noor, W. S. W. M., Isa, M. F. M., & Salleh, S. S. M. M. (2016). Developing human capital for sustainable competitive advantage: The roles of organizational culture and high performance work system. *International Journal of Economic Perspectives*, *10*(4), 655–673. https://www.researchgate.net/publication/319304634

Fedurek, P., Asiimwe, C., Rice, G. K., Akankwasa, W. J., Reynolds, V., Hobaiter, C., & Goldberg, T. L. (2024). Selective deforestation and exposure of African wildlife to bat-borne viruses. *Communications Biology*, *7*(1), 470. PMID: 38649441

Fields, D. M. (1993). Institutions for the 21st century. *The Futurist*, *27*(1), 33.

Findlater, A., & Bogoch, I. I. (2018). Human Mobility And The Global Spread Of Infectious Diseases: A Focus On Air Travel. *Trends in Parasitology*, *34*(9), 772–783. Https://Doi.Org/Https://Doi.Org/10.1016/J.Pt.2018.07.004 PMID: 30049602

Fischer, K., & Zink, K. J. (2012). Defining elements of sustainable work systems - a system-oriented approach. *Work (Reading, Mass.)*, *41*, 3900–3905. PMID: 22317318

Folger, R., & Skarlicki, D. P. (1999). Unfairness and resistance to change: Hardship as mistreatment. *Journal of Organizational Change Management*, *12*(1), 35–50. DOI: 10.1108/09534819910255306

Follett, C. (2023). *Globalization and Growing Global Equality*. Globalization.

Frame, D. J. (2013). *Framing decisions: Decision making that accounts for irrationality, people, and constraints*. Jossey-Bass.

Gianakos, D. (2019). Emotional intelligence: Build by reading poetry. *Physician Leadership Journal*, *6*(4), 74–75.

Global Covid-19 Response (Reactive vs Proactive) IHR 1969 vs IHR 2005, proactive to reactive? *International Health Regulations (1969)*. (1982, January 1). PAHO/WHO | Pan American Health Organization. https://www.paho.org/en/documents/international-health-regulations-1969

Gostin, L. O. (2021). The Coronavirus Pandemic 1 Year On—What Went Wrong? *Journal of the American Medical Association*, *325*(12), 1132–1133. DOI: 10.1001/jama.2021.3207 PMID: 33755061

Grace, D. (2023). Burden of foodborne disease in low-income and middle-income countries and opportunities for scaling food safety interventions. *Food Security*, *15*(6), 1475–1488. DOI: 10.1007/s12571-023-01391-3

Grace, D. (2023). Burden Of Foodborne Disease In Low-Income And Middle-Income Countries And Opportunities For Scaling Food Safety Interventions. *Food Security*, *15*(6), 1475–1488. Https://Doi.Org/10.1007/S12571-023-01391-3

Gronhaug, K., & Olson, O. (1999). Action research and knowledge creation: Merits and challenges. *Qualitative Market Research*, *2*(1), 6–14.

Gupta, M. (2018). Consensus building process in group decision making-an adaptive procedure based on group dynamics. *IEEE Transactions on Fuzzy Systems*, *26*(4), 1923–1933. DOI: 10.1109/TFUZZ.2017.2755581

Gustavsen, B. (1993). Action research and the generation of knowledge. *Human Relations*, *46*(11), 1361.

Hair, J. F.Jr. (2007). Knowledge creation in marketing: The role of predictive analytics. *European Business Review*, *19*(4), 303–315. DOI: 10.1108/09555340710760134

Hall, A.D., & Fagen, R.E. (1956). Definition of system. General Systems, Yearbook of the Society for General Systems Research (SGSR - now ISSS)

Halladay, S. D. (2013). Using predictive analytics to improve decision making. *The Journal of Equipment Lease Financing (Online)*, *31*(2), B1–B6.

Halladay, S. D. (2013). Using predictive analytics to improve decisionmaking. *The Journal of Equipment Lease Financing*, *31*(2), B1–B6.

Hall, D. J., Skipper, J. B., Hazen, B. T., & Hanna, J. B. (2012). Inter-organizational IT use, cooperative attitude, and inter-organizational collaboration as antecedents to contingency planning effectiveness. *International Journal of Logistics Management*, *23*(1), 50–76. DOI: 10.1108/09574091211226920

Hanson, K. (2025). When Should You Apply Pre-Emergent To Your Lawn? *Southern Living*. Https://Www.Southernliving.Com/When-To-Apply-Pre-Emergent-11679145 ?Utm_Source=Chatgpt.Com

Hawthorne, P. (2004). Redesigning library human resources: Integrating human resources management and organizational development. *Library Trends*, *53*(1), 172–186.

Heymann, D. L., & Rodier, G. (2004). SARS: A global response to an international threat. *The Brown Journal of World Affairs*, *10*(2), 185–197. http://www.jstor.org/stable/24590530

Heymann, D. L., & Rodier, G. (2004). SARS: A Global Response To An International Threat. *The Brown Journal of World Affairs*, *10*(2), 185–197. Http://Www .Jstor.Org/Stable/24590530

Hoffmann, S., & Havelaar, A. (2019). Measuring The Burden Of Global Foodborne Disease From Animal And Fish Sources. *Amber Waves: The Economics Of Food, Farming, Natural Resources, And Rural America, 2019*(10).

Hofstede, G. (1980a). Culture and organizations. *International Studies of Management & Organization*, *10*(4), 15–41.

Hofstede, G. (1980b). Culture's Consequences. *Sage (Atlanta, Ga.)*.

Hofstede, G. (1991). *Cultures and organizations: Software of the mind*. McGraw-Hill.

Hofstede, G. (2011). Dimensionalizing cultures: The Hofstede model in context. *Online Readings in Psychology and Culture*, *2*(1), 2307–0919.

Hofstede, G., & Minkov, M. (2010). Long-versus short-term orientation: New perspectives. *Asia Pacific Business Review*, *16*(4), 493–504.

Holling, C. S. (1986). The resilience of terrestrial ecosystems: local surprise and global Change. In: Clark, W.C., & Munn, R.E., editors. *Sustainable development of the biosphere*. Cambridge University Press/IIASA Laxenburg

Holman, P., Devane, T., & Cady, S. (2007). *The change handbook: The definitive resource on today's best methods for engaging whole systems* (2nd ed.). Berrett-Koehler Publishers.

Holmes, J. D., Nelson, G. O., & Stump, D. C. (1993). Improving the innovation process at Eastman Chemical. *Research Technology Management*, *36*(3), 27. https://www.jstor.org/stable/24128245

Horgan, J., & Netchev, S. (2022). *Columbian Exchange*. World History.

House, R. J., Hanges, P. J., Javidan, M., Dorfman, P. W., & Gupta, V. (Eds.). (2004). *Culture, Leadership, and Organizations: The GLOBE Study of 62 Societies*. Sage.

House, T. W. (2022). *National Biodefense Strategy And Implementation Plan For Countering Biological Threats, Enhancing Pandemic Preparedness, And Achieving Global Heatlh Security*. The United States Retrieved From., Https://Www.Whitehouse.Gov/Wp-Content/Uploads/2022/10/National-Biodefense-Strategy-And-Implementation-Plan-Final.Pdf

Igwama, G. T., Olaboye, J. A., Maha, C. C., Ajegbile, M. D., & Abdul, S. (2024). Integrating electronic health records systems across borders: Technical challenges and policy solutions. *International Medical Science Research Journal*, *4*(7), 788–796.

Indexmundi. (2020). *Democratic Republic Of The Congo Major Infectious Diseases*. Https://Www.Indexmundi.Com/Democratic_Republic_Of_The_Congo/Major_Infectious_Diseases.Html

Jafar, A. J. N., Patel, S., Mitchell, R., & Redmond, A. (2024). Redefining global health and shifting the balance: The ARC-H principle. *BMJ Global Health*, *9*(2), 1–4. DOI: 10.1136/bmjgh-2023-014487

Jamieson, D. W., & Davidson, J. E. (2019). Advancing thinking and practice on use of self. *Organization Development Journal*, *37*(1), 39–53.

Janssen, M. (1998). Use of complex adaptive systems for modeling global change. *Ecosystems (New York, N.Y.)*, *1*(5), 457–463. DOI: 10.1007/s100219900041

Javidan, M., Dorfman, P.W., de Luque, M.S., House, R.J. (2006). In the eye of the beholder: Cross-cultural lessons in leadership for project GLOBE. *The Academy of Management Perspectives*, February, *20*(1), pp. 67–90.

Jayanti, E. B. (2013). *An investigation of the internal corporate factors of organizational learning and innovation*. (3600937 Ph.D.), ProQuest Dissertations & Theses Global database.

Jeffries, M., Salema, N., Laing, L., Shamsuddin, A., Sheikh, A., Avery, T., Chuter, A., Waring, J., & Keers, R. N. (2023). Using sociotechnical theory to understand medication safety work in primary care and prescribers' use of clinical decision support: A qualitative study. *BMJ Open*, *13*(4), e068798–e068798. DOI: 10.1136/bmjopen-2022-068798

Jobs, C. G., Aukers, S. M., & Gilfoil, D. M. (2015). The impact of big data on your firms marketing communications: A framework for understanding the emerging marketing analytics industry. *Academy of Marketing Studies Journal*, *19*(2), 81–92.

Johns Hopkins University. (2023). Covid-19 data timeline through 2023.0 https://coronavirus.jhu.edu/region/united-states

Jones, G. R. (2013). *Organizational theory, design, and change*. Pearson.

Joseph, E. C. (2007). Discovering the anticipatory sciences. *Futurics*, *31*(3/4), 2–20.

Jurik, N. C., & Cavender, G. (2016). Sustainable workplaces as innovation. *The Journal of Applied Management and Entrepreneurship*, *21*(1), 53–71. DOI: 10.9774/GLEAF.3709.2016.ja.00006

Kadakia, K. T., & Galea, S. (2023). Urbanization and the Future of Population Health. *The Milbank Quarterly*, *101*(S1), 153–175. DOI: 10.1111/1468-0009.12624 PMID: 37096620

Katella, K. (2023). *Omicron, Delta, Alpha, and more: What to know about the Coronavirus Variants*. Yale Medicine.

Kaur, J. (2024). Smart solutions for health: Computational intelligence reshaping the Industry 4.0 healthcare paradigm. In Shah, I. A., & Sial, Q. (Eds.), *Advances in computational intelligence for the healthcare Industry 4.0*. IGI Global Scientific Publishing.

Kezar, A. (2013). Understanding sensemaking/sensegiving in transformational change processes from the bottom up. *Higher Education*, *65*(6), 761–780. DOI: 10.1007/s10734-012-9575-7

Khang, A. (2023). *AI and IoT-based technologies for precision medicine*. IGI Global Scientific Publishing.

Kılıç, R. (2022). The problem of hunger in the world and a new model proposal to solve this problem. *Balkan Sosyal Bilimler Dergisi*, *11*(21), 63–68.

Koc, H. C., Xiao, J., Liu, W., Li, Y., & Chen, G. (2022). Long COVID and its Management. *International Journal of Biological Sciences*, *18*(12), 4768–4780. DOI: 10.7150/ijbs.75056 PMID: 35874958

Koestler, A. (1967). *The ghost in the machine*. Arkana.

Koestler, A. (1978). *Janus: A summing up*. Random House.

Kolachi, N., & Akan, O. (2014). HRD role in organizational development (a case of corporate thinking at ETISALAT, UAE). *International Business Research*, *7*(8), 160–167.

Kotter, J. P. (2012). *Leading change*. Harvard Business Review Press.

Kotter, J. P., Akhtar, V., & Gupta, G. (2021). *Change: How organizations achieve hard-to-imagine results in uncertain and volatile times*. John Wiley & Sons, Inc.

Koufteros, X., Peng, X., Lu, G., & Peters, R. (2014). The impact of organizational structure on internal and external integration. *Journal of Organization Design, 3*(2), 1–17. DOI: 10.7146/jod.7386

Kumar, B., Suneja, M., & Swee, M. (2023). When I say… appreciative inquiry. *Medical Education, 57*(11), 1006–1007. DOI: 10.1111/medu.15140

Kumar, V. (2013). *101 design methods: A structured approach for driving innovation in your organization*. Wiley.

Labonte, R., Wiktorowicz, M., Packer, C., Ruckert, A., Wilson, K., & Halabi, S. (2021). A pandemic treaty, revised international health regulations, or both? *Globalization and Health, 17*(128), 1–4. DOI: 10.1186/s12992-021-00779-0 PMID: 34742296

Lai, K. Y., Webster, C., Kumari, S., & Sarkar, C. (2020). The nature of cities and the Covid-19 pandemic. *Current Opinion in Environmental Sustainability, 46*, 27–31. https://doi.org/https://doi.org/10.1016/j.cosust.2020.08.008 PMID: 32874374

LangChain. (2024, October 16). Conceptual guide: Multi agent architecture [Video]. YouTube. https://www.youtube.com/watch?v=4nZl32FwU-o

Lawler, E. E., III. (2011). *Sustainability must be a top priority*. Retrieved from https://www.forbes.com/sites/edwardlawler/2011/10/26/sustainability-must-be-a-top-priority/#5f8b8b9312cc

Lawler, E. E., III. (2012). *Sustainability: It should be about more than the bottom line*. Retrieved from https://www.forbes.com/sites/edwardlawler/2012/03/15/sustainability-it-should-be-about-more-than-the-bottom-line/#65a1712522c8

Lawler, E. E.III, Worley, C. G., & Creelman, D. (2011). *Management reset: organizing for sustainable effectiveness*. Jossey-Bass.

Lee, A. J. P. (2015). Predictive analytics: The new tool to combat fraud, waste, and abuse. *Journal of Government Financial Management, 64*(2), 12–16.

Lee, V. J., Ho, M., Kai, C. W., Aguilera, X., Heymann, D., & Wilder-Smith, A. (2020). Epidemic preparedness in urban settings: New challenges and opportunities. *The Lancet. Infectious Diseases, 20*(5), 527–529. PMID: 32224312

Lehner, R., & Hight, D. L. (2006). Appreciative inquiry and student affairs: A positive approach to change. *College Student Affairs Journal, 25*(2), 141-151,135.

Levasseur, R. E. (2004). Open system theory and organizations. *Futurics*, *28*(1/2), 79–85.

Lewin, R., & Regine, B. (2000). *The soul at work: Listen…respond…let go*. Simon & Schuster.

Lilja, J., & Richardsson, D. (2012). Putting appreciative design into practice. *International Journal of Quality and Service Sciences*, *4*(1), 4–15. DOI: 10.1108/17566691211219698

Lin, Y., Chen, H., Brown, R. A., Li, S., & Yang, H. University of Arizona, Southern Arizona VA Health Care System, National Taiwan University, Florida State University, & Stanford University. (2017). Healthcare predictive analytics for risk profiling in chronic care: A Bayesian multitask learning approach. *MIS Quarterly, 41*(2), 473-496. https://doi.org/DOI: 10.25300/MISQ/2017/41.2.07

Lincicome, S. (2023, September 12). *Globalization isn't going anywhere.* CATO Institute. https://www.cato.org/publications/globalization-isnt-going-anywhere

Lincicome, S. (2023, September 12). *Globalization Isn't Going Anywhere*. Cato. Org. Https://Www.Cato.Org/Publications/Globalization-Isnt-Going-Anywhere

Llopis, G. (2024, July 2). *Healthcare leadership in crisis: Time for reinvention.* Forbes.com. https://www.forbes.com/sites/glennllopis/2024/07/02/healthcare-leadership-in-crisis-time-for-reinvention/

Mack, T. C. (2005). Profits and nonprofits: Looking for and finding value in the future. *Futures Research Quarterly*, *21*(4), 55–61.

Madir, J. (2020). *HealthTech: Law and regulation*. Elgar Commercial Law and Practice.

Maggs, P., & Chelin, J. (2013). Scenario planning for an uncertain future? *Library Management*, *34*(8/9), 664–676. DOI: 10.1108/LM-02-2013-0017

Marketing consulting services industry (NAICS 541613). (2017). *United States Marketing Consulting Services Industry Report*, 1-195.

Martens, H., & Dehaes, R. (2008). Integrating diversity management into the management of the organisation: Multiple case study with the 7s-instrument. *The International Journal of Diversity in Organisations, Communities and Nations*, *8*(4), 161–169.

Masch, V. A. (2013). Extensions of stochastic multiscenario models for long-range planning under uncertainty. *Environment Systems & Decisions*, *33*(1), 43–59. DOI: 10.1007/s10669-013-9433-x

Mason, D. (2003). Tailoring scenario planning to the company culture. *Strategy and Leadership*, *31*(2), 25–28.

McChrystalgroup.com. (2025). Teams of Teams®: New rules of engagement in a complex world. https://www.mcchrystalgroup.com/capabilities/team-of-teams

McChrystal, S., Collins, T., Silverman, D., & Fussell, C. (2015). *Teams of teams: New rules of engagement for a complex world*. Portfolio/Penguin.

McClernon, T. R., & Swanson, R. A. (1995). Team building: An experimental investigation of the effects of computer-based and facilitator-based interventions on work groups. *Human Resource Development Quarterly*, *6*(1), 39–58. https://doi.org.coloradotech.idm.oclc.org/10.1002/hrdq.3920060105

Mccloskey, D. N. (2023, September 12). *Globalization Creates A Global Neighborhood, Benefiting All.* Cato.Org. Https://Www.Cato.Org/Publications/Globalization-Isnt-Going-Anywhere

McElyea, B. E. (2003). Organizational change models. *Futurics*, *27*(1/2), 57.

McIntyre, P. (2016). General Systems Theory and creativity. In *The Creative System in Action* (pp. 13-26). Palgrave Macmillan UK.

Merianos, A., & Peiris, M. (2005). International Health Regulations (2005). *Lancet*, *366*(9493), 1249–1251. DOI: 10.1016/S0140-6736(05)67508-3 PMID: 16214586

Merson, M. H., Black, R. E., & Mills, A. J. (2018). *Global health: Diseases, programs, systems, and policies* (4th ed.). Jones & Bartlett Learning.

Milgroom, M. G. (2023). Epidemiology and SIR Models. In Milgroom, M. G. (Ed.), *Biology of Infectious Disease: From Molecules to Ecosystems* (pp. 253–268). Springer International Publishing., DOI: 10.1007/978-3-031-38941-2_16

Millett, S. M. (2006). Futuring and visioning: Complementary approaches to strategic decision making. *Strategy and Leadership*, *34*(3), 43–50. DOI: 10.1108/10878570610660591

Millett, S. M., & Staley, D. J. (2009). Does future thinking need a philosophy? [World Future Society]. *World Futures Review*, *1*(5), 23–30.

Miranda Silva, G., & Gomes, J., P., Filipe Lages, L., & Lopes Pereira, Z. (2014). The role of TQM in strategic product innovation: An empirical assessment. *International Journal of Operations & Production Management*, *34*(10), 1307–1337.

Mishra, R., Dwivedi, V., & Saxena, S. (2024). *Computational convergence and interoperability in electronic health records (EHR)*. IGI Global Publishing.

Mishra, R., Dwivedi, V., & Saxena, S. (2024). Computational Convergence And Interoperability. In *Electronic Health Records (EHR)*. IGI Global.

Molinari, N. M., Leblanc, T. T., & Stephens, W. (2018). The Impact Of A Case Of Ebola Virus Disease On Emergency Department Visits In Metropolitan Dallas-Fort Worth, TX, July, 2013-July, 2015: An Interrupted Time Series Analysis. *PLoS Currents*, *10*, •••. Https://Doi.Org/10.1371/Currents.Outbreaks.E62bdea371ef5454d56f71fe217aead0 PMID: 29623242

Moon, S. (2019). Power in global governance: An expanded typology from global health. *Globalization and Health*, *15*(Suppl 1), 74. DOI: 10.1186/s12992-019-0515-5 PMID: 31775779

Morente, F., & Ferràs, X. (2017). Innovation management from the inside: An approach from attention and everyday praxis. *Intangible Capital*, *13*(3), 640–667. DOI: 10.3926/ic.1004

Morrison, E., Hutcheson, S., Nilsen, E., Fadden, J., & Franklin, N. (2019). *Strategic doing: Ten skills for agile leadership*. Wiley.

Morse, T. D., Masuku, H., Rippon, S., & Kubwalo, H. (2018). Achieving An Integrated Approach To Food Safety And Hygiene—Meeting The Sustainable Development Goals In Sub-Saharan Africa. *Sustainability*, *10*(7), 2394. Https://Www.Mdpi.Com/2071-1050/10/7/2394

Mufungizi, I., Okon, I., Nkundakozera, M., & Akilimali, A. (2024). Supporting Health Systems And Environment In The Democratic Republic Of Congo: A Call For Action. *Health Science Reports*, *7*(7), E2257. PMID: 39027365

Munteanu, C., & Schwartz, B. (2022). The relationship between nutrition and the immune system. *Frontiers in Nutrition*, *9*, 1082500. PMID: 36570149

Nadler, D., & Tushman, M. (1997). *Competing by design*. Oxford University Press.

Nassar, A. (2024, December 19, 2024). *D617 Public Health Core Functions and Essential Services: Task 3: Public Health Strategies*. https://wgu.hosted.panopto.com/Panopto/Pages/Viewer.aspx?id=0062fa01-13a2-441b-ab7d-b1d801216963

Natarajan, T., & Pichai, S. (2024, March 27). Transition from waterfall to agile methodology: An action research study. *IEEE Access : Practical Innovations, Open Solutions*, *12*, 49341–49362. DOI: 10.1109/ACCESS.2024.3384097

Naude, L., van den Bergh, T. J., & Kruger, I. S. (2014). Learning to like learning: An appreciative inquiry into emotions in education. *Social Psychology of Education*, *17*(2), 211–228. DOI: 10.1007/s11218-014-9247-9

Neumann, J. E., Lau, C. M., & Worley, C. G. (2009). Ready for consideration: International organizational development and change as an emerging field of practice. *The Journal of Applied Behavioral Science*, *45*(2), 171–185. DOI: 10.1177/0021886309335429

Ngcamu, B. S. (2016). Conceptualizing transformation in the post-merger and incorporation environment era. *The International Journal of Sociology and Social Policy*, *36*(5/6), 270–288.

Nickols, F. (2020). SWOT/PESTLE. *Odnetwork.org*. https://nickols.us/SWOTPESTLE.jpg

Norrie, P. (2016). *A History Of Disease In Ancient Times: More Lethal Than War*. Springer International Publishing AG. Https://Doi.Org/10.1007/978-3-319-28937

Norrie, P. (2016). *A History of Disease in Ancient Times: More Lethal Than War*. Springer International Publishing AG., DOI: 10.1007/978-3-319-28937

Norrie, P. (2016). A History of Disease. In *Ancient Times More Lethal Than War*. Springer International Publishing.

Northouse, P. (2022). *Leadership: Theory and practice* (9th ed.). Sage.

Nouri, B. A., Ghorbani, R., & Soltani, M. (2017). The effect of knowledge management on organizational innovation with the mediating role of organizational learning (Case study: Agricultural bank in Iran). *Journal of Applied Economics & Business Research*, *7*(3), 194–211.

Nyuur, R. B. (2015). Unlocking the potential barriers on SMEs' uptake of scenario planning. *Journal of Strategy and Management*, *8*(2), 139–154. DOI: 10.1108/JSMA-01-2014-0007

O'Flaherty, B., & Heavin, C. (2015). Positioning predictive analytics for customer retention. *Journal of Decision Systems*, *24*(1), 3–18.

ODnetwork.org. (2025). *Global OD Competency Framework*. https://www.odnetwork.org/page/global-framework

Ohlemacher, J. (2015). Fostering meaningful dialogue can improve success in learning. *Assessment Update*, *27*(2), 5–13.

Okoli, C., & Pawlowski, S. D. (2004, March 27). The Delphi method as a research tool: An example, design considerations and applications. *Information & Management*, *42*, 15–29. https://snazlan.wordpress.com/wp-content/uploads/2015/11/the-delphi-method-as-a-research-tool-an-example-design-considerations-and-applications.pdf

Paraschivescu, A. O., & Cotîrlet, P. C. (2015). Quality continuous improvement strategies Kaizen strategy — comparative analysis. *Economy Transdisciplinarity Cognition, 18*(1), 12–21.

Parker, D. J. (1999). Y2K-OK? *EMedia, 12*(12), 80.

Pavlov, A., & Micheli, P. (2023). Rethinking organizational performance management: A complexity theory perspective. *International Journal of Operations & Production Management, 43*(6), 899–915. DOI: 10.1108/IJOPM-08-2022-0478

Perrow, C. (1986). *Complex organizations: A critical essay* (3rd ed.). McGraw-Hill.

Pesut, D. J. (2013). Creativity and innovation: Thought and action. *Creative Nursing, 19*(3), 113–121. DOI: 10.1891/1078-4535.19.3.113 PMID: 24400465

Pires, S. M., Desta, B. N., Mughini-Gras, L., Mmbaga, B. T., Fayemi, O. E., Salvador, E. M., Gobena, T., Majowicz, S. E., Hald, T., & Hoejskov, P. S. (2021). Burden of foodborne diseases: Think global, act local. *Current Opinion in Food Science, 39*, 152–159. PMID: 34178607

Pohl, H. R., Wohlers, D., Chou, C.-H., Citra, M. J., Fay, M., Coley, C., Harper, C., Ingerman, L., Buser, M. C., & Ingber, S. Z. (2019). Toxicological Profile For Glyphosate: Draft For Public Comment.

Polifko, K. A. (2007). *Concepts of the nursing profession*. Change Agent Leadership, Theories Transformational Leadership. Thomson Delmar Learning.

Prakash, A., Jha, S. K., & Rajendra, P. M. (2012). Scenario planning for service quality: A monte carlo simulation study. *Journal of Strategy and Management, 5*(3), 331–352. DOI: 10.1108/17554251211247599

Pryor, M., Humphreys, J. H., Oyler, J., Taneja, S., & Toombs, L. A. (2011). The legitimacy and efficacy of current organizational theory: An analysis. *International Journal of Management, 28*(4), 209–228.

Rabine, A., & Faber, S. (2025). *Trump EPA May Threaten State And Local Use Of Toxic Weekkiller Glyphosate*. Https://Www.Ewg.Org/News-Insights/News/2025/02/Trump-Epa-May-Threaten-State-And-Local-Bans-Toxic-Weedkiller-Glyphosate?Utm_Source=Chatgpt.Com

Rahman, M. T., Sobur, M. A., Islam, M. S., Ievy, S., Hossain, M. J., El Zowalaty, M. E., & Ashour, H. M. (2020). Zoonotic diseases: Etiology, impact, and control. *Microorganisms, 8*(9), 1405. PMID: 32932606

Raimi, M. O., Vivien, O. T., & Oluwatoyin, O. A. (2021). Creating The Healthiest Nation: Climate Change And Environmental Health Impacts. In *Nigeria: A Narrative Review. Morufu Olalekan Raimi, Tonye Vivien Odubo & Adedoyin Oluwatoyin Omidiji (2021) Creating The Healthiest Nation: Climate Change And Environmental Health Impacts In Nigeria: A Narrative Review.* Scholink Sustainability In Environment. ISSN.

Rasmussen, S. A., & Goodman, R. A. (2018). *The CDC field epidemiology manual.* Oxford University Press.

Ravn Boess, E., Kørnøv, L., Lyhne, I., & Partidário, M. R. (2021). Integrating Sdgs In Environmental Assessment: Unfolding SDG Functions In Emerging Practices. *Environmental Impact Assessment Review, 90*, 106632. Https://Doi.Org/Https://Doi .Org/10.1016/J.Eiar.2021.106632

Raza, S. A., & Standing, C. (2011). A systemic model for managing and evaluating conflicts in organizational change. *Systemic Practice and Action Research, 24*(3), 187–210. DOI: 10.1007/s11213-010-9186-0

Relman, D. A., Chofnes, E. R., & Mack, A. (2010, January 1). *Infectious Disease Movement in a Borderless World: Workshop Summary.* The National Academies Press. https://nap.nationalacademies.org/read/12758/chapter/6

Robbins, S. P., & Judge, T. A. (2023). *Organizational behavior* (19th ed.). Pearson.

Rothwell, W. J., Stavros, J. M., & Sullivan, R. L. (eds), Sullivan, A. (2010). *Practicing organization development: A guide for leading change* (3rd ed.). Pfeiffer.

Sanz-Valle, R., Naranjo-Valencia, J. C., Jiménez-Jiménez, D., & Perez-Caballero, L. (2011). Linking organizational learning with technical innovation and organizational culture. *Journal of Knowledge Management, 15*(6), 997–1015. DOI: 10.1108/13673271111179334

Sawka, K. A. (2007). Strategic planning in volatile industry conditions. *U.S. Banker, 117*(2), 40.

Scheifele, F. (2024). *Green Industrial Policy in Renewable Energy: Insights from Developing Countries.* Technische Universitaet Berlin.

Schirmer, M., Arichi, T., & Chung, A. W. (2023). *Connectome analysis: Characterization, methods, and analysis.* Academic Press.

Schroeder, P., Parisi, L. L., & Foster, R. (2019). Healthcare quality improvement: Then and now. *Nursing Management, 50*(9), 20–25. DOI: 10.1097/01. Numa.0000579004.87116.35 PMID: 31460894

Schwarm, B. (2013, May 2). The well-tempered clavier. *Encyclopedia Britannica*. Retrieved from https://www.britannica.com/topic/The-Well-Tempered-Clavier-BWV-846-893

Scott, G. (2001). 'Seeing the Forest for the Trees': Towards a framework for effective change research in education. *Innovations in Education and Teaching International*, *38*(1), 86–92.

Selin, S. W., Pierskalla, C., Smaldone, D., & Robinson, K. (2007). Social learning and building trust through a participatory design for natural resource planning. *Journal of Forestry*, *105*(8), 421–425.

Setty, K., & Ferrero, G. (2021). Water Safety Plans. In *Oxford Research Encyclopedia Of Global Public Health*.

Sevilla, N. L. (2017). *Germs on a plane: The transmission and risks of airplane-borne diseases* [Ph.D., George Mason University]. ProQuest Dissertations & Theses Global.

Sevilla, N. L. (2017). *Germs On A Plane: The Transmission And Risks Of Airplane-Borne Diseases* [Ph.D., George Mason University]. Proquest Dissertations & Theses Global., Https://Proxy.Cecybrary.Com/Login?Url=Https://Search.Proquest.Com/Docview/1958954996?Accountid=26967

Sevilla, N. L. (2018). Germs on a plane: The transmission and risks of airplane-borne diseases. *Transportation Research Record: Journal of the Transportation Research Board*, *2672*(29), 93–102. PMID: 34285452

Shah, I. A., & Sial, Q. (2024). *Advances in computational intelligence for the Healthcare Industry 4.0*. IGI Global Publishing.

Shukla, A. (2017, July 2). *What is Innovation? Why Innovation is important* Retrieved from paggu: http://www.paggu.com/getting-into-roots/what-is-innovation-why-innovation-is-important/

Shukla, R., Bagotia, H., Satish, P., Kamath, H. S., Chatterjee, S., Savariah, D., Kaulgud, V., Gobburi, H., & Acharya, S. (2025). Fintech and healthtech synergism: Pioneering a digital healthcare revolution for accessible, affordable, and effective patient-centered care. *Journal of Family Medicine and Primary Care*, *14*(3), 820–824. DOI: 10.4103/jfmpc.jfmpc_999_24 PMID: 40256084

Sicilia, M.-A., & Balazote, P. S. (2013). *Interoperability in healthcare information systems: Standards, management, and techology*. IGI Global Scientific Publishing.

Siegel, E. (2016). *Predictive analytics: The power to predict who will click, buy, lie, or die*. Wiley.

Siegel, E. (2016). *Predictive Analytics: the Power to Predict Who Will click, buy, lie, or Die*. Wiley. (Original work published 2013)

Simpkins, R. A. (2009). How great leaders avoid disaster: The value of contingency planning. *Business Strategy Series*, *10*(2), 104–108. DOI: 10.1108/17515630910942241

Smaczny, T. (2001). Is an alignment between business and information technology the appropriate paradigm to manage IT in today's organisations? *Management Decision*, *39*(10), 797–802.

Srinidhi, B. (1998). Strategic quality management. *International Journal of Quality Science*, *3*(1), 38–70. http://search.proquest.com.proxy.cecybrary.com/docview/211982714?accountid=26967

Staykova, M. P. (2019). Rediscovering the Delphi technique: A review of the literature. *Advances in Social Sciences Research Journal*, *6*(1), 218–229. DOI: 10.14738/assrj.61.5959

Steiber, A., & Alänge, S. (2015). Organizational innovation: Verifying a comprehensive model for catalyzing organizational development and change. *Triple Helix (Heidelberg)*, *2*(1), 1–28. DOI: 10.1186/s40604-015-0026-1

Steil, G.Jr, & Gibbons-Carr, M. (2005). Large group scenario planning: Scenario planning with the whole system in the room. *The Journal of Applied Behavioral Science*, *41*(1), 15–29.

Stephens, J., Barton, J., & Haslett, T. (2009). Action research: Its history and relationship to scientific methodology. *Systemic Practice and Action Research*, *22*(6), 463–474. DOI: 10.1007/s11213-009-9147-7

Strand, R. (2014). Strategic leadership of corporate sustainability. *Journal of Business Ethics*, *123*(4), 687–706. DOI: 10.1007/s10551-013-2005-7

String, G., & Lantagne, D. (2016). A Systematic Review Of Outcomes And Lessons Learned From General, Rural, And Country-Specific Water Safety Plan Implementations. *Water Science and Technology: Water Supply*, *16*(6), 1580–1594.

Stuckelberger, A., & Urbina, M. (2020). WHO international health regulations (IHR) vs COVID-19 uncertainty. *Acta Biomedica*, *91*(2), 113. PMID: 32420935

Sukumar, S. R., & Ferrell, R. K. (2013). Big Data collaboration: Exploring, recording and sharing enterprise knowledge. *Information Services & Use*, *33*(3/4), 257–270. DOI: 10.3233/ISU-130712

Sullivan, R. L., Rothwell, W. J., & Balasi, M. J. B. (2013). Organization development (OD) and change management (CM): Whole system transformation. *Development and Learning in Organizations*, *27*(6), 18–23. DOI: 10.1108/DLO-08-2013-0060

Sun, C., Zhang, Z., Vochozka, M., & Vozňáková, I. (2022). Enterprise digital transformation and debt financing cost in China's A-share listed companies. *Oeconomia Copernicana*, *13*(3), 783–829. DOI: 10.24136/oc.2022.023

Suthar, A. B., Allen, L. G., Cifuentes, S., Dye, C., & Nagata, J. M. (2018). Lessons learnt from implementation of the International Health Regulations: A systematic review. *Bulletin of the World Health Organization*, *96*(2), 110–121E. https://doi-org.library.capella.edu/10.2471/BLT.16.189100 PMID: 29403114

Sweet, S. (2011). Which is Best for Us? Top Down, Bottoms Up, or Middle Out. Retrieved from http://www.i4process.com/publications/which-is-best-for-us-top-down-bottoms-up-or-middle-out/

TechAdvisory.org. (2015). *Why use predictive analytics?* TechAdvisory.org. https://www.techadvisory.org/2014/05/why-use-predictive-analytics/

Teoh Kae, N., & Rashad, Y. (2015). The general review of how different leadership styles cause the transformational change efforts to be successful. *International Journal of Management. Accounting & Economics*, *2*(9), 1130–1140.

The World Bank In DRC. (2025). Https://Www.Worldbank.Org/En/Country/Drc/Overview#1

The World Café. (2025, June 25). History. Theworldcafe.com. https://theworldcafe.com/about-us/history/

Thietart, R. A., & Forgues, B. (2011). Complexity science and organization. In Allen, P., Maguire, S., & McKelvey, S. (Eds.), *The Sage Handbook of Complexity and Management* (pp. 53–64). Sage.

Thomas, J. C., Sage, M., Dillenberg, J., & Guillory, V. J. (2002). *A Code Of Ethics For Public Health* (Vol. 92). American Public Health Association.

Thomas, M., & McGarry, F. (1994). Top-down vs. bottom-up process improvement. *IEEE Software*, *11*(4), 12–13. DOI: 10.1109/52.300121

Thoradeniya, T., & Jayasinghe, S. (2021). COVID-19 and future pandemics: A global systems approach and relevance to SDGs. *Globalization and Health*, *17*(1), 59. PMID: 34020654

Turner, J. R. (2019). Complexity Theory: An overview with potential applications for the social sciences. *Systems*, *7*(1), 4. DOI: 10.3390/systems7010004

Turnock, B. J., Birkhead, G. S., Morrow, C. B., & Pirani, S. (2022). *Turnock's public health: what it is and how it works.* Jones & Bartlett Learning.

Turnock, B. J., Birkhead, G. S., Morrow, C. B., & Pirani, S. (2022). *Turnock's Public Health: What It Is And How It Works.* Jones & Bartlett Learning.

UN. (2025). *Intergovernmental Negotiating Body to draft and negotiate a WHO convention, agreement or other international instrument on pandemic prevention, preparedness and response.* United Nations. Retrieved 2025 from https://www.who.int/news/item/20-05-2025-world-health-assembly-adopts-historic-pandemic-agreement-to-make-the-world-more-equitable-and-safer-from-future-pandemics

United Nations. (2025, June 22). *Sustainable Development Goals.* UN.org. https://unosd.un.org/content/sustainable-development-goals-sdgs

Uop. (2023). *Public Health Vs. Medicine.* University Of Pittsburgh. Retrieved 6/13/2025 From Https://Www.Publichealth.Pitt.Edu/Public-Health-Vs-Medicine

UoP. (2023). *Public Health vs. Medicine.* University of Pittsburgh. Retrieved 6/13/2025 from https://www.publichealth.pitt.edu/public-health-vs-medicine

Urrestarazu, H. (2015). Towards a consistent constructivist general systems theory. *Constructivist Foundations, 10*(2), 180–183.

Using Technology to Predict Workplace Injuries. (2014).. . *Professional Safety, 59*(6), 18. https://ehsworks1.blogspot.com/2014/02/using-technology-to-predict-workplace.html

Valavanidis, A. (2018). Glyphosate, The Most Widely Used Herbicide. *Scientific Review (Singapore).*

Valikangas, L., Gibbert, M., Nair, L. B., Paukku, M., & Peixoto, I. (2016). *Strategic innovation: The definitive guide to outlier strategies.* Pearson Education, Inc.

Van Assche, K., Verschraegen, G., Valentinov, V., & Gruezmacher, M. (2019). The social, the ecological, and the adaptive. von bertalanffy's general systems theory and the adaptive governance of social-ecological systems. *Systems Research and Behavioral Science, 36*(3), 308–321. DOI: 10.1002/sres.2587

Van Tulder, R., & van Mil, E. (2023). *Principles of sustainable business: Frameworks for corporate action on the SDGs.* Routledge.

Vărzaru, A. A. (2022). Assessing digital transformation of cost accounting tools in healthcare. *International Journal of Environmental Research and Public Health, 19*(23), 15572. DOI: 10.3390/ijerph192315572

Vogelsang, J., Townsend, M., Minahan, M., Jamieson, D., Vogel, J., Viets, A., Royal, C., & Valek, L. (2013). *Handbook for strategic HR: Best practices in organization development from the OD network.* OD Network. AMACOM.

Von Hippel, E. (1982). Get new products for customers. *Harvard Business Review, 60*(2), 117–122.

Wachter, R. (2015). *The digital doctor: Hope, hype, and harm at the dawn of medicine's computer age.* McGraw-Hill Education.

Wade, W. (2012). *Scenario planning: A field guide to the future.* John Wiley & Sons, Inc.

Wahl, D. C. (2019). A brief history of systems science, chaos, and complexity. *Resilience.*

Waldman, D., & Javidan, M. (2020). *The false dichotomy between globalism and nationalism.* Harvard Business Review.

Waller, M. A., & Fawcett, S. E. (2013). Click here for a data scientist: Big Data, Predictive Analytics, and Theory Development in the era of a Maker Movement Supply Chain. *Journal of Business Logistics, 34*(4), 249–252. DOI: 10.1111/jbl.12024

Warzynski, C. C. (2004). Future-search conferences at Cornell University. *New Directions for Institutional Research, 2004*(123), 105–112.

Watkins, J. M., Mohr, B., & Kelly, R. (2011). *Appreciative inquiry: Change at the speed of imagination* (2nd ed.). Pfeiffer.

Weick, K. E., & Quinn, R. E. (1999). Organizational change and development. *Annual Review of Psychology, 50*, 361–386.

Weitzman, F. (2014). Organizational longevity as a predictor of organizational learning, organizational identity, organizational innovation, and fiscal conservatism. (3624405 Ph.D.), Colorado State University, Ann Arbor. ProQuest Dissertations & Theses Global database.

Weitzman, F. (2014). *Organizational longevity as a predictor of organizational learning, organizational identity, organizational innovation, and fiscal conservatism.* (3624405 Ph.D.). ProQuest Dissertations & Theses Global database.

WGU. (2020). *Environmental Health: Lesson 1:1 Environmental Health As Interconnectedness Of Risks [MOOC].* Https://Apps.Cgp-Oex.Wgu.Edu/Wgulearning/Course/Course-V1:Wgux+OEX0355+V01/Block-V1:Wgux+OEX0355+V01+Type@Sequential+Block@A6abd0761688459bba15ffe73a977ebd/Block-V1:Wgux+OEX0355+V01+Type@Vertical+Block@Fea22b1e58da4c1eb6ef136a4518b70e

WGU. (2020b). *Lesson 2:1 Environmental Toxicology [MOOC]*. Https://Apps.Cgp-Oex.Wgu.Edu/Wgulearning/Course/Course-V1:Wgux+OEX0355+V01/Block-V1:Wgux+OEX0355+V01+Type@Sequential+Block@662276f3ef464de1ac3982501619e38b/Block-V1:Wgux+OEX0355+V01+Type@Vertical+Block@0c7456123f3e41cdb15dde01f8e15ea6

WGU. (2024). *Western Governors University: D-618 Environmental Health*. Western Governors University.

Whitehead, R. (1994). *Ground Water Atlas Of The United States: Segment 7, Idaho, Oregon, Washington* (060776757X).

Whitney, D., & Fredrickson, B. L. (2015). Appreciative inquiry meets positive psychology. *AI Practitioner*, *17*(3), 18–26. DOI: 10.12781/978-1-907549-24-3-3

Wills, M. J. (2014). Decisions through data: Analytics in healthcare. *Journal of Healthcare Management*, *59*(4), 254–262.

Wilson, H. J., & Daugherty, P. R. (2025, January-February). The secret to successful AI-driven process redesign: Strong leaders put business transformation in the hands of all employees. *Harvard Business Review*, *103*(1), 45–51.

Winslett, G. (2023). Digital Trade. In *Services: Globalization's Exciting New Frontier*. Globalization.

Wirtenberg, J., Abrams, L., & Ott, C. (2004). Assessing the field of organization development. *The Journal of Applied Behavioral Science*, *40*(4), 465–479. DOI: 10.1177/0021886304270246

Wong, J., Young, E., Hung, L., Mann, J., & Jackson, L. (2023). Beyond Plan-Do-Study-Act cycle – staff perceptions on facilitators and barriers to the implementation of telepresence robots in long-term care. *BMC Health Services Research*, *23*, 1–16. DOI: 10.1186/s12913-023-09741-9 PMID: 37468953

World Health Organization. (2019). Global strategy on digital health 2020-2024.

World Health Organization. (2025, May 20). *World Health Assembly adopts historic Pandemic Agreement to make the world more equitable and safer from future pandemics* [News Release]. Geneva. https://www.who.int/news/item/20-05-2025-world-health-assembly-adopts-historic-pandemic-agreement-to-make-the-world-more-equitable-and-safer-from-future-pandemics

World Health Organization. (n.d.). *The true death toll of COVID-19 estimating global excess mortality*. World Health Organization. https://www.who.int/data/stories/the-true-death-toll-of-covid-19-estimating-global-excess-mortality The World Health Organization (1983) International Hth Regulation 1969 Regulations 1969 3rd ed.

Worren, N. A. M., Ruddle, K., & Moore, K. (1999). From organizational development to change management: The emergence of a new profession. *The Journal of Applied Behavioral Science*, *35*(3), 273–286. DOI: 10.1177/0021886399353002

Worsley-Tonks, K. E., Bender, J. B., Deem, S. L., Ferguson, A. W., Fèvre, E. M., Martins, D. J., Muloi, D. M., Murray, S., Mutinda, M., & Ogada, D. (2022). Strengthening global health security by improving disease surveillance in remote rural areas of low-income and middle-income countries. *The Lancet. Global Health*, *10*(4), e579–e584. PMID: 35303467

WSDA. (2019). Washington Pesticide Laws And Related Regulations Handbook. In W. S. D. O. A. P. M. Division (Ed.).

Xu, P. (2012). Architectural and landscape design: A new synthesis major proposed with interdisciplinary and general models. *The International Journal of the Arts in Society*, *5*(6), 369–388.

Yadav, A. K., Kumar, S., Singh, G., & Kansara, N. K. (2021). Demystifying R naught: Understanding what does it hide? *Indian Journal of Community Medicine : Official Publication of Indian Association of Preventive & Social Medicine*, *46*(1), 7–14. PMID: 34035567

Zanon, C. J., Alves, F. A. G., Chiappetta, J. C. J., & Lopes de Sousa, J. A. B. (2013). Alignment of operations strategy: Exploring the marketing interface. *Industrial Management & Data Systems*, *113*(2), 207–233. DOI: 10.1108/02635571311303541

Zhang, L., Miranskyy, A., & Rjaibi, W. (2021). Quantum advantage and the Y2K bug: A comparison. *IEEE Software*, *38*(2), 80–87. DOI: 10.1109/MS.2020.2985321

Zhang, Q., Li, Y., Kroeze, C., Xu, W., Gai, L., Vitsas, M., Ma, L., Zhang, F., & Strokal, M. (2024). A Global Assessment Of Glyphosate And AMPA Inputs Into Rivers: Over Half Of The Pollutants Are From Corn And Soybean Production. *Water Research*, *261*, 121986. PMID: 38924948

About the Authors

Sterling K. Carter is an academic researcher, writer, and the Chief Executive Officer of SBC Global Consulting in Vancouver, WA, USA. SBC Global Consulting is a global research and consulting firm devoted to helping organizations improve productivity, efficiency, and reduce waste. Sterling holds a Doctorate in Management with a concentration in Global Leadership, a Master of Business Administration with a concentration in Logistics and Supply Chain Management, and a Bachelor of Science in Information Technology from Colorado Technical University. Sterling is also a Lean Six Sigma Master Black Belt, a Certified Agile Leader, a Certified Scrum Master, and is certified in Data Analytics. He has over a decade of experience consulting in multiple verticals, including healthcare. After completing his doctorate and publishing his dissertation, The Strategies Global Leaders Need to Improve Interoperability of an EHR System, he has devoted his life to global health and health systems integration and interoperability. Publications

Christina Anastasia is a college professor and professional businesswoman with a passion that focuses on small business and economic development. Her specialization is in business plan preparation for acquisition of funds and has counseled for the SBDC helping start- up companies write business plans. As a business owner, she is a strong supporter that small business is the backbone of American society and that economic development relies on the Mom and Pop businesses that dot the American landscape. One of her own companies, a graphic design and sign business, fits into this demographic. She has been doing business in the sign industry since 2001. In addition, Dr. A owns an RV Park, and a successful wholes business that jobs products to smaller gift stores and outlets throughout the country. In addition to being and educator and business owner, Dr. A has published three books and has been a contributing author for a textbook in Organizational Behavior and have written course content for doctoral, graduate, and undergraduate courses.

Barbara Mae Carter is a professor at Colorado Technical University, teaching leadership and organizational development classes. Barbara serves on the dissertation committee for doctoral research at Colorado Technical University and presents at Doctoral Symposia. She is an experienced Instructional Designer with a demonstrated history of consulting and facilitating adult learning. Barbara completed a Doctor of Management with a concentration in Organizational Development and Change from Colorado Technical University. In December 2019, she published her dissertation, The Leadership Practices Female ODC Managers Use to Improve Change Initiatives. Barbara holds a Master of Arts in Organizational Leadership and a Bachelor of Arts in Management from George Fox University. She is also a Certified Agile Leader and a Certified Ruth Clark Instructional Designer. Publications

Index

A

C

D

E

F

G

H

I

127, 147, 182

www.ingramcontent.com/pod-product-compliance
Ingram Content Group UK Ltd.
Pitfield, Milton Keynes, MK11 3LW, UK
UKHW052002041026
15590UKWH00008B/2107